Stone Tool Traditions in the Contact Era

Stone Tool Traditions in the Contact Era

Edited by
CHARLES R. COBB

THE UNIVERSITY OF ALABAMA PRESS
Tuscaloosa

To dad and the memory of my mother, for their unfailing support and endless barrage of bad puns about chert

The University of Alabama Press
Tuscaloosa, Alabama 35487-0380

Manufactured in the United States of America

Typeface: Goudy and Goudy Sans

∞
The paper on which this book is printed meets the minimum requirements of American National Standard for Information Science-Permanence of Paper for Printed Library Materials, ANSI Z39.48-1984.

Library of Congress Cataloging-in-Publication Data

Stone tool traditions in the contact era / edited by Charles R. Cobb.
p. cm.
Includes bibliographical references and index.
ISBN 0-8173-1372-9 (alk. paper) — ISBN 0-8173-1373-7 (pbk. : alk. paper)
1. Indians of North America—Implements. 2. Indians of North America—First contact with Europeans. 3. Indians of North America—Antiquities. 4. Stone implements—North America. 5. North America—Antiquities. I. Cobb, Charles R. (Charles Richard), 1956–
E98.I4 S76 2003
621.9'0089'97—dc21

2003002156

British Library Cataloguing-in-Publication Data available

Contents

Illustrations

Tables

1
Introduction
Framing Stone Tool Traditions after Contact

Charles R. Cobb

The Columbian quincentennial in 1992 played a key role in prompting an interest in Contact-period research, but archaeology has had a history with the topic long before that date—even if the appellation "Contact" has only recently begun to enjoy widespread currency as a discrete field of study. Yet, for various reasons, Contact studies still defy easy categorization. As Lightfoot (1995) points out, the field bridges a liminal historical arena that neither specialist in prehistoric nor historical archaeology comfortably lays claim to, and it encompasses divergences in method and theory between the two groups of practitioners that are difficult to reconcile. Further, Contact research has become very broad in scope. It may be dominated by the era of European expansionism beginning in the A.D. 1400s, but it spans a tremendous variety of premodern settings as well—from the Roman frontier (Wells 1998) to the fringes of Tiwanaku expansionism (Goldstein 1993). Nevertheless, amid all of this variability in Contact-period archaeology, there is one common thread: a concern with how Contact situations transformed the material culture of the societies involved and, in turn, how those transformations were linked with the reproduction of those societies in new ways.

Studies about the spread of European exploration and colonialism—particularly in the Americas—have paid relatively little attention to the shifts in the role of stone technology among indigenous groups. In part, this neglect can be attributed to the empirical generalization that stone tools and objects tended to drop out relatively rapidly compared to other classes of material culture. Plus, there is always the lingering suspicion by lithic researchers that the somewhat mundane aesthetic appeal of stone tools and debitage relegates those artifacts to a category of "data *habitus*"—empirical taken-for-granteds that are unremarkable when compared to silver gorgets among the Choctaw or the ubiquitous glass beads churned out by factories in Venice, Amsterdam, and Bohemia. Compared to stone artifacts, even plain Colono wares have managed to generate some excitement among Contact-period archaeologists.

But if just one lesson is to be learned from Contact studies, it is that we must be extremely wary of any generalizations about these culturally volatile situations, and this is particularly true of lithic technology. The idea that groups began using metal tools simply because they were superior to stone is largely untested. Further, the decline in stone tool use was not immediate (Bamforth 1993:49–50). Lithic technologies witnessed a diverse—and often protracted—history in the Americas following Columbus's landing. The contributions to this volume underscore this diversity. Ranging across North America and into Hawai'i, these studies outline the continuity in flake- and ground-stone technologies in a wide variety of settings. The reasons for the persistence of stone technologies are as varied as their occurrences. In some cases, even with wide access to metal objects, certain stone tool types still seemed to be the best implements for carrying out traditional tasks. In others, reliance on lithic technology represented a commitment to maintaining traditional practices amidst a rising tide of imported commodities. Simply put, there is no single answer or predictable nature to either the decline or persistence of stone tools in the Contact era.

Lithic researchers typically rely upon a common pool of methods to explore the production and use of stone tools, and the chapters in this volume reflect such familiar techniques such as low-magnification functional analysis and stage-reduction approaches. Together, the authors employ a wide spectrum of theoretical perspectives in considering how lithic technologies were embedded within social relations in the Contact era. With their concern for both utilitarian and social dimensions, it is not surprising to see in many of the studies both functional and economic aspects of material culture considered alongside symbolic and ritual aspects. Also juxtaposed are ground-stone and flaked-stone technologies, with three of the eight studies focusing on the former. Although lithic analysts draw distinctions, quite rightly, between the two technologies, both are seen to suffer early on from the adoption of European metal tools.

Although every chapter in this book has different points to make about understanding the uses of culturally modified stone in the Contact era, when read as a whole two essential issues emerge. First, what we often refer to as the Contact era involved a long period of time when the political economies of Europe, and attendant relations with Native Americans and local groups elsewhere, were changing rapidly. Second, stone scrapers, pipes, and other objects were more than just things that reflected social relationships; they embodied those relationships and were crucial to the reproduction of everyday practices and belief systems. Both of these issues must be taken into account as we attempt to develop more richly textured and historically nuanced frameworks for understanding Contact situations.

EVOLVING POLITICAL ECONOMIES

Native groups in eastern North America in the 1600s and 1700s were being drawn into a form of merchant capitalism very different from the nascent industrial capitalism faced by Plains tribes in the 1800s. Likewise, mercantile policies driving the competition between European powers in the 1400s and 1500s sometimes were more reminiscent of feudal political economies than capitalist ones. Any attempt to address indigenous responses to the European presence must first be cognizant of the *longue durée* of global economies in order to understand European objectives and actions and the ways they changed over time. Native groups varied widely in their responses to the European presence, and their respective worldviews and practices strongly shaped localized relationships. As a result, the social terrain of Contact was very uneven across space and through time. As Cusick (1998b:6) observes, "contact situations are structured, but not deterministic." It is thus useful to examine European contact and lithic technology in terms of three arbitrarily set major structures: first contact, mercantilism or merchant capitalism, and capitalism. If, indeed, a constant exists throughout all of these periods, it is that the lines between colonizer and colonized were much more hazy than we are wont to appreciate in our archaeological studies (e.g., Comaroff and Comaroff 1992; Stoler and Cooper 1997). Marriage practices, racial categorizations—and even technologies—were blurred in everyday practice, despite the edicts emanating from policymakers anxious to impose distinctions between Westerner and non-Westerner in far-flung holdings. A temporal trajectory of lithic technologies after Contact will bring some understanding of the dynamic nature of this interaction.

First Contact

Studies dealing with the initial period of exploration in the Americas often assume a Janus profile, setting a baseline for looking backward in the attempt to reconstruct what "unadulterated" indigenous societies looked like just prior to European contact (e.g., Fried 1979; Stahl 2001:27–31). Or, as is more often the case, they look forward in order to explore the subtle changes wrought by first contact in anticipation of major changes to follow. In either case, studies set in this interval deal with a period when the playing field was fairly level. In North America, European technological advantages were offset by the small numbers of people precariously perched along the coast or along major drainages in an alien environment. Ironically, their most potent weapons were epidemic diseases brought from the Old World.

This is a period when European material culture must have been viewed as highly exotic, if not bizarre, and utilitarian applications of it were not always clear-cut. And even if an application was obvious, as in the case of functionally familiar knives or celts, for instance, there seems to have been some reluctance to incorporate familiar shapes if they were rendered in strange raw materials. Nevertheless, both indigenous groups and Europeans relied on their folk taxonomies in an attempt to render new peoples, places, and things into intelligible categories. Hamell (1983) argues that glass beads and copper alloys were readily accepted early on in the Northeast primarily because they were recognized as broadly analogous to similar materials (e.g., translucent stones such as quartz and native copper) that had strong metaphorical connotations in the indigenous worldview. Thus, while functional attributes of exotic objects might have been recognizable, symbolic translations of material culture might have been necessary to make it acceptable.

This may explain why many categories of stone tools were slow to be supplanted in the dawn of the Contact era. At the King site in Georgia, lithic technology was relatively untouched by the Spanish presence in the mid–sixteenth century (see Cobb and Ruggiero, chapter 2); the same is true for the early-eighteenth-century Wichita in eastern Oklahoma who occupied the Lasley Vore settlement (see Odell, chapter 3). Only a handful of European objects emerged from the King site, and they are additions to the mortuary assemblages rather than replacements of local technology. These burials, some of which apparently represent flintknappers, contain iron tools that appear to be functional equivalents of stone tools (also found with the burials), such as celts. Presumably, this is the onset of the selective incorporation of European material culture that typifies the Contact period. Yet even at the Lasley Vore site where European goods are much more abundant, stone tool technology continued unabated. Nevertheless, Native Americans did not take long to begin actively incorporating functionally superior European tools. Cutting tools, for example, were eagerly sought, and iron knives were rapidly adopted by a wide variety of groups, ranging from the Iroquois (Bradley 1987:140–141) to the Plains Indians (Hudson 1993; Odell, chapter 3).

The growing presence of Europeans was not only felt in the realm of manufacturing technology, but it also affected the area's access to a wide variety of raw materials. In the eighteenth century, traditional sources of salt for the Cherokee were severely disrupted by European encroachment (Hatley 1989), and similar problems moved westward with the establishment of the United States, often involving lithic sources. Groups east of the Pawnee in the Central Great Plains were displaced westward in the nineteenth century, forcing the

Cree to shift their settlements and to rely more heavily on stone quarry sources to the west (Holen 1991). Likewise, Silliman's (chapter 9) study suggests that in the same era a reorientation of choices in regional lithic sources at the Rancho Petaluma in California may be due to changing patterns of mobility, but in this instance Native Americans had become tethered to an agricultural and ranching enterprise. Clearly, raw material identification is an important, and not always systematically addressed, component for identifying changes in the organization of lithic technology in the Contact era.

With the subtle technological changes that were occurring in the early Contact era, we may find that indirect lines of evidence may tell us just as much as the stone tools themselves. For example, attempts have been made to distinguish faunal butchering marks made by metal versus stone tools based upon the profile of the cut (v-shaped versus u-shaped, respectively) (Binford 1981:110–114; Guilday et al. 1962; Lyman 1987:294–295). Clark (2003) has evaluated these patterns on a protohistoric Oneida faunal assemblage in central New York and suggests that bone and metal tools were used for butchering, while stone tools possibly were preferred for disarticulation and filleting. Whether such differences can be attributed solely to functional characteristics of the various tool types is still uncertain.

The initiation of culture contact appears to have been a time of experimentation for Native and European alike. Goods and technologies were exchanged, appropriated, and often transformed according to categories comprehensible to the receiving culture. Because this process was of necessity structured by worldview, it stands to reason that there was considerable variability in the way that lithic technologies were impacted. When the European presence accelerated, lithic technologies began to recede—but again, not in necessarily predictable ways.

Mercantilism

As European positions solidified and became more secure, colonies and their patron countries were able to embark on much more systematic extensions of political and economic policy. This period of mercantilism or merchant capitalism is characterized by a strong reliance on exchange relations, with Europeans strongly committed to extracting raw materials, particularly furs, from North America. In some regions, expanding colonial enclaves dealt with indigenous groups that were becoming "forest proletariats" (Hickerson 1973:39)—they were still in possession of the means of production but become increasingly entangled in European trade networks and rivalries. In other areas, particularly those under Spanish control and the mission system, many Indians fell under direct colonial governance. Still, mercantilism was not a monolithic policy or practice. The broad goals of exploiting colonies for raw goods, obtaining bullion, and developing export industries might have been widely held by Europeans, but the differing forms of indigenous social and economic organization and the variation in implementation among European nation-states caused those goals to have many outcomes (e.g., Lightfoot 1995; Stoler 1989; Wolf 1982).

Archaeological studies can make an important contribution toward addressing this variability and moving us away from facile generalizations about the Contact period, as can be seen in the debates over Frederich Engels's (1972 [1884]) seminal observation on the development of the state, which is often cited as a key contribution toward a feminist understanding of the modern era by linking the rise of female oppression to the loss of communality and the rise of private property (Leacock 1972; Muller 1985). Karen Sacks (1974) maintains that Engels's work is flawed because it does not recognize the reasons underlying this transition. She argues that in class societies males become more involved in production for exchange, whereas females become more tied to the household and to production for use. However, Contact-period situations present gray areas that defy such broad characterizations. As indigenous societies routinized their external economic ties with European groups, they engaged in many of the activities associated with class-based societies, yet they often veered off in unpredictable permutations. The fur trade offers a classic case in point.

The explosion in the fur trade in the 1600s, so often referenced as the Iroquois "beaver wars" (see Carmody, chapter 5), continued elsewhere long after the beaver had played out in the Northeast. The Hudson Bay Company and other enterprises continued their trade in a wide variety of pelts in Canada well into the twentieth century. Deerskins became a major trade item in the 1700s and into the 1800s in the southeastern United States, and bison became increasingly important in the Plains during the 1800s.

Jay Johnson (1997; chapter 4) observes that one stone tool type that thrived in certain regions of the South in the 1700s, probably because of the fur trade, was a formal, keeled chert scraper (see also Odell, chapter 3; Cassell, chapter 10). The type was somewhat common in the Upper Mississippi Valley prior to Contact (among the Oneota, for example) and might have been commonly used in bison processing. Its efficacy for hide processing apparently led to a wider dissemination into the South as the deer fur trade surged. Johnson (1997) points out that the lithic "Oliver Complex" found in the Lower Mississippi Valley, involving such scrapers and other tools (Brain 1988:396–399), is probably a manifestation of this process.

Who were the individuals using these tools? All historic accounts indicate that women were the primary hide producers. This often led to acute intracommunity tensions when demands on female labor upsurged as men sought to take advantage of the lucrative trade in skins with Charleston and other European towns (Braund 1993; Hatley 1989).

In this historic instance we find that, *contra* Sacks (1974), women's labor became intimately tied to external exchange networks as certain Indian groups strengthened their ties with class-based (viz. European) societies and began to undergo internal transformations themselves. A key point of tension was that women were not allowed to forego traditional duties but were assuming new and equally onerous ones associated with hide preparation. Lines of economic exploitation based on ethnicity and class radiating out of European centers were transformed locally into forms of dominance founded on gender. Similar tensions were felt in the Contact Northeast, where matrilineal societies shifted more power to males, and material culture was realigned to new associations of gender (Nassaney and Volmar, chapter 6). Stone tools became some of the instruments of these new forms of exploitation (see also Cobb 2000:113–115) and thus played an important role in the cultural transformation.

During the age of mercantilism, the Spanish, through the institutions of *encomienda, repartimieto,* and *reduccion*, developed some of the most restrictive and oppressive (and effective) strategies for controlling Native-American labor. Missions served a crucial role by forcing Indians to live on compounds and to work fields or other enterprises in order to produce surpluses that were intended to keep the local colony afloat as well as to enrich the Spanish Crown. Yet all missions were not equal. Their policies and practices varied widely depending upon which religious order was in charge and which indigenous groups were being missionized. Even relative wealth and location created distinctions among missions. Many missions truly were on the frontier of colonial expansion and did not have ready access to European supplies. At Mission Tucmacacori in southern Arizona, the relative isolation and irregular access to metal apparently led to a strong continuity in stone tool production and use (primarily projectile points and scrapers) (Whittaker and Fratt 1984), whereas the widespread persistence of stone technology at missions in southern Texas and northeastern Mexico likely reflects the continued importance of traditional hunting and gathering practices (Hester 1989).

With the steady encroachment of European settlements following the sixteenth century, native societies remained astute observers of the political terrain and were very attuned to the various strategies implemented by different European powers. The Iroquois in particular displayed considerable adroitness in playing off continued incursions by Dutch, French, and English agents, recognizing—and taking advantage of—cycling tactics of cajolery and demands peculiar to each nationality and their objectives in the New World. Similar patterns were seen elsewhere in the age of mercantilism, but the consolidation of the United States and Canada, along with the birth of industrial capitalism, had profound ramifications for indigenous societies and their relationship to material culture.

Capitalism

The nineteenth century ushered in the birth of industrial capitalism and the explosive spread of wage labor. Several researchers have observed that documenting and explaining the growth of capitalism and its impacts should comprise a central focus for historical archaeology (Leone 1995; Orser 1996; Paynter 1988). There is little question that over the past decade or two archaeologists have made major strides in evaluating the recursive relationship between material culture and the imposition of capitalist tenets. As examples, archaeologists have addressed enclosure of the landscape and privatization (Johnson 1996), the roles of architecture and landscape in the imposition of modernist worldviews (Deetz 1977; Leone et al. 1987), and the increasing commodification of material culture (Beaudry et al. 1991; Shackel 1993).

Like mercantilism, capitalism has assumed many forms as it has penetrated indigenous societies. The fragmented nature of this process is exemplified by the United States, where East Coast economic development symbolized the manifest destiny that justified westward movement and the purging of native cultures that remained in an innate, "underdeveloped" state. This despite the fact the Indian groups in the Southeast, for example, had proven remarkably adept at adapting to the rapid economic and political changes following the Revolutionary War—a success that was perceived as sufficiently threatening to result in their removal in the 1830s. Similarly, Native Americans elsewhere typically fused variants of capitalism and traditional practices to forge remarkably resilient synergistic economies. For instance, the decline of the lumber boom in Minnesota, Wisconsin, and Michigan at the turn of the twentieth century led the Chippewa to successfully combine wage labor with traditional cooperative strategies in order to market timber products (Cleland 1993).

Hawai'i and Alaska are powerful reminders that engagement with processes of capitalism could strongly impact societies even where outright European and North American colonization was stymied by ecological, social, and other conditions. Sahlins (1990) has observed that Hawaiian elites were able to greatly enrich themselves through monopolization of local sandalwood resources that became highly desirable as Pacific trade opened up in the nineteenth century. In places like Hawai'i, European technologies entered political-economic systems that were already class-based. There, the ability of the elite to procure access to foreign goods might have coincided with strategies to force the less-privileged to continue to rely on indigenous traditions. Bayman (chaper 7) shows that Hawaiian elites monopolized control of metal tools so that lower classes continued using stone adzes well after Contact. His study is a particularly important cautionary tale for those who draw inferences about the nature and degree of contact based simply on the frequency of European items. The placement of test units solely in elite domiciles on a Hawaiian site could give a sense of strong acculturation due to the likelihood of encountering European artifacts. In contrast, units biased toward commoner houses could lead to statements about either lack of contact or the pursuit of resistance.

The lag time in the development of the Arctic allowed "mature" capitalist tactics such as the substitution of goods for wages to still be imposed on workers in the latter part of the nineteenth century (Cassell, chapter 10). In northern Alaska, the Iñupiat were seduced into whaling, and later the fur trade, in return for European and indigenous goods. North-American whalers imposed discipline parameters of Western time and space under the guise of the traditional system of whaling and debt obligations. Stone tools enter this drama once again in an exploitative sense, as scrapers for preparing hides for the fur trade, thereby reducing the risks of placing all bets on the erratic nature of whaling.

In contrast, Silliman (chapter 9) and Wagner (chapter 8) show that lithic technology could be a path of negotiation or even resistance between indigenous and capitalist economies (see also Bamforth 1993:68–69). In California's Rancho Petaluma we see that by the nineteenth century Native Americans were still being drafted into the service of Spanish-American institutions that bore a strong resemblance to the mission system. Even as laborers in a form of agrarian capitalism, however, they apparently chose to rely on stone tools for a variety of domestic tasks. As Silliman suggests, in this instance native technology appears to have been a key avenue for promoting notions of identity outside of the traditional community and within the multi-ethnic setting of the rancho. Likewise, the ground-stone pipe production Wagner documents among the early-nineteenth-century Potawatomi appears to be strongly tied to a resurgence of concern with identity. It coincided with a wave of revitalization movements in the Midwest and represents one of the last bastions of indigenous technology in the region.

It is perhaps a misconception to see capitalism as penetrating indigenous societies, because this view connotes two entities with essential characteristics clashing with one another. In reality, capitalism is a dynamic process defined by its mutability. The empire-building and move toward political and economic dominance by Western nation-states in the nineteenth century were met with a range of indigenous strategies to circumvent wage labor and related practices, leading to a capitalist pastiche rather than a monolithic enterprise. Since archaeologists can place indigenous technologies in the social contexts that trace out the historical unfolding of the late colonial project, they occupy a particularly strong vantage point for comprehending this process.

ROCKS AS RELATIONS

The various uses of stone objects in Contact situations speak to more than just the articulation of indigenous societies with the evolving world economy and the expansion of modernism. The studies in this volume also demonstrate how items rendered in stone were part of the social world conceived as material culture. In various ways, stone implements contributed to the continuity of shifting practices and worldviews that comprised Contact situations. For that reason, lithic studies must transcend form and raw material if they are to make substantive contributions to the body of Contact-period research (or that of any period, for that matter). This is not to say that residues, edge angles, polishes, and so forth are unimportant. But these attributes are points of departure for moving lithic studies more toward the center of anthropological understandings of technology rather than constituting simple reflections of design and use. If we look at stone tools solely in a behavioral way, then they become mere fetishes. We must also consider the underlying relationships that they help to reproduce.

By the 1800s, for example, smoking had become widespread outside of Native American groups, and it seems to have become more secularized within native societies, as well (e.g., Nassaney and Volmar, chapter 6). Both Indian men and women smoked, and quite often Euro-American kaolin pipes were used as this behavior became increasingly commodified. Nevertheless, there were important instances when indigneous smoking vessels continued to be used in ritual contexts, as exemplified by the Potawatomi and nearby groups such as the Fox and Sauk (Wagner, chapter 8) and by groups in the Northeast (Nassaney and Volmar, chapter 6).

So, while the superficial fact that pipes were used for smoking might be true, it only tells part of the story. Although tobacco use became less confined to specific interest groups, some control was still exerted over its ceremonial use through the context and means of smoking. Tobacco has enjoyed a remarkable persistence in ceremonial life throughout the Americas—which still continues—and in many cases the pipe was a central component to ritual, almost as necessary as the tobacco itself (Rafferty 2001). Ritual is removed from time and society (Bloch 1989:80; Bourdieu 1977:163); ritualized practices such as the smoking of tobacco constitute a part of the naturalized order that, in the Contact era, served as a haven from the penetration of Euro-American ways and beliefs. Similarly, ritual objects like pipes became important metaphors for tradition and identity. Nassaney and Volmar (chapter 6) observe that stone ritual objects could even take on gendered connotations (pipe=male; pestle=female). As Nassaney and Volmar demonstrate, stone objects not only constituted strategies for maintaining identity against European encroachment, but they also mediated tensions between indigenous interest groups as traditional roles underwent dramatic changes.

Cassell's (chapter 10) whaling station study presents a mix of indigenous, mercantile, and capitalist practices in which our standard typologies and concepts fail us. The Iñupiat might have used stone scrapers for centuries, yet when the tool became central to the fur trade it was transformed (socially) into part of the technology of exploitation—but not in a direct way since the Iñupiat had unfettered access both to the means of making the tools and to the natural resources upon which the tools were used. Thus the scrapers could not be construed simply as capital. Yet the Iñupiat were living in a community structured according to Western economic needs and were bartering their labor, if not selling it. Further, the manipulation of the traditional economic order by American whalers placed a native worker in a network of social and economic obligations from which one did not easily walk away. In this instance, stone scrapers could perhaps be viewed as a form of *subsumed capital* in that they contributed to the transferal of surplus labor in the absence of both surplus value based on wages and restricted access to the means of production. The term "subsumed class" (taken from Resnick and Wolff [1987]) was introduced to the archaeological literature by Saitta (1994), and describes an interest group that distributes surplus labor or product that has already been appropriated by a different group. Saitta argues that subsumed classes in small-scale societies are not exploitative in the traditional sense because they do not directly extract surplus from others. I use the term "subsumed capital" here to convey the notion of technology dedicated to the appropriation of surplus in small-scale societies in the absence of wages—but potentially involving some degree of exploitation and power inequality, even if subtle.

As the studies in this book emphasize, lithic technology involves more than just a way of doing things with stone. It also is a tangible way of acting out culture. During the Contact era, objects in stone had functional uses, but they were further used to manipulate, to signify, to resist, and to negotiate. If we view pipes as only vessels for smoking or scrapers as merely involved in hide preparation we only scratch the surface of the various relationships they might have mediated in the past.

CONCLUSION

Any study dealing with the Contact period must recognize the two-way nature of interactions. Clearly, societies in both European states and emerging colonies were profoundly transformed by their mutual interactions. In addition to fueling the growth of the glass bead industry in Europe, indigenous consumer demand for cloth in Africa and the Americas strongly spurred textile industries in England and elsewhere. The tremendous impact of precious metals from the New World on the European political economy is well-known. At a smaller scale, everything from European language to fashion was altered by the give-and-take of everyday life on the frontier of far-flung colonies. Lithic technology probably did not play a major role in this larger picture, but that might be the viewpoint of "big man" history rather than that of anthropology. The production, trade, and consumption of stone objects did have significant implications for the quotidian dimension of cultures in contact—which is where anthropology has made a major contribution to the study of the birth of the modern era.

The historical complexity of European expansion around the globe stymies any blanket generalizations about the replacement or persistence of native technologies. When we consider the case studies in this volume, social contexts of lithic use varied widely because local histories comingled with regional trends that were tied into a global competition for influence, wealth, and power. Stone tool technology played a role in both directions of change.

The order of the contributions to this volume reflects the diverse, time-transgressive nature of the Contact era. I have tried to seriate them based upon relative degree of interaction between indigenous and European or Euro-American societies. While this perhaps reflects the influence of older, acculturation models, there is little question that protracted interaction will have quite different consequences than brief brushes between groups. Nevertheless, I recognize that a brief brush in the sixteenth century was very likely to leave very different cultural, political, and economic imprints than a brief brush during the eighteenth century. That being said, the first two studies in the volume (Cobb and Ruggiero, chapter 2; Odell, chapter 3) represent instances of short or intermittent contact in the Southeast and Plains, respectively. The next four papers (Johnson, chapter 4; Carmody, chapter 5; Nassaney and Volmar, chapter 6; Bayman, chapter 7) examine societies in North America and Hawai'i with ongoing, though not necessarily consistent, interactions with European or Euro-American groups. The final three cases are set in the nineteenth-century Midwest (Wagner, chapter 8), California (Silliman, chapter 9), and the Arctic (Cassell, chapter 10), as industrial capitalism began to take shape. While the social contexts and labor relations surrounding lithic technology varied for all of the situations in this collection, together they demonstrate that the importance of "mundane" items in enculturation and social reproduction cannot be overemphasized (Hodder 1986:71–72; Keesing 1987).

2

Lithic Technology and the Spanish Entrada at the King Site in Northwest Georgia

Charles R. Cobb and Dino A. Ruggiero

The de Soto expedition (1539 to 1542) marked the first major, organized Spanish incursion into the interior Southeast of the present-day United States. Although it stands as a watershed event in the Contact era, smaller European forays had touched down numerous times along coastal areas prior to de Soto. From his landing onward, however, European material culture became increasingly available to Native Americans of the Southeast as processes of exploration and colonization accelerated. Most of the interaction early on was with the Spanish, although the French made an ill-fated attempt to colonize eastern Florida at Fort Caroline in 1562. It took well over a century after de Soto before the French and English began their successful penetration into the Southeast.

Indigenous societies encountered by the Spanish in northern Georgia are recognized by archaeologists as part of the Lamar Culture that also covered portions of Alabama, Tennessee, South Carolina, and Florida (Hally and Rudolph 1986; Williams and Shapiro 1990). From a typological viewpoint, Lamar constitutes a late (A.D. mid–1300s onward) Mississippian regional expression. In other words, Lamar groups were dependent upon corn-beans-squash agriculture, were often—though not always—organized into chiefdoms, and participated in long-distance exchange networks for the acquisition of ceremonial objects that display widely shared iconographies. Old World diseases would rapidly deplete these groups in the latter sixteenth and seventeenth centuries, but until that time the Spanish found themselves dealing with hierarchical polities sustaining relatively significant population levels.

The King site in northwest Georgia is one of the most thoroughly documented village-sized Lamar occupations. It dates to the mid–sixteenth century and might have been the settlement of Piachi in the Coosa chiefdom. There is some question as to whether de Soto himself actually passed through the King site. In any event, European goods from the settlement are very limited in number and restricted to mortuary contexts.

In the Southeast, the King site sits at the chronological threshold of the Contact period. For this reason, it represents a valuable case for examining initial changes in material culture resulting from the influx of European objects. Our study of the lithic assemblage from the site incorporates both household and mortuary contexts. It demonstrates that early access to European goods, primarily tools that had functional equivalents in stone, were found only with burials and had negligible impact on lithic technologies. Interestingly, though, European objects were restricted to so-called flintknapper burials, indicating some form of privileged access for those individuals.

THE COOSA POLITY

The King site is located on the Coosa River in northwest Georgia (Figure 2.1). Although the attribution of the King site to the town of Piachi may be problematic, there is little doubt that this occupation falls well within the confines of the polity the Spaniards referred to as Coosa. Marvin Smith (2000) points out that the term "Coosa" has three referents: a large alliance of chiefdoms as described here; the core chiefdom of Coosa within this confederation; and the paramount town in the chiefdom.

Archaeological and ethnohistorical research indicates that at its fullest extent Coosa represented a paramount chiefdom encompassing smaller polities extending from eastern Tennessee into central Alabama (Hudson et al. 1985; M. Smith 2000). Three major Spanish excursions came into contact with Coosa: 1) Hernando de Soto's expedition in 1540; 2) a detachment from Tristán de Luna's effort to colonize the Gulf Coast in 1560; and 3) Juan Pardo's extended expedition of 1567–1568. None of these visits was intended as an effort to colonize the Coosa area, and their most dramatic effect cumulatively was likely the decimation of Native Americans by European-borne diseases. The de Luna group, which included veterans of de Soto's journey, found towns much more reduced and impoverished than their memory allowed (Swanton 1922:231), perhaps reflecting the spread of pathogens from both de Soto's expedition twenty years earlier and from intermittent Spanish contact with coastal groups.

After Pardo's exploration, the Spaniards ended their efforts at systematic exploration of the interior Southeast. It is not until the late seventeenth and eighteenth centuries that the documentary record picks up again in any great detail, with the Creek, Cherokee, and other well-known historical groups. By that time Coosa had ceased to exist as a formal polity and many of the towns described by the Spanish (including the King site) had been abandoned. Given this history, we can anticipate that residents of the King site became well acquainted

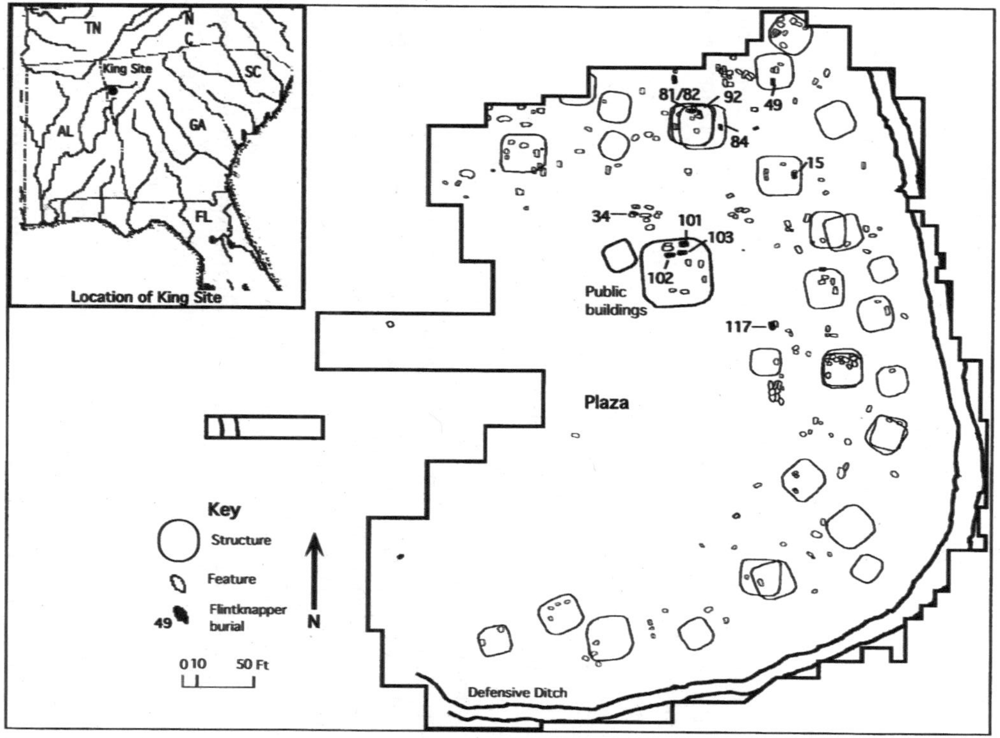

Figure 2.1. Eastern portion of the King site, showing location of the flintknapper burials. Inset shows geographic location of the King site

with the Spanish, either first-hand or by reputation, but they were never subject to the processes of colonization or missionization that evolved in other areas of Spanish Florida. Nevertheless, goods of European manufacture occur commonly on sixteenth-century sites in the interior, and they appear to have been readily adopted into the utilitarian and symbolic realms of groups constituting the Lamar Culture.

A question has arisen over the nature of possible wounds on skeletons recovered from the King site and whether they were a result of the de Soto passage (cf. Blakely and Mathews 1990; Milner et al. 2000). The resolution of this question may shed some light on which town described in the de Soto chronicles may actually be represented by the King site. This issue holds less importance with regard to the European artifacts that occur in the site assemblage, because the Spanish made repeated visits to the Coosa chiefdom in the sixteenth century. Thus there were a number of opportunities for European material culture to wind up in a local town (including the possible trade of European objects from coastal areas).

ORGANIZATION OF THE KING SITE

The King site was excavated in its entirety (except for that lost to riverbank erosion) in two major phases in the 1970s and 1990s (Hally 1988, 1993). The eastern portion of the site was the best preserved (Figure 2.1). Based on this work Hally (1988) suggests that the King site consisted of about 45 to 50 single-post structures lining the interior of a substantial stockade. An outlying defensive ditch surrounded three sides of the site, and the Coosa River formed a northern boundary. A central plaza contained two (presumed) public buildings, the larger of which contained several burials. The overall size of the site is estimated at 2.3 ha. The site appears to have been differentiated into public and private spheres (Hally 1988; Seckinger 1972), with the public sphere incorporating the large, central plaza and the private sphere defined by the zone of domestic structures and space lining the interior wall of the palisade.

LITHIC ASSEMBLAGES

The more fine-grained excavations at the King site occurred within the structures and in mortuary contexts. These particular associations thus provide the best resolution on the organization of lithic technology during the town's occupation. We discuss the lithics associated with one of the domestic structures (from Ruggiero 2000) and with the mortuary assemblages (from Cobb and Pope 1998).

Household Context

Two possible types of domestic structures, winter and summer houses, have been identified at the King site (Hally 1988). Winter houses were semi-subterranean, square or rectangular features. These were fairly substantial wattle-and-daub buildings, with four major interior support posts around a central hearth. Structure sizes range between 6 and 10 m^2. Most of these were rebuilt at least once. Summer houses are reflected by rectangular clusters of posts, representing single-post walls that might have been open in a ramada style. They ranged in size from 3 m × 1.5 m to 7 m × 4 m.

The domestic lithic assemblage in our study is associated with Structure 8, presumed to be one of the winter houses (Figure 2.2). The building measured about 10 m × 10 m. An entryway is represented by a wall-trench passage in the southwest corner. Like the overall site plan, interiors of the houses apparently were segregated into public and private spaces (Hally 1988; Pohlemus 1990). Public space in the central area around the hearth consisted of food processing, food consumption, and various manufacturing activities. The private area along the interior walls was used for storage and held the sleeping benches.

Lithic artifacts and debitage were found throughout the floor of the structure. The most common formal tools were complete and broken triangular projectile points. Other tools (sorted by morphology) included scrapers, gravers, and a drill (Table 2.1). From a total of 96 unifacial and bifacial tools recovered from the floor, a sample of 77 was examined for patterns of edge damage (Hundertfund 1996). As Odell (chapter 3) observes, functional analyses of protohistoric lithic assemblages are scarce and have much to offer in terms of assessing patterns of site and intrasite tool use, as we found in our study (see also Carmody, chapter 5). The King site low-magnification analysis was conducted with a stereoscope at 30× magnification, and edge damage was assessed using criteria developed by several researchers (Ahler 1971; Lawrence 1979; Odell and Odell-Vereecken 1980; Tringham et al. 1974). Of the 77 tools analyzed, 86 percent (*N*=66, excluding utilized cores) showed evidence for use-wear related edge damage (e.g., Figures 2.3–2.5). The use-wear was indicative of boring, chopping, cutting, projectile use, scraping, slicing, and wedging (Table 2.1). Multiple uses were recorded for some tools. Because no European tools were recovered from domestic contexts, we can surmise that the range of functional activities presumably carried out with stone tools are reasonably well represented in this sample.

A total of 1,713 waste flakes was recovered from the floor of the structure. Most of the raw material was Fort Payne chert (*N*=1405, 82.0 percent), locally available as small river cobbles and pebbles. Retouch or edge-damage was evident

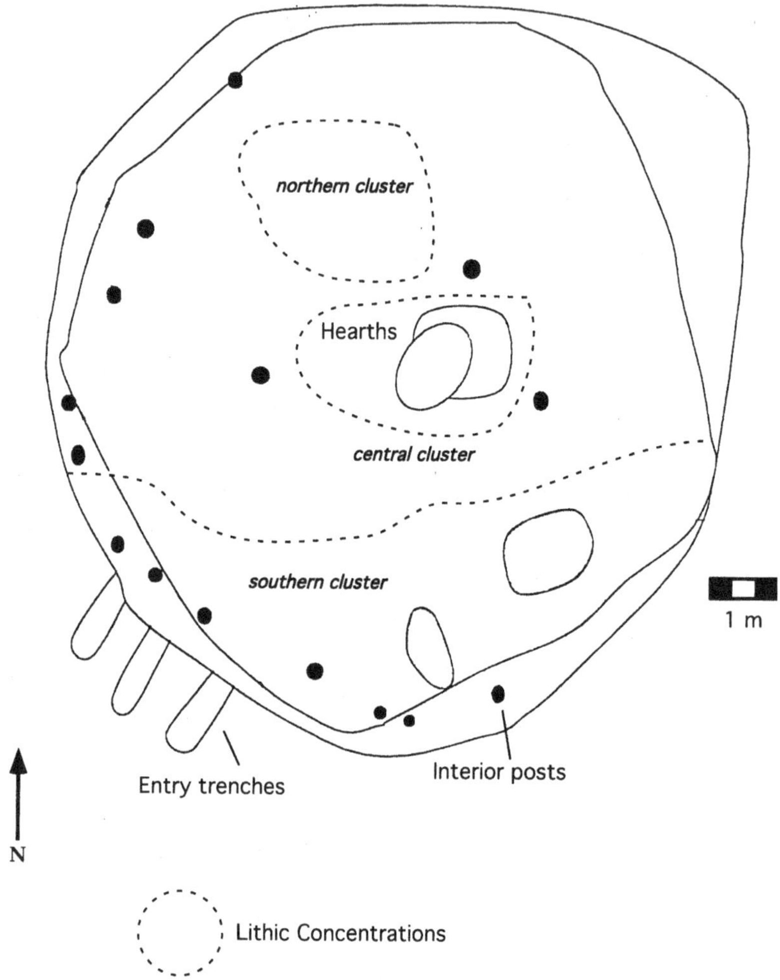

Fig. 2.2. Structure 8 on the King site

on 7.9 percent of the debitage (*N*=135), indicating that flake tools were an important complement to unifacial and bifacial ones (although post-depositional damage might have inflated this number). A large proportion of the flake assemblage (*N*=1116, 65.1 percent) consisted of complete flakes (Table 2.2), which might suggest that soft hammer percussion was widely practiced (e.g., see Mauldin and Amick 1989; Tomka 1989). Both bifacial and expedient technologies were carried out in the house, as reflected in flake attributes: 65.4 percent of the flakes with at least partial platforms (*N*=1344) displayed the acute-angle platform often (although not universally) associated with bifacial thinning flakes

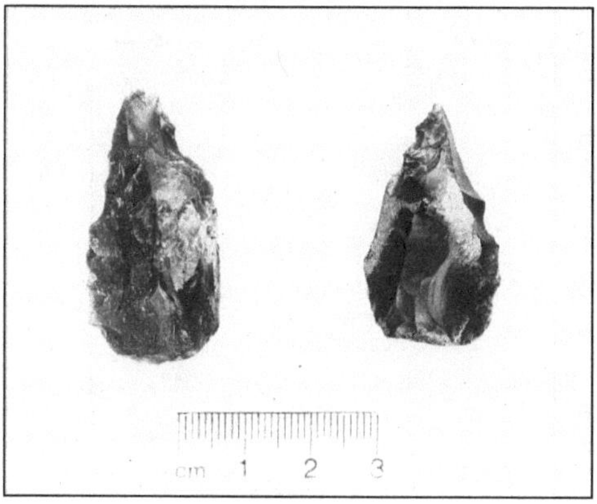

Fig. 2.3. Preform-gravers from the King site

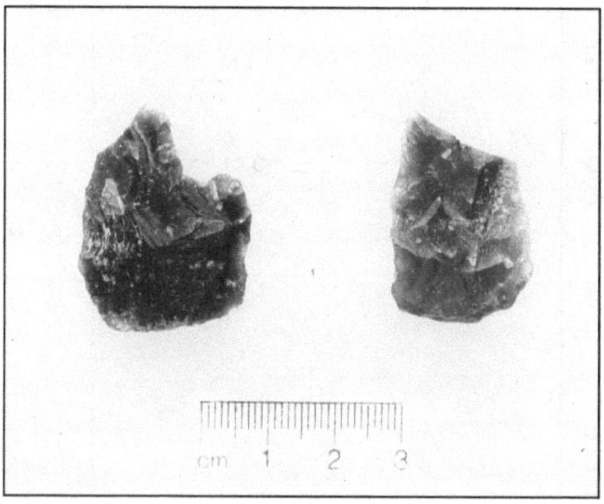

Fig. 2.4. Scrapers from the King site

Fig. 2.5. Triangular projectile points from the King site

Table 2.1 King Site Tool Types by Morphology and Function

Function	Triangular Point I[1]	Triangular Point II[2]	Point Frag.	Bipointed Biface	Dallas Point	Biface Frag.	Drill	Biface Preform	Point Preform	Scraper	Graver	Total
Boring							1					1
Chopping			1					1				2
Chop./Scraping		1				1				1		3
Cutting	3	3	5			7		2		1	2	23
Cut./Projectile						1						1
Cut./Scraping	1		1			1						3
Cut./Slicing			1									1
Projectile	1	1				4						6
Scraping	2	2	3		1	2		1		5		16
Scrap./Slicing						1						1
Slicing	2			1		1		1	1			6
Wedging	1											1
Total Analyzed	10	7	11	1	1	18	1	5	1	7	2	64
Structure Total	14	8	15	1	1	36	1	9	2	7	2	96

[1]Straight to incurvate sides.

[2]Straight to excurvate sides, more finely made

Table 2.2 Selected Debitage Characteristics

Condition of Flake	N	%	Platform Attribute	N	%	Platform Facets	N	%
Complete	1116	65.1	Crushed	170	12.7	Cortex	276	20.4
Broken	236	13.8	Right angle	295	21.9	One	922	68.3
Fragment	313	18.3	Acute angle	879	65.4	Two	150	11.1
Debris	48	2.8				Three	1	0.1
						Four+	2	0.1
Total	1713			1344			1351	

and over 11 percent of the flakes (*N*=153) with complete platforms were multifaceted; whereas 12.7 percent of the flakes (*N*=170) had the crushed platforms often associated with bipolar detachment.

The flakes with platforms displaying acute angles and multiple facets are indicative of late-stage tool manufacture, but early-stage debris is strongly represented: 20.4 percent of the platform-bearing flakes have cortex on the platform, a particularly common trait for traditions where tools are manufactured from pebbles. Further, the low platform facet counts (Table 2.2) also indicate a strong emphasis on core reduction. Such flakes could be associated with either early-stage biface reduction or the expedient removal of flakes from amorphous cores.

The tools and debitage occurred in three distinct spatial clusters on the floor of Structure 8. Technological analyses of the debitage, as well as typological and low-magnification functional studies of the tools, demonstrate that the clusters were associated with relatively discrete activities (Ruggiero 2000).

Lithic materials from the public, central hearth area were relatively sparse compared to the other clusters, consisting of six bifaces (broken and intact) and one flake. This location probably was a high-use area that was cleaned on a regular basis. The functional analysis of the bifaces indicates that they were used for cutting and slicing.

A second cluster of twelve tools and flakes was restricted to a northern segment of private space. Tools in this area were used for cutting, scraping, and slicing. The prevalence of high-quality raw materials, particularly fine-grained specimens from Fort Payne chert indicate that this zone might have had some special significance beyond typical domestic activities. Further, the area was unusual in that only intact lithic tools were found, compared to the broken and partial tools elsewhere on the floor.

The third and largest lithic cluster, in the southern and southeastern (private) perimeter of the house, seems to have been used for a number of domestic tasks and might also represent the storage of stone tools and flakes intended for potential tools. This area is distinguished by two nearby deposits of tools and debris, representing well over 90 percent of the lithic artifacts recovered from the structure. Most of the formal tools show evidence of use, and there is a substantial quantity of expedient flake tools (8 percent of the debitage in the two deposits). The content and location of the lithics in the two concentrations is suggestive of the purposeful caching of materials near one wall of the house, perhaps under a bench. The two accumulations also have very discrete boundaries, suggesting that they are secondary rather than primary deposits (see Behm 1983). At the same time, an analysis of a sample of standardized flotation units from the house floor (six from the north half of the house; nine from the south) revealed a higher average density of micro-debitage (24 g/sample) from the southern samples than in the northern ones (17 g/sample). Since small flakes have a high likelihood of being deposited and remaining near a production locus (Kvamme 1997), stone tool production and maintenance might have complemented the caching of tools in the southern portion of the structure.

The general lithic technologies represented in the winter structure are very similar to those documented for Mississippian sites elsewhere in the Southeast, as well as Lamar sites (e.g., Hally 1970; Koldehoff 1987; Teltser 1991). An expedient technology was commonly used, as manifested in the recovery of bipolar and amorphous cores, in addition to the flakes with crushed platforms. Bifacial technology focused to a large degree on the production of triangular points and the occasional manufacture of finely crafted bi-pointed bifaces. That no European artifacts have been recovered from domestic contexts (Smith 1975:63) and that lithic technology appears to have been little affected—if at all—by early encounters with Europeans is important. We see the first impacts of the encounter between two worlds in the mortuary assemblages.

Mortuary Contexts

Over 250 burials were excavated at the King site. The mortuary artifact assemblage was relatively rich and diverse, pointing to several axes of social differentiation not easily subsumed under a vertical model of social ranking (Cobb and Pope 1998). Burials occurred in the public buildings in the plaza. The private zone also contained burials, typically (though not always) within the floors of structures. Structure 8, for example, had two burials in the northern half of the floor.

Although interment in public space might have conferred some degree of status (Seckinger 1972), public burials did not always contain the most abundant mortuary artifacts. The two richest burials on the site in terms of artifact abundance and diversity are both found in domestic contexts. Goods found with those burials included a shell mask, shell gorgets, copper objects, and similar items that are often taken as symbols of rank in Mississippian studies. The fact that the two burials accorded the highest rank based on artifact wealth were placed in private space does not deny the potential importance attributed to interment in public space. Rather, it merely emphasizes that individuals holding elevated positions might have received varying treatments in spatial location and burial accoutrements based on the very different roles they held in society—roles not always easily compared along an axis of rank.

Particularly noteworthy for our purposes is the fact that ten of the burials appear to represent flintknappers (see Figure 2.1 for the location of flintknapper burials on the King site). They were identified as such by their association with tight clusters of artifacts—probably originally in bags—that appear to represent flintknapping kits. Although the kits varied somewhat in content, at the least they held a number of hammerstones and accumulations of debitage and/or stone tools. The flaked-stone tools were similar to those found in the structure: triangular projectile points, unifacial scrapers, and the like. Whether the handfuls of debitage reflect the full array of lithic reduction activities found elsewhere on the site is questionable, but they do contain the amorphous and bifacial cores typical of both expedient and more formal lithic technologies also found on the house floor.

Other common objects in the kits included—but were not limited to—beaver incisors, small celts, and sandstone abraders. Many of these items are not necessarily related to stoneworking and suggest that the individuals crafted other raw materials as well. Beaver incisors, for instance, could have been used to groove arrow shafts for fletching, and the celts presumably were somehow related to woodworking. Furthermore, the flintknapper burials had funerary items aside from the tool-working kits. On one end of the spectrum, these included only a few common objects such as projectile points or clay pipes. At the other end, one of the richest burials on the site (Burial no. 92) was represented by a flintknapper interred with two iron celts and an iron spike, two copper plates, red ochre, a number of shell beads, and 31 projectile points (Garrett 1988:40).

The number of European objects securely associated with documented mortuary contexts at the King site is quite small—only eight (Hally 1988). One sword was found by pot hunters in a burial, but little is known of its precise context. The other eight items of known provenience are limited to one iron spike or rod, three celts, one wedge or tapered celt, what appear to be two (badly corroded) knives that were interred in an unmodified condition, and one fragment of a possible spike (Smith 1975). What is particularly intriguing is that the eight European items are distributed among five burials, and three of those burials, containing six of the iron objects, are flintknappers (Table 2.3).

Why would flintknappers want European iron goods at the King site, and why, compared to other segments of society, would they have been in a favorable position to obtain them? That the iron artifacts appear to have been the types of objects that could easily have been accommodated with the indigenous

Table 2.3 Flintknapper Burials and Iron Implements

Burial	Age[1]	Sex[1]	Burial Space	Iron Tools[2]	European Tool Descriptions[2]
15	Unknown	Unknown	domestic	1	celt
34	50-60	Male	public		
49	45-50	Male	domestic		
81/82	60-70	Male/Female	domestic		
84	40-50	Male	domestic		
92	45-50	Male	domestic	3	2 celts, 1 spike
101	50-60	Male	public		
102	50-60	Male	public		
103	50-60	Male	public		
117	28-30	Indeterminate	margin	2	1 celt, 1 spike

[1]From appendix, Blakely (1988).
[2]From Smith (1975).

worldview and lifestyle, particularly that of a flintknapper and craftsman is noteworthy. Stone celts were already interred with many of these individuals, and, except for raw material, the European ones are very similar. The iron spikes are more problematic, but they conceivably would have been useful for a number of familiar applications, such as pressure flaking.

It is doubtful whether special access to European items was strongly linked to flintknapping abilities alone. As noted, several of the individuals who were flintknappers also appeared to hold some special status, given the abundance and variety of associated mortuary goods. But not all flintknappers were so richly appointed, and it would be difficult to argue that high status was somehow founded on flintknapping prowess. The flintknapper burials that do have metal objects are found in both domestic and public space (Table 2.3), and these include both rich and relatively impoverished burial assemblages. More likely, artisanship might have been one variable among many contributing to a person's position in society. A few of these favored individuals presumably were able to leverage their influence to gain first access to the unusual items carried by the foreign visitors. By and large, the King site flintknapper burials fit the general profile of those described elsewhere in North America (Seeman 1984): they tend to be adult males and their "kits" include a range of finished products and tools that are not restricted to the working of flaked stone.

IRON AND FLINTKNAPPERS

At this time it is difficult to say how extensive or prolonged the contacts were between Europeans and King site residents. Although the small number of

European objects may point to limited exchange, many studies have now shown that it is dangerous to use the number of European goods as a proxy for degree of contact or acculturation (e.g., Lightfoot 1995; Loren 1999). Nevertheless, changes in stone tool technology appear to have been slight, if at all, emphasizing the very limited impact of European influence in the community.

How does the King site assemblage of European artifacts compare with contemporary sites in eastern North America? An examination of contemporary Iroquois sites sheds some light on the potential significance of iron. Bradley (1987) has documented that protohistoric Onondaga Iroquois sites (A.D. mid–1500s) in New York reflect a preference for glass beads, iron, and especially copper alloy, which occurs the earliest and is the more abundant of these three materials. Further, the metal items, such as copper kettles, typically were broken down into fragments and recycled into more familiar objects. It took several decades at least before Iroquois groups began to replace indigenous utilitarian objects with those of European manufacture on a significant scale. Iron artifacts are less common than copper ones among the Onondaga sites, and in early protohistoric contexts are so reworked that it is often difficult to discern the original, European form of the tool. This pattern is quite distinctive from intact iron tools interred at the King site.

Contrasts between the King site and Onondaga villages with regard to the degree of modification of iron tools emphasize the importance of exploring differences in indigenous receptions to European material culture. Such variation might have been rooted in divergent cultural views of (and/or nature of interaction with) Europeans. Copper stands as another interesting case in point. This metal was widely valued throughout the Eastern Woodlands for a number of millennia, probably for reasons related to color and its source. There is widespread documentation of the importance of the color red to Native-American groups in the South and elsewhere (e.g., Dye 1995; Hudson 1976; Knight 1986; Swanton 1928). Assuming that copper was maintained in its reddish state when worked into objects such as plates, tinklers, and so forth, this could explain its desirability. Likewise, the distant origin of copper might have contributed to its value, imbuing it with a mysterious and powerful quality (*sensu* Helms 1988). European copper alloys were widely worked into projectile points, tinkler cones, and the like, but there is considerable variation across the Eastern Woodlands that may be tied to group ethnicity or other aspects of identity (e.g., Bradley and Childs 1991; Waselkov 1989).

That metals on Iroquoian sites turn up in domestic contexts as opposed to the funerary contexts for the King site is also noteworthy. It is difficult to say, however, if this difference is purely a function of access and the subsequent "deglamorization" of European goods. The Oneida Cameron site, which dates to the 1500s (or early–1600s at the latest), has a relative abundance of metal items and glass beads in midden contexts—despite the fact that it was deep in the interior of New York and quite likely had no direct contact with Europeans (Carmody, chapter 5).

Considerations of the selection and context of European raw materials may shed new light on the King site flintknappers. Although the iron tools potentially had functional applications in native technology, it should not be overlooked that their color—black—also might have been of considerable significance in the same way that copper was linked to red. George Hamell (1983) argues that northern Iroquois groups viewed metal as a generic substance and differentiated materials largely on the basis of color. Among the Cherokee, black was associated with the moon, souls of the dead, and death (Hudson 1976: 132). For some Southern groups, the color black played a prominent role in warfare and ballgame symbolism, both traditional provinces of men.

The restriction of European objects to those made only of iron suggests a process of selection based on both symbolic and practical value. Indeed, to some degree the King site stands out even in the Southeast for its narrow range of acquisitions from Spaniards. Within the "core" of the Coosa province around the King site a much wider variety of European goods has been recovered from contemporary sites, including glass beads, Clarksdale bells, and fragments of weapons such as swords and crossbow tips (Langford and Smith 1990). Elsewhere, sixteenth-century settlements in the Choctawhatchee Bay area of northwest Florida were bypassed by the major Spanish expeditions, but the sites have yielded "glass beads and finger rings, objects of iron, brass and copper bells, and a single copper coin" (Scarry 1990:94–95). A coastal location possibly contributed to a greater flow of European goods at the Florida sites, but even sixteenth-century sites in Arkansas have yielded more diversity and abundance of such items than the King site (Morse and Morse 1990), and these would have been dispersed by a de Soto expedition that had lost much of its matériel after the Mabila debacle in Alabama.

Even given the small sample taken from the King site, the thorough excavation of the site indicates that the absence of non-iron materials does not appear to be accidental. Further, if we accept that King site residents were actively incorporating and rejecting elements of European culture, then the flintknappers with iron artifacts appear to have been involved in that decision-making process. To speculate somewhat, we would suggest that individuals were interred with those European objects that were more readily equated with a facet of the deceased person's identity—and this was the role of male flintknapper. That would explain in part the objects that happened to be selected and why they were not recycled. The association of the novel iron tools with a foreign and obviously powerful group, combined with the color, might also have served to endow the somewhat familiar shapes with an exotic and powerful essence.

Acquisition of the iron tools might not have been so straightforward, however.

If we accept the proposition that a massacre at the hands of Spaniards did not occur at the King site (Milner et al. 2000), it is quite possible that Europeans never directly visited the community in the 1500s (as Smith [1975:66] has suggested). Thus the tools might have come into the hands of King site residents through some form of exchange. According to the prestige-goods model that is often applied to Mississippian societies (Brown et al. 1990; Cobb 1989; Welch 1991), the exotic items might have been directly bestowed to the flintknappers from elites at the paramount town of Coosa, or another high-rank community. The paramount chiefdom of Coosa incorporated seven archaeological site clusters (consisting of five to thirteen sites within 20–30 km of one another), each with a mound site that likely represented an administrative center (Hally 1994:246). The King site was a lesser community in this hierarchy, and, barring direct contact with the Spanish, might have had its access to European objects filtered through the workings of the prestige-goods economy.

Whichever model is closer to the truth, it is apparent that the association of flintknapper burials with iron objects represents part of a larger, longstanding pattern of exchange and social obligations. Like stone tool technology, this social network was subject to limited European impact at the mid–1500s; whatever social or geographic mechanisms served to hinder the flow of European goods into the King site, as compared to contemporary sites elsewhere, these same mechanisms likely promoted the insularity and stability of indigenous technologies such as stone working. Bayman's (chapter 7) description of Hawaiian elites monopolizing trade with Europeans perhaps is a good analogy for the manner in which Mississippian chiefs in Spanish Florida, their power as yet undiminished by the Spaniards, might have directed the flow of trade in the new wealth of objects. All this would quickly change as the sixteenth century drew to a close.

CONCLUSION

The restricted number and range of European items at the King site when compared to nearby, contemporary settlements, may indicate that, outside of direct European contact, towns in the Coosa polity might have received such goods chiefly via distributive networks. Perhaps stone tool manufacture and other technologies at the King site appear little changed with the first blush of European contact because interaction with the newcomers and their materials were possibly limited by social mechanisms. Given the short duration of occupation, the King site lithic assemblage presents a relatively clear-cut case of late Mississippian, largely expedient, stone-working technology before it was strongly impacted by Europeans. Although it would not be judicious to extrapolate lithic practices from this single site to protohistoric occupations throughout the Southeast, it does perhaps serve as a useful baseline to begin comparative explorations of European influences on technology (as Odell, chapter 3, argues for the Wichita).

What influence there was appears to have been felt most by individuals recognized as flintknappers. The condition and context of the interred iron tools suggest that the social roles interlaced with flintknapping might have led to the acquisition and reworking of European objects that were peculiar to Lamar culture, or even the King site itself. This reinforces the notion that the links between social roles, lithic technology, and European material culture must be framed in terms of cultural appropriation by specific groups rather than universal statements about processes of culture contact.

ACKNOWLEDGMENTS

We would like to thank David Hally and the Department of Anthropology at the University of Georgia for generously making the King site collections available for analysis.

3
Wichita Tools on First Contact with the French

George H. Odell

ACCULTURATION

The clash of worldviews that results from contact between widely divergent cultural groups has served for years as grist for the mills of history and anthropology. The desire to generalize the results of this experience has stimulated the production of models that seek to explain the phenomenon or at least to describe it. The best known of these is Wallerstein's (1974, 1980) "World System" model, which is centered on the capitalist economy that was evolving in the fifteenth and sixteenth centuries and which situated participating groups into a core-periphery structure. This and other acculturation models have been critiqued extensively (see Rice 1998:45–46), and my purpose here is not to discuss this literature; for a recent comprehensive review, see Cusick (1998a). Rather, I will select common themes that are useful in interpreting the contact situation between Native Americans and invading Europeans, especially the French.

Many of the models that have been proposed are Euro-centric in structure (Cusick 1998a:135) and commonly envision American Indians as passive reactors to dominant European invaders (Grumet 1995:22; Rogers 1990:10; Smith 1987:113–114). Recent revisions of these ideas have stressed the proactive nature of Native-American responses. That is, cultural groups that retained some degree of integrity following the onslaught of disease and dislocation were not merely passive receptors of stimuli provided by militarily and technologically dominant forces but full participants in interactions with outsiders, whether they were coming from another tribe or another continent (Cobb, chapter 1; Foster 1960; Wagner 1998:432–434).

Examples of the autonomous nature of native populations have proliferated in the past few years. For instance, in Chiapas, Mexico, Gasco (1993:175) has documented "Spanish-Indian interaction observed in colonial Sonusco, in which natives maintained control of production of a valuable export commodity and in which the primary form of economic interaction was trade." Further north, archaeological research into the interaction between Euro-Americans and the Potawatomi of the Great Lakes shows that it was less one-sided than originally believed. Despite concerted attempts to acculturate the tribe through missions and other means, the Potawatomi retained traditional values, made minimal use of Euro-American goods except those specifically associated with the fur trade, and consistently refused inferior goods (Wagner 1998). And in the Great Plains, a detailed study of the Arikara documented their largely successful efforts to control their own destiny in the face of rapid Euro-American expansion (Rogers 1990).

The success of tribal units in retaining their autonomy depended upon several factors. Crucial, of course, were the effects of outside influences such as diseases (Hill 1998:153–154; Ramenofsky 1987; Smith 1987:chapter 4) and territorial pressure from invading forces of Europeans or displaced Indian migrants (Smith 1987:21–22, 131–139). But equally important was a society's internal cohesion, which could be fostered, as in the Arikara case, by an elaborate system of social obligations and ritual governing all aspects of social life (Rogers 1990:214–216, 1993:78). This element was also crucial for the Potawatomi, who retained the manufacture of stone smoking pipes longer than any other traditional technology because these items facilitated most of their other important social, religious, and political activities (see Wagner, chapter 8). Given the broad variability of Native responses to outside influences, it has become clear that the mere availability or technical superiority of European goods does not explain the depth of acculturation of these influences or the manner in which they were integrated (Bamforth 1993; Rogers 1993).

Thus acculturation depended on a complex intermingling of external and internal factors that may be difficult to predict in any individual case. The effect of these factors on the material objects that people used are equally difficult to hypothesize for any individual culture. Stone tools were eventually replaced by metal in most of the world's societies, but little has been written about the process of replacement. The baseline for interpreting acculturation and the effects of cultural contact are the conditions that prevailed at the time the first contact was made (see Cobb, chapter 1). This paper attempts to establish that baseline for the lithic technology of one cultural group on the eastern Plains of North America. From this database, future research may be able to provide more information on the nature and trajectory of the acculturative process.

CULTURE CONTACT ON THE SOUTHERN PLAINS

Much is known about Arikara acculturation on the Northern Plains because of the accumulation of a large database of excavated earth lodges and the syntheses of Daniel Rogers (1990, 1993), who has pulled disparate strands of evidence into an interpretable body of information. Most other tribal entities have not benefited from this level of attention, though information on the contact situation that their histories may provide could be substantial.

Such archaeologically understudied entities include a group of loosely affiliated tribal units that later coalesced into the Caddoan Wichita tribe, who were relatives of the Arikara and Pawnee. These people maintained villages that were often paired and that were located along major watercourses. The villages consisted of beehive-shaped grass houses (usually containing a matrilineally organized extended family) between which open storage structures were often built. From these villages the occupants produced pottery and farmed maize, gourds and/or squash, beans, and tobacco, which they stored in granaries and underground caches. Horticulture was primarily a spring and summer activity that produced some surplus for trade. In the fall/winter and often in mid-summer, the Wichita organized a bison hunt in which the entire village participated. Meat was dried or smoked, hides were used for mats, tepees, and clothing, and bone was fashioned into hoes, awls and other tools (Gunnerson and Gunnerson 1988:17–20; Newcomb and Field 1967:310–314; F. Smith 2000:4–5; Wedel 1982). In the sixteenth to eighteenth centuries the Wichita were located on the Arkansas River and its tributaries, primarily in the present-day states of Kansas and Oklahoma (Wedel 1959; Wedel 1982).

THE LASLEY VORE SITE

In 1988 I undertook the investigation of a Wichita village of the sixteenth to eighteenth centuries as part of archaeological mitigation prior to the construction of a tissue facility by the Kimberly-Clark Paper Company. Located 13 miles south of Tulsa, Oklahoma, the approximately 2–4 ha settlement overlooked the Arkansas River (Figure 3.1). It was named the Lasley Vore site after a Creek Indian gentleman who moved to the locale in 1892 and built a house on the property. Because the site was situated on land that was to be leveled for construction of the plant, it would be totally destroyed in the process. We negotiated an agreement that left us two months to excavate everything of importance.

Methods of inquiry involved pedestrian survey, testing with a Ditch Witch (Odell 1992), excavating a series of 2 m × 2 m test pits, stripping the plowzone, and hand excavating subsurface features. These combined techniques yielded a total of 81 features, mostly hearths and pits. They were not distributed randomly, but were aggregated into 10 clusters, of which five contained enough material to be amenable to quantitative analyses.

The features contained an abundance of Native-American objects: ceramic containers; animal bone waste from food preparation; modified bone and retouched chipped-stone tools; and large rough stone grooved abraders, manos,

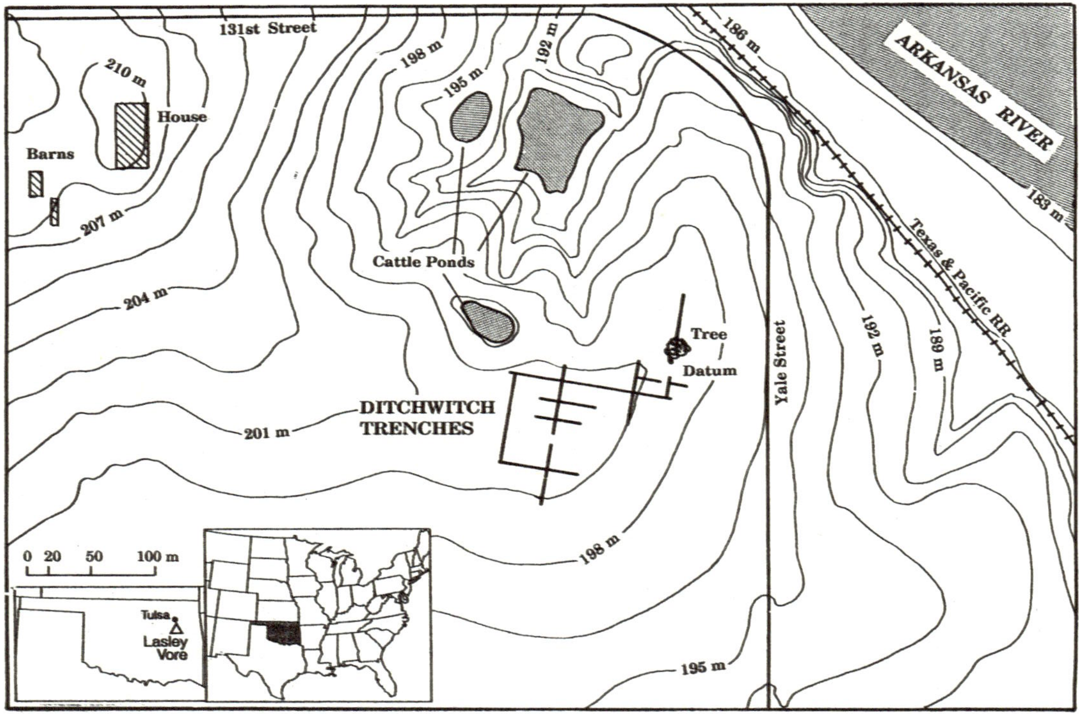

Fig. 3.1. Location and plan of the Lasley Vore site in eastern Oklahoma (from Odell 1999:Figure 1)

and metates. In association with these were European trade goods: glass beads, iron axeheads, iron and brass gun parts, brass tinkling cones, and an assortment of other objects. Although considerable attention was paid to the issue, no house patterns were discerned—indeed, only one questionable posthole was observed. Despite the lack of evidence for structures, other clues from the settlement suggest that its occupants lived in houses. These clues include the presence of daub, the patterning of the features, and the evidence for permanent or semipermanent occupation, discussed below.

The available evidence, discussed in Odell (1999), indicates that Lasley Vore was a substantial village. Its overall size is quite large for this area, and part of another settlement of identical age, which might have been occupied contemporaneously, was discovered about 400 m away during a later survey of the Arkansas bluff line (Odell et al. 1990). Several large storage and cooking pits, which contained a wide variety of paleobotanical remains and animal bones (especially bison, deer, and turtle) were situated at various locations around the site. Pottery, especially storage jars, was abundant, and some of the pits contained large grinding stones. Two of the pits were filled with charred corn kernels, indicating that this cultigen was grown in the area (Odell 1998).

That the various parts of the site were occupied simultaneously is probable. The features clustered cleanly, and in only one instance was one pit dug into another. Had palimpsests of occupation occurred, they would have resulted in multiple overlapping of individual features and considerably less feature patterning.

The Native-American pottery and abundant Fresno points suggest a very late prehistoric or protohistoric date for the occupation—a contention supported by the trade goods, which are consistent with a French presence in the area during the first half of the eighteenth century. This contention is also supported by six radiocarbon dates, but anomalies in the radiocarbon technique itself in such a recent settlement do not allow much precision. Taken together, the Lasley Vore site represents a substantial village occupied late in the regional prehistoric sequence, and it contains evidence of contact with Europeans.

THE FRENCH CONNECTION

The first recorded European in eastern Oklahoma was Jean-Baptiste Bénard, Sieur de la Harpe, who traveled from St. Malo, France, to Louisiana in 1718. While there he received a commission to establish a trading post up the Red River among resident Caddoan tribes. The small French band succeeded in setting up their post among the Nasoni Indians not far from present-day Texarkana (Miroir et al. 1973; Villiers du Terrage 1934:21–22; Wedel 1978). La Harpe's mandate was to engage in commercial relations with the Indians and the Spanish, an activity that occasionally amounted to contraband (Folmer 1941). Trade with the Caddo progressed well, but trade with the Spanish hit a few roadblocks, so la Harpe determined to try his hand with distant cousins of the Caddo to the north. In August, 1719, la Harpe and nine men, accompanied by several packhorses laden with merchandise, set forth on an 18-day journey that terminated on the banks of a major river called the "Alcansas"—probably the Arkansas. Here they encountered a large village of Tawakoni Indians (Smith 1958–59), one of a number of cultural groups later known as Wichita.

La Harpe and his men remained for 10 days in the Tawakoni village, where they were honored with the Calumet Ceremony, traded numerous material items, and exchanged vows of alliance. Following several mishaps, most of la Harpe's party eventually made it back to their trading post. La Harpe returned to France in 1720, but came back to Louisiana later that year as "Commandant of St. Bernard Bay," a somewhat nebulous designation. While residing in North America, la Harpe made one more attempt to contact the Tawakoni village but failed and returned to Biloxi. He boarded a ship for France in 1723 and never returned to the New World (Villiers du Terrage 1934:26–36; Wedel 1971).

La Harpe's visit in 1719 was the last formal contact the Wichita people had with the French while the Wichita resided in Oklahoma. By the 1750s hostilities with the Osage, Missouri, and Skidi Pawnee had forced most of the tribal units south of the Red River (Wedel 1981:32, 1982:128), after which disease and conflicts with Euro-Americans precluded them from reclaiming their ancient hunting grounds.

The exact location of the Tawakoni village that la Harpe visited has eluded scholars for years, and divergent opinions on the matter have placed it on the Canadian River, the Cimarron River, the Arkansas River near Haskell, or further south near Muskogee (Lewis 1924; Smith 1958–59; Vehik 1992; Villiers du Terrage 1934). The most concerted effort to find it occurred in 1972, ending up on the Arkansas River at Wealaka Ridge near Leonard, Oklahoma, about 10–15 km south of the Lasley Vore site (Wedel 1981:28, 1982:124). Unfortunately, no protohistoric archaeological material has been recorded at this locale, suggesting that—due to the vagaries of preservation and ambiguities in la Harpe's diaries that record these events (Margry 1879–88)—we will never know exactly where this village was located.

What is certain is that Lasley Vore represents a large, semi-permanent, late prehistoric village containing abundant European trade goods. It was probably inhabited by Wichita Indians and was contemporaneous with, or existed shortly after, la Harpe's visit to the Tawakoni (i.e., in the first half of the eighteenth century). Given the typology and chronological specificity of the trade goods and the limited contact the Wichita had with the French, it is probable that the European objects discovered at this site originated with the la Harpe expedition.

The archaeological analyses conducted on the Lasley Vore assemblage provide an ideal opportunity to inspect a Wichita settlement at the cusp of contact with French interlopers, so let us turn to the lithic material objects the Wichita possessed at this important juncture.

THE LASLEY VORE LITHIC ASSEMBLAGE

Analysis of the various Lasley Vore data sets, from which the tables in this paper derive, has been presented in Odell (2002). Most of the typological and raw-material-sourcing tabulations reported here are taken from the entire excavated assemblage, but other analyses, such as breakage patterns, heat alteration, and debris class, derive from samples isolated for use-wear analysis. Sampled pieces originated in undisturbed context from the five feature clusters that contained the largest quantities of features and material. Definitions of the lithic terms used here can be found in Odell (1996).

Typology and Technology

Lasley Vore Assemblage

The modified stone tools, known as the "type collection," recovered from the Lasley Vore site are listed in Table 3.1. Numerically the chipped-stone component dwarfs the rough/ground-stone component, though the latter includes some impressive tools, especially the three large metates and the abraders, some of which are illustrated in Figure 3.2. The largest single category is the scrapers, registering almost 30 percent of the type collection. Of these, end scrapers (39.5 percent) and distolateral scrapers (i.e., retouched on the end and on at least one of the sides: 43.7 percent) constitute the lion's share, followed at a great distance by side-, spurred, and thumbnail scrapers. The next most frequent stone tool class, at slightly less than 20 percent of the type collection, is the retouched piece. Almost all of these are flakes, and more than 80 percent were unifacially retouched.

Projectile points were also frequently encountered, in almost the same frequency as retouched pieces. More than 80 percent of these are small triangular Fresno and Maud types, clear typological markers of a late prehistoric assemblage (Figure 3.3). The Nodena point also probably belongs to this period, but the 5 Gary and lone Langtry, Ellis, and Williams points, as well as many of the 22 indeterminate points, might have been deposited by occupants of earlier sites recorded nearby, or picked up and taken back by inhabitants of the Lasley Vore settlement.

The rest of the lithic types are each represented by less than 10 percent of the type collection. The most plentiful of these, at 8.6 percent of the total, are

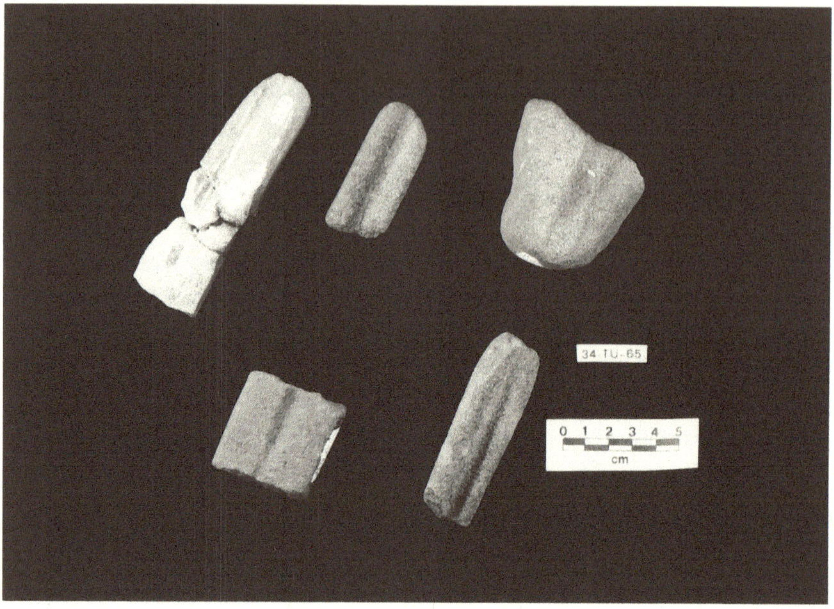

Fig. 3.2. Sample of grooved abraders from the Lasley Vore assemblage

bifaces, which have been categorized and defined within Callahan's (1979) three-stage system. Almost half of these are comprised of fragments for which stage cannot be determined and non-reduction bifaces, which apparently were never on a reduction trajectory. Of those bifaces whose stage can be determined, more than half are initial stage bifaces, the remainder comprised equally of stage 2 and stage 3 pieces. Manos and unifaces register at about 4 percent of the type collection and the rest at very reduced quantities.

The vast majority of the raw material types for chipped-stone tools originated in the Reeds Spring, Keokuk, and Moorefield Formations of the Ozark Plateau. About 60 km east of the Lasley Vore settlement, these Mississippian limestone formations yield cherts of various colors that can be quite vitreous and isotropic and that submit well to heat treatment. The next most abundantly represented source is Florence A (or Kay County) chert located about 140 km northwest of the settlement in the southern Flint Hills of north-central Oklahoma and south-central Kansas. A fine-grained chert in its natural state, it becomes vitreous and rosy-colored when submitted to heat. The Florence A chert location has been a favored source for centuries, as attested by the numerous prehistoric quarry pits in the region.

Other than these two areas, the assemblage contains a smattering of materials from southeastern Oklahoma (e.g., Johns Valley chert, Cotter dolomite),

Fig. 3.3. Sample of Fresno and Maud points from the Lasley Vore assemblage

novaculite from Arkansas, Alibates agatized dolomite from Texas or the Canadian River beds of western Oklahoma (Wyckoff 1993), and Knife River flint from North Dakota. Thus some material for individual chipped-stone tools originated from great distances away, but the occupants' tool procurement areas were principally the Ozarks and secondarily the southern Flint Hills. The sandstone from which grinding tools were made was probably collected locally, but the granite, quartz, and quartzite might also have originated in the Ozarks.

The paucity of local cherts in the Cherokee Prairie biotic province, where the site lies, had a noticeable effect on the way people treated their tools. The occupants maximized their tool-manufacturing efficiency by heat treating much of their flint—as about three-quarters of both type collection and debitage samples exhibit heat alteration. Heat treatment was highest for projectile points and lowest for scrapers/unifaces, but even for the latter it affected two-thirds of the type (Table 3.2).

In addition, the lack of local chipped-stone material induced the occupants to use their tools more intensively than they would have on sites with more readily available workable stone. This caused severe breakage among certain categories, especially bifaces, retouched pieces, and specialized, generally unifacial,

Table 3.1 Modified Stone Tools in the Lasley Vore Lithic Assemblage

Type	N	%
I. Chipped Stone		
1. Adze	2	0.2
2. Biface	76	8.6
3. Burin	6	0.7
4. Chopping Tool	3	0.3
5. Combination Tool	1	0.1
6. Core (flake)	4	0.5
7. Denticulate	21	2.4
8. Drill	13	1.5
9. Graver	8	0.9
10. Gunflint	6	0.7
11. Notched Piece	4	0.5
12. Projectile Point	165	18.6
13. Retouched Piece	174	19.7
14. Scraper	263	29.7
15. Uniface	39	4.4
16. Wedge	13	1.5
II. Rough/Ground Stone		
1. Abrader	18	2.0
2. Hammerstone	19	2.1
3. Mano	41	4.6
4. Metate	3	0.3
5. Worked Piece	5	0.6
6. Ground Stone Indeterminate	1	0.1
Total	885	100%

Table 3.2 Heat Alteration within Types or Type Combinations in the 5-Cluster Sample

Type	Not Heat Altered	%	Heat Altered	%	Total
Biface	7	22.6	24	77.4	31
Projectile point	9	17.0	44	83.0	53
Retouched piece	12	22.6	41	77.4	53
Scraper/uniface	27	33.3	54	66.7	81
Burin/Drill/Graver Denticulate/ Notched piece	4	16.7	20	83.3	24
Total	59	24.4	183	75.6	242

Table 3.3 Complete vs. Broken Pieces among Several Types or Type Combinations in the Combined 5-Cluster Type Collections

Type	Complete	%	Broken	%	Total
Biface	2	6.5	29	93.5	31
Projectile point	30	56.6	23	43.4	53
Retouched piece	6	11.3	47	88.7	53
Scraper/Uniface	47	58.0	34	42.0	81
Burin/Drill/Graver/Denticulate/ Notched piece	7	29.2	17	70.8	24
Total	92	38.0	150	62.0	242

types such as burins, gravers and denticulates. Projectile points and scrapers/ unifaces did not suffer quite the degree of breakage of the other types, but more than 40 percent of these were also fragmented (Table 3.3). This situation also resulted in a paucity of cores in the assemblage (only four), as most cores were simply fragmented into oblivion in attempting to extract every last bit of usable toolstone. Although a bipolar knapping technique was probably practiced occasionally, the assemblage bears few obvious traces of it.

Parry and Kelly (1987) established that the most recent, i.e., most sedentary, populations in North America produced lithic assemblages characterized by expediency and lack of strict formality. The Lasley Vore assemblage, like the King site assemblage in Georgia (Cobb and Ruggiero, chapter 2), fits this pattern in its strong emphasis on a flake technology. For instance, in a sample of eight common tool types excluding bifaces and projectile points (i.e., burins, denticulates, gravers, notched and retouched pieces, scrapers, unifaces, and wedges), more than 90 percent were manufactured on flake blanks and only one was made on a biface. A sample of unretouched lithic debris from the Lasley Vore assemblage supports this scenario, as it contains 70 percent flakes (Table 3.4:total of all categories except blocky fragments). The other large debris category is blocky fragments, which include potlidded, fire-crazed, and frost-fractured pieces that do not exhibit a flake fracture surface. Three pieces have been termed blades, but these are pseudo-blades, as no blade cores or other evidence of a true blade technique has been uncovered.

The lack of formal lithic technological organization is supported by the paucity of evidence for corrective measures, such as sharpening or core rejuvenation flakes. Bifacial reduction was certainly practiced, as demonstrated by the 20 percent of the debris sample that was classified as biface reduction flakes, but 27 percent were classified as interior flakes. The presence of 12 percent flakes possessing some cortex suggests that at least some of the lithic material was transported

Table 3.4 Technological Debris Classes in the Utilized and Nonutilized Debris Samples for each Cluster

	Cluster											
	2		4		5		7		8		Total	
Debris Class	N	%	N	%	N	%	N	%	N	%	N	%
Primary decortication flake	50	15.3	36	5.5	39	5.9	40	8.0	13	2.5	178	6.7
Secondary decortication flake	66	20.2	89	13.6	110	16.6	97	19.4	45	8.6	407	15.3
Interior flake	90	27.6	179	27.3	179	27.1	152	30.4	124	23.8	724	27.2
Biface reduction flake	91	27.9	124	18.9	117	17.7	172	34.4	48	9.2	552	20.7
Blade	3	0.9	3	0.5	1	0.2	1	0.2			8	0.3
Sharpening flake	1	0.3	1	0.2					1	0.2	3	0.1
Core rejuvenation flake							1	0.2			1	0.1
Blocky fragments	25	7.7	223	34.0	215	32.5	37	7.4	291	55.7	791	29.7
Total	326	99.9	655	100	661	100	5	100	522	100	2664	100.1

to the site in nodular or tabular form, rather than as already-reduced blanks. The relative frequency of cortex, as well as the large proportion of initial stage bifaces (more than half), mentioned previously, suggest that the occupants might have been stockpiling their lithic material.

Some Comparisons

Most of the traits discussed above can also be noted in related sites of supposedly Wichita affiliation. The most well-known of these in Oklahoma is the Deer Creek site, located up the Arkansas River from Lasley Vore near Ponca City and formerly known as Ferdinandina (Wedel 1981). Lithic artifacts collected from this locale show an abundance of two types that are also the most plentiful at Lasley Vore: scrapers and projectile points. Scrapers vary in their characteristics, but appear to consist of the same range of morphological variation as those at Lasley Vore; and most of the points are Fresno arrowheads (Sudbury 1975:97–104). Other lithic implements are generally omitted from Sudbury's report, which concentrates on the European trade goods, but the collections include several manos and grooved abraders, both frequently represented at Lasley Vore.

Similar patterns can be discerned in the lithic assemblage from the protohistoric village of Bryson-Paddock, near Deer Creek, which was partially excavated in 1974 and 1975. At this site the most abundant chipped-stone tool type by far is the scraper, and Fresno points dominate the projectile class. A small bifacial presence was noted, of which a significant component consisted of "large, crude bifaces"—probably analogous to the relatively abundant stage 1 bifaces at Lasley Vore. Gravers, notched pieces, denticulates and retouched pieces from the site are illustrated but are termed "utilized debitage" (Hartley and Miller 1977:Figure 4). Grinding stones are also relatively frequent, as at Lasley Vore.

Further up the Arkansas River in Kansas, the traits described above were first synthesized by Wedel (1959) following excavations at Little River focus sites such as Thompson, Tobias, Malone and Paint Creek, and on Lower Walnut focus sites such as Larcom-Haggard, Elliott, and Arkansas City Country Club. At the Tobias site, for example, Wedel (1959:265) reported that 64.1 percent of the projectile points were small, unnotched arrowheads (i.e., Fresno points)—not quite as high a proportion as at Lasley Vore, but dominant nonetheless. Of the endscrapers, Wedel (1959:273) wrote, "Upward of 250 of these ubiquitous little objects were found; they came to light wherever we dug on the site." Observations such as these were also made for other related sites, but I will spare the redundancies. The abundance of scrapers appears to have been widespread throughout the Southeast in the eighteenth century, due to the influence of the fur trade (see Johnson, chapter 4). Interestingly, this trend seems to have started earlier in Kansas, prior to the existence of the European fur trade.

A few types were present at these Kansas sites that were not recovered from

Lasley Vore. These include the beveled-edge (including Harahey) knife and what Wedel (1959:267) termed "plain-shafted [i.e., rods] and T-shaped drills." Beveled knives and rodlike drills were also discovered on late prehistoric sites near Marion, Kansas (Rohn and Emerson 1984:132–140). The endscrapers photographed for the Marion publication are all very uniform and invasively retouched—what I would call "unifaces," though they have a scraper form. It is difficult to tell from the text whether or not the 10 endscrapers illustrated are technologically typical of the total of 273 reported from Marion sites, but I doubt it. If they are, the extensive surficial retouch on scrapers from this region would constitute a major deviation from both the Oklahoma protohistoric sites and the other Great Bend aspect sites that Wedel and others have analyzed. In any case, most typo-technological aspects of these Kansas lithic assemblages are similar to those found in Oklahoma. The differences noted in knife, drill, and possibly scraper technology may relate to their purported slightly greater antiquity (Hawley and Haury 1994:14; Vehik 1992:327, 1994:248; Wedel 1959:585).

Function

Stone tool form and technology can provide a substantial range of information on certain aspects of prehistoric behavior, but they are not particularly accurate indicators of how tools were actually used (Ahler 1971; Odell 1981; Wylie 1975). The latter question requires a technique that is specifically suited to questions of tool function. Use-wear analysis, the study of wear on tool edges and surfaces resulting from utilization, has proven adequate for this task (Bamforth et al. 1990; Keeley and Newcomer 1977; Odell and Odell-Vereecken 1980).

The prehistoric situation at the Lasley Vore settlement presented two areas of inquiry for which use-wear analysis appeared particularly well suited: 1) the function of the settlement as a whole, or what people were doing there; and 2) the spatial distribution of activities, or what people were doing in specific areas of the site. Although evidence for residential structures was not observed, it is likely that the feature clusters relate in some way to specific household units. But even if this assumption is in error, most of the features ended up as garbage dumps that surely relate to the specific area of the site in which they were located, and this is good enough for our purposes.

Results of the Lasley Vore use-wear analysis have been reported in Odell (1999) and will be summarized here. In general, the analysis demonstrated that a wide variety of activities was conducted at the site, which is consistent with patterns expected of a large habitation area. It also indicated that the substantial quantity of typological scrapers in the assemblage did have functional import, i.e., the largest single activity at the village was hide scraping. Equally important activities were hunting and warfare, as evidenced from impact damage on projectile points that were brought back to the site in the bodies of animals or for repair. These projectile tips included not only the anticipated Fresno and Maud points, but also unmodified debitage and other typed classes such as retouched pieces. Other important activities at the site were the cutting, shaving, and drilling of a large variety of substances, flat grinding, grooved grinding (perhaps for the shaping of bone tools), chopping/wedging, pounding, and graving.

To ascertain where on the site these activities were conducted, the data were analyzed using the five feature clusters yielding the greatest amount of archaeological material. Comparing these areas using typological and technological indicators of the lithic assemblage showed no differences among any of the clusters. Only through use-wear techniques were the areas able to be individually characterized and discriminated.

The results of the use-wear analysis, encapsulated in Figure 3.4, show an undercurrent of hide scraping in four of the five clusters tested. In addition, the two clusters at the center of the settlement, 4 and 8, were functionally similar to one another in other ways. Dominant activities of mano grinding and percussive activities such as chopping and wedging indicate that these were the principal domestic areas of the village. Flat grinding using a mano and metate would have constituted one of the principal subsistence activities at the settlement—whether of corn or of nuts, both of which were abundantly represented among the paleobotanical remains. The river and stream valleys abounded in hickory, walnut, pecan, and oak trees, and the flat alluvial terrace just below the site would have been ideal for farming and indeed had been used for this purpose before the Kimberly-Clark Company bought the land. Construction activities in this area involving wedging, chopping, and other percussive tasks probably reflect the buildings and facilities that must have existed but that left no trace in the archaeological record.

Use-wear results from the other areas of the site underscore the diversity of activities conducted in the village. Except for the similarities between domestic units 4 and 8 noted above, each of the clusters exhibits a specific functional profile. Perhaps the most distinctive was the northern area (Cluster 2), which contained little evidence for domestic tasks and was the only locale in which hide scraping was not an important concern. Abundant impact damage indicates that projectiles were taken to this area for repair. In addition, tool users refurbished their bone and antler equipment here, as seen in the preponderance of hard material wear on drilling and graving tools.

The southeastern sector (Cluster 7) also served as a locus of weapon repair, but other functional characteristics found here are different from those further north. This area emphasized cutting and shaving of a variety of materials,

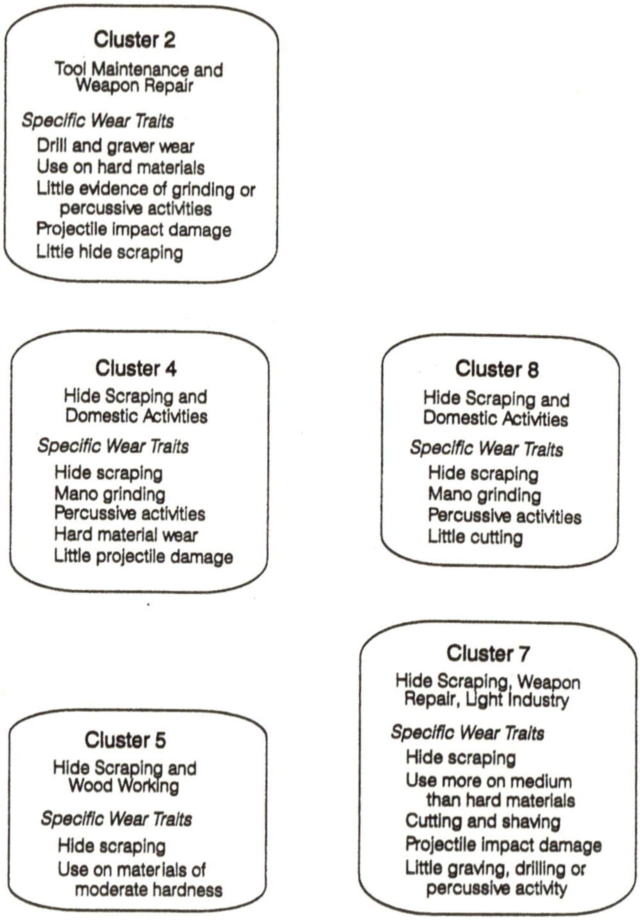

Fig. 3.4. Activities conducted in the five largest feature clusters, shown in the approximate locations at which these clusters occurred on the site (from Odell 1999:Figure 7)

suggesting a sort of light industry. The southwestern unit (Cluster 5) showed a high percentage of utilization on substances of moderate resistance (i.e., a woodworking area).

The lithic variables that most completely characterize the activities performed on the Lasley Vore settlement and that serve as the best discriminators among internal portions of the village are functional in nature and were recognized through use-wear analysis. Comparing these parameters to other relevant analyses is difficult, as few use-wear studies of North American protohistoric assemblages have ever been attempted. The only other of which I am aware was Doug Bamforth's (1993) analysis of stone tools from the Chumash village of

Helo' in southern California. Bamforth documented a cottage industry in the drilling of shell beads that has no counterpart in the Lasley Vore assemblage. Hide scraping was a dominant activity at Lasley Vore, but it can hardly be termed a cottage industry as almost all households appear to have engaged in it and its customers (the people for whom the finished product was intended) were probably either the tool users themselves or members of the same community.

TOOL REPLACEMENT AND ACCULTURATION

The Lasley Vore settlement was occupied for a maximum of only about 30 years after European trade goods were first introduced into this region in substantial quantities with la Harpe's visit. Wichita abandonment of the region by the mid–eighteenth century precludes any modern archaeological study, in the state of Oklahoma, of their acculturation and the replacement of Native-American tools, containers, and ornaments by European ones. To ascertain this aspect of Wichita lifeways, one would have to investigate the places where the Wichita moved after abandoning the Arkansas basin—primarily in Texas. Unfortunately, for this group of Native Americans a study of this kind has never been conducted. But in the absence of investigations of later acculturation period sites, one may still be able, using specific artifacts from the Lasley Vore assemblages and data from other contact situations, to predict the general course that tool replacement probably took. These considerations have already been presented in a study of Lasley Vore metal artifacts (Odell 2001) and will be summarized here.

Metal artifacts from Lasley Vore include gun parts; tools and weapons such as axe and knife blades; and miscellaneous utensils such as iron pot rims, spoon handles, and tinkling cones. The settlement was never reprovisioned, as subsequent attempts by la Harpe to revisit it came to naught (Villiers du Terrage 1934:31–33; Wedel 1971:54–56) and the Wichita had moved south before any permanent European presence was established in the area. Lack of reprovisioning had certain predictable outcomes. Tools that retained their usefulness for tasks for which they were originally intended were apparently utilized to the absolute maximum. An example of this situation is the lone axehead that retained its socket for attachment to a wooden handle. In this case the blade was worn and sharpened almost to the socket itself, well beyond its optimal utility for cutting down a tree.

Other metal implements were useless for their original functions without constant reprovisioning. A case in point is the musket, which must have been a little difficult to fire once the original ammunition was used up. It might have taken some time to run out of ammunition, as the lithic assemblage contains six gunflints, four of which are battered on all edges Native-American style. But once ammunition was depleted, guns were dismembered and their parts reused for

Table 3.5 Principal activities discerned in the Lasley Vore artifact assemblage.

Activity	Stone Tool	Appropriate Metal Tool	Substituted Metal Tool
scraping	scraper, uniface		butt plate
cutting/shaving	biface, flake	knife blade	
chopping/adzing	chopper, axe, adze, biface	axehead	
drilling/graving	drill, graver, burin		reused gun part(?)
pounding	hammerstone		gun barrel
wedging	biface, uniface, flake, wedge		broken axehead, iron pot rim
dancing/fashion		kettle scrap	ornaments, tinklers
weapon: firearm		musket, fusil	
weapon: bow and arrow/dart	projectile point		
grinding	metate, mano, grooved grinder		

Above the horizontal line are those activities observed in the lithic assemblage for which some metal counterpart has been identified—either as an intended function (column 3) or from a refashioned implement (column 4). Below the line are those tools that had no counterpart in the other material class (taken from Odell 2001:Table 3).

specific tasks. Gun barrels became hammers and picks; brass butt plates became scraping tools; and other brass accoutrements were shaped into drills, reamers, and other useful objects. And the reuse of metals was not exclusive to guns: iron pot rims were reused as wedges, brass kettles became tinkling cones, and so forth. Native Americans were ingenious in their re-employment of scrap metal once it became obvious that European trade goods would not be resupplied.

Objects of metal and stone at Lasley Vore that exhibit functional overlap are documented in Table 3.5. Above the dashed line are cases in which an introduced metal tool has assumed the function of a stone implement, either in the same functional mode, as in knives and axes, or recycled from a different functional mode, as in the butt plate scraper, the gun barrel hammer, the refashioned brass reamer, and the wedges made from iron pot rims and broken axeheads. Below the line are cases in which no exact counterpart has been identified in the other material. Among metal implements, these include muskets and kettle scrap made into tinkling cones; among stone tools, they include projectile points and grinding tools. These relationships are important in predicting the nature and direction of tool replacement among the Wichita.

Studies of tool replacement in indigenous societies do not abound in the archaeological literature, but the few that have been conducted illustrate that stone tools were not replaced all at once when metal became available. They were replaced in piecemeal fashion, depending upon tool-specific factors such as cost and efficiency and external factors such as the existence of trade routes to raw material sources and the integration of new technologies into administrative structures and the existing cultural fabric (Ramenofsky 1998; Rogers 1990; Rosen 1996, 1997).

External factors have not been researched sufficiently to be interpretable in most cases, but the relative cost and efficiency of specific tool types can be approximated using indicators from the Lasley Vore site and other ethnographic and archaeological situations. For instance, it has been noted that stone grinders, scrapers, and projectile points had no immediate counterparts among eighteenth-century European trade goods. This suggests that for the tasks in which these tools were involved the efficiency of stone relative to metal was quite high.

At the other end of the spectrum, the only metal axehead at Lasley Vore that continued to function as an axehead was not discarded until it was worn to the very maximum, well past its effectiveness for most tasks. It continued to be employed because it held an edge better and was more durable than a stone axe. Knowing how much effort it took to produce a ground-stone axe, the Wichita continued to utilize a still functional (though barely) metal axe rather than manufacture a new one of stone.

To compare the cost and efficiency of specific metal and stone implements, I used indicators from the Lasley Vore assemblage, as well as pertinent ethnographic and archaeological data from other regions. Cost was defined as the relative amount of energy expended in procurement or manufacture; efficiency included the effective performance of a task with minimal energy, minimal resharpening requirements, and edge durability. Stone tool types were judged subjectively on these qualities and are compared to one another in Figure 3.5.

As indicated above, the stone axe is very costly to produce, especially in its abraded, ground-stone form, and is not as efficient as its metal counterpart. This would be the first stone tool type to be replaced. Drills, gravers, and knives are not as costly as axes to produce, but they need to be sharpened frequently and are much more brittle and prone to damage than their metal counterparts. The presence of seven metal knife blades in the Lasley Vore assemblage attests to the popularity of this trade item.

Stone grinding tools, arrowheads, and scrapers, on the other hand, were cheap to produce and relatively efficient in their appointed tasks. One recycled brass butt plate does show scraping wear, but the popularity of the stone scraper

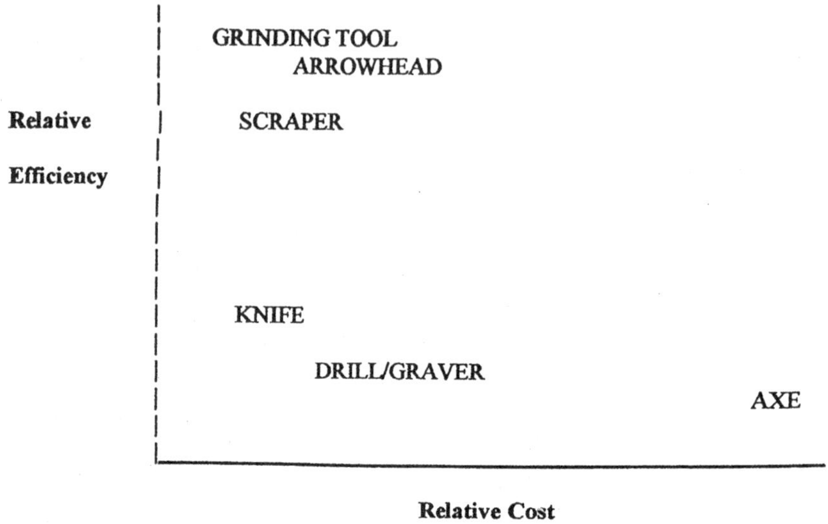

Fig. 3.5. Hypothetical cost and efficiency of certain common stone tools in relation to their metal counterparts (from Odell 2001:Figure 8)

remained undiminished for years. The same is true of stone Fresno and Maud points, for which no metal counterpart was discovered at Lasley Vore. Metal arrowheads would appear on subsequent contact sites and would ultimately replace stone points, but I suspect that—because of the wounding efficiency and relative ease of manufacturing stone arrowheads—replacement was widespread only when metal scrap became common on Native-American sites. Grinding stones had no metal counterpart at all, and people continue to employ whetstones to sharpen metal tools to this day. Grinding stones ultimately declined in importance through massive changes in industrial organization that made it more economical to buy flour from a large mill than to grind it oneself.

CONCLUSION

Contact between two fundamentally different cultures has occurred at different times and in different places throughout the history of the world. The period of acculturation that followed initial contact has been studied archaeologically among several groups, using a variety of artifact classes. Stone tools are particularly subject to change and replacment by incoming metal technologies and can shed a considerable amount of light on the general process of acculturation that occurred within that society.

This paper has concentrated on a tool assemblage from the protohistoric

Wichita, who inhabited eastern Oklahoma in the first half of the eighteenth century. Little research on acculturation has been attempted with this tribe, because the Wichita remained in the region only 30–40 years after their first formal contact with a French entourage led by la Harpe in 1719, thus providing little time depth in which to study the phenomenon. The la Harpe visit was momentous for both parties, though it was not to result in a permanent French presence in the region for another century. The trade goods that la Harpe disseminated were undoubtedly distributed to allies throughout the Arkansas drainage.

The Lasley Vore settlement, contemporary with la Harpe's visit and probably containing items that he had brought, was excavated in 1988. A suite of techniques applied to the lithic assemblage documented a largely expedient, flake-based tool kit characterized by abundant scrapers and small Fresno points. Chert suitable for stone tool production was not available locally, so tool users were forced to procure their materials in the Ozarks and secondarily in other areas. This situation caused them to rely heavily on techniques of heat treatment in manufacturing these tools and on economizing the material at hand. Like other very early contact sites (e.g., the King site, see Cobb and Ruggiero, chapter 2), European technology had little impact on the manufacture or form of tools that were produced.

A use-wear analysis of the assemblage demonstrated the existence of hide-scraping activities in almost all parts of the settlement. But five feature clusters, analyzed separately, showed specific functional profiles (i.e., people were conducting different activities at specific locations within the village). These included areas for weapons repair, bone/antler tool maintenance, woodworking, light industry, and various domestic activities.

Although the Lasley Vore archaeological remains do not possess enough time depth to achieve a very clear idea of the nature of Wichita acculturation and tool replacement, their use and recycling of metals provides an indication of the most likely directions that these trajectories would have taken. A cost-efficiency model suggests that stone axes and chopping tools would have been replaced early, followed by knives and then drills and gravers. Scrapers, grinding tools, and arrowheads were cheap and, in some ways, just as efficient as their metal counterparts (if they had any). Replacement of these stone types would have occurred later and for other reasons, such as massive changes in industrial organization and the eventual ubiquity of metals on Native-American habitations.

The Lasley Vore assemblage has provided a glimpse of Wichita tool use at the cusp of contact. The tribe's departure from eastern Oklahoma shortly after contact has precluded local documentation of their eventual adaptation and acculturation to these new influences, data that will have to be acquired from Texas sites. However, protohistoric villages such as Lasley Vore provide a baseline for indigenous lithic technologies that may facilitate subsequent interpretation of Wichita acculturation.

ACKNOWLEDGMENTS

My study benefited from the assistance of too many people in the fieldwork and analysis stages to enumerate here, but they know who they are and have my utmost gratitude. I appreciate Charlie Cobb's invitation to participate in the SAA symposium in which the papers in this volume were presented, as well as the comments of two anonymous reviewers. The Kimberly-Clark Corporation funded the initial fieldwork and the inventorying of Lasley Vore artifacts, and the Research Office of the University of Tulsa supported the analytical process with several grants. Frieda Vereecken-Odell drew the site plan and took the artifact photos. I am very grateful for all of this help and support.

4
Chickasaw Lithic Technology: A Reassessment

Jay K. Johnson

My first exposure to a Contact-period lithic assemblage came when I volunteered to analyze the stone tools from the Orchard site, an early-eighteenth-century Chickasaw site in northeast Mississippi. The collection contained many surprises (Johnson 1997). I had expected that the access to European trade goods would have resulted in the complete replacement of stone tools with metal ones. Not only was there a large number of stone tools in the collection from the Orchard site, but the lithic industry of this site is one of the most elaborate and structured assemblages to be found in the Midsouth.

Perhaps the most interesting of the stone tools are the thumbnail scrapers. The analyses of the Orchard site scrapers showed them to be uniform in size, shape, and technology. Strong evidence also suggests that the production demands of these tools forced the Chickasaws to exploit a new source of raw material, the Fort Payne tabular cherts which outcrop in the Tennessee River valley to the northeast. This material was of sufficient size to allow the production of the sort of flake blank that is critical in making a sharp but broad working-edge angle (Figure 4.1). The Chickasaw stone tool kit at the Orchard site also contains Dallas points which must have been arrowheads, broad bifacial knives, and awls.

The question was, if the Chickasaw had access to the obviously superior European tools, why were they using arrows and stone scrapers? A close examination of the spatial and temporal distribution of similar early historic tools in the Southeast led to a likely explanation. The Chickasaws' location at the western extreme of the British trade network and their isolation as the result of hostilities from the French trade out of Mobile meant that they had relatively less access to metal tools. In order to participate in the deer skin trade, they were forced to supplement their tool kit with stone tools. In fact, scrapers also become more common at the edges of the early historic European trade network

Fig. 4.1. Chickasaw lithic artifacts: a) British gun spall; b) French gun spall; c–d) Native gun spall; e–h) Dallas Triangular points; i–j) Edwards Stemmed, *var. Sunflower* points; k–l) awls; m) bifacial knifed; n–q) thumbnail scrapers, dorsal and side views

in northern Alabama and central Tennessee (Johnson 1997). It seems likely that in these frontier locations, several days' journey from the European ports of trade, other items assumed priority to the Indians. For example, glass beads, likely markers of status differentiation, are abundant on early-eighteenth-century Chickasaw sites in northeastern Mississippi.

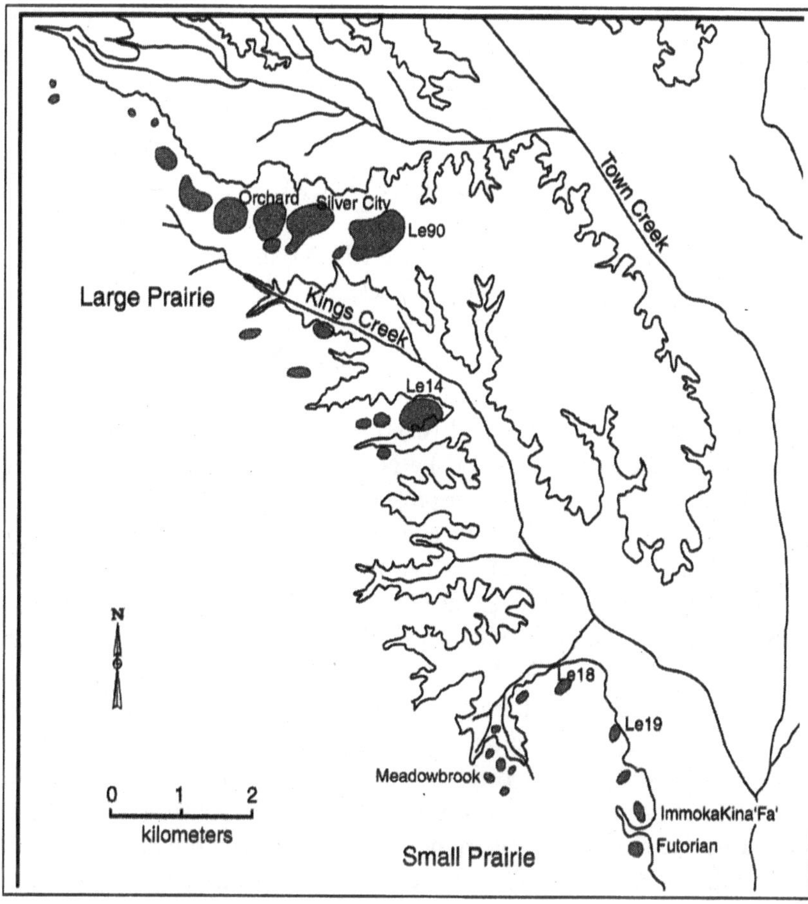

Fig. 4.2. Map of Chickasaw sites in northeastern Mississippi

The distribution of scrapers within the area that was occupied by the Chickasaws throughout the eighteenth century also proved interesting. The Chickasaw divided themselves into moieties. The red clans occupied villages in an area designated by the French as the Large Prairie (Atkinson 1985; Galloway 1996). These war villages were located north of present-day Tupelo, Mississippi, along Beldon Ridge (Figure 4.2). The white clan villages were situated in an area known as the Small Prairie that is now covered by the subdivisions and malls of downtown Tupelo. They were led by the peace chief who resided in the village of Ackia. Thumbnail scrapers and other elements of the Chickasaw stone tool kit are much more common in Large Prairie assemblages than they are at Small Prairie sites. This pattern was interpreted to be the result of the documented trade relations that the Small Prairie villages had with both the French and the English (Johnson 1997). As a consequence, the peace villages had better access to trade goods than did the war villages, whose European trade seems to have been largely restricted to the English. Stone tools were not needed to supplement metal tools once the production demands of the deer skin trade began to be felt in the Small Prairie villages.

THE CHICKASAW PROJECT

Unfortunately, this hypothesis about trade relations and stone tool production would be difficult to test by excavating Chickasaw village sites in the Large and Small Prairies, since most of them have been destroyed by the growth of Tupelo. Therefore, John O'Hear and I initiated a joint Mississippi State University–University of Mississippi project to reanalyze the collections from the Chickasaw sites excavated by Jesse Jennings and Albert Spaulding between 1939 and 41 in preparation for the construction of the Natchez Trace Parkway. The Chickasaw Nation is an equal partner in the project, and the National Park Service has made the collections available for study. In addition, the Museum of Man at Louisiana State University has loaned us the collections for the 1938 Moreau Chambers excavations at MLe14, one of the Large Prairie sites. The project was funded by the National Endowment for the Humanities with cost share support from Ole Miss and MSU. We have a sizeable collection of mostly eighteenth-century Chickasaw artifacts from both Large and Small Prairie villages.

This project was designed specifically to measure the way in which the internal social structure of the Chickasaws impacted their relationship with the French, English, and other Indians. While the metal artifacts will be more useful in measuring the relative importance of the French and the English as trade partners and the glass beads will be better in developing fine-grained chronological control, the stone tools can tell us a good deal about the rate at which the indigenous technology was replaced and how that can be related to social organization and other factors.

This paper will concentrate on the lithic artifacts from two of the sites in our sample. The MLe14 village site, located in the Large Prairie, was originally thought to have been Ackia, the village which was the focus of one of the French attacks in 1736. As a result, it received a good deal of attention, having been excavated by Moreau Chamber, Henry Collins, and Jesse Jennings. Jennings (1941) determined that it was not the village of Ackia. This is a reasonable conclusion since we know that Ackia was one of the Small Prairie villages. Recently, James Atkinson (1985) has proposed that MLe18, another of the sites excavated by Jennings and Spaulding is a likely candidate for the main village of the Peace Chief. This will be the second assemblage to be examined in this analysis (Table 4.1).

One class of stone tools was, for the most part, manufactured by Europeans.

Table 4.1 Stone Tools from Two Chickasaw Sites

	MLe14	MLe18
Gun Spalls		
British	10	3
French	—	6
Native	2	1
Dallas Points	36	9
Edwards Points	2	—
Knives	2	—
Awls	2	1
Scrapers	22	15
Pipe Preforms	—	2
Pipes	—	5

This is, of course, the gun spalls (Figure 4.1). Following the standard terminology, these are designated as spalls rather than flints because they were made from flake blanks rather than segments of blades. This matches the other chronological diagnostics which indicate that the two sites were occupied during the early part of the eighteenth century, since gun flints were not introduced until the second half of the century (Witthoft 1966). Gun spalls can also be classified by raw material and, therefore, country of origin. Of the twelve spalls from MLe14, all but two were made from the dark grey chert, which is likely to have been derived from the chalk deposits at Dover, England, and were ultimately brought to the Southeast by the British, likely through Charlestown, fitting our expectations of a primarily English–Large Prairie trade relationship. The two non-British spalls are of native manufacture. As predicted from the ethnographic accounts, the people of the Small Prairie village located at MLe18 traded with both the French and the English; three of ten gun spalls are British, six are French, and one is native made.

Bifaces were found at both sites, but only MLe14 produced examples of the large, broad, well-made tools that are interpreted to have been knives. The MLe14 collection contained two of the three awls in the present sample. Arrowheads make up slightly more than half of the finished stone tools at MLe14 and most of these are the elongated, excurvate "triangular," Dallas points that characterize Protohistoric and Historic assemblages from this region. There are two examples of Edwards Stemmed, var. Sunflower points, which may be significant because this form is much more common in the Yazoo Basin and in the Natchez Hills region of western Mississippi. It is considered by some to occur late in the sequence (Williams and Brain 1983) and is frequently found on sites with historic period Natchez occupations (Brown 1985). We know from both the archaeology and the documents that the Large Prairie was the refuge of the Natchez who fled their homeland following the French reprisals for the Natchez uprising in 1729. The occurrence of these arrowheads in the MLe14 collection along with Fatherland Incised, the major diagnostic of the Natchez ceramic complex, is suggestive of the presence of the Natchez in the Large Prairie region.

Historic-period finished bifaces make up slightly more than a quarter of the assemblage at MLe18 and consist exclusively of triangular points. This is in keeping with our expectation that, because of the fact that Small Prairie Chickasaws traded with both the French and the English, they had better access to trade goods. While there are about equal numbers of arrowheads and gun spalls at MLe18, three times as many arrowheads as gun spalls were found at at MLe14, the Large Prairie site.

Scrapers, on the other hand, do not fall into expected patterns. They are an important component of both site collections. Perhaps traditional men's tools, like weapons, were replaced by metal tools before the hide-working tools, which were likely used by women. Gender must certainly have been a factor in stone tool replacement during this period of time.

The one class of lithic artifact found at MLe18 but not at MLe14 is that of native-made stone smoking pipes (Figure 4.3). This is all the more interesting because the MLe14 collection is considerably larger than the one from MLe18. The pipes from MLe18 are remarkable in their diversity. At least two were unfinished and they were made from several kinds of raw material. The only ones that are similar are those which appear to have been copies of European kaolin pipes. The fact that long narrow bifaces are relatively rare at MLe18 supports the conclusion, based on the lack of evident wear, that these tools were not used as pipe drills and are likely to have been awls used in the preparation of skins. Without making too much of the correlation, if MLe18 is Ackia, the peace chief might have made use of these pipes in formal settings. Incidently, in keeping with the extreme distance from ports of trade and the fragile nature of kaolin pipes, they are rare at Chickasaw sites.

CONCLUSION

This first look at the Park Service collections from the Tupelo area Chickasaw sites suggests that, in broad outline, the earlier characterization of the two settlement areas and their relationship to European trade partners is correct. Because considerably more excavations were conducted at MLe14, the collection from that site is larger than the one from MLe18. Ultimately it will be interesting to examine the ratio of stone tools to potsherds in order to answer questions about the rate of replacement for the lithic industries. Until those data are available, proportions within the lithic assemblages from the two sites are informa-

Fig. 4.3. Stone pipes from MLe18

tive. So, the fact that the ratio of arrowheads to European gun spalls is 1.0 for MLe18 and 3.6 for MLe14 indicates that the people of Small Prairie village might have had better access to metal artifacts, which allowed them to abandon lithic tool production earlier in the eighteenth century. Also, the fact that the Small Prairie collection contained both British and French gun spalls while only British gun spalls appear to have been imported into the Large Prairie village fits our expectations.

The results from the analysis of other classes of artifacts are beginning to come in. Metal (the gun parts in particular) indicates that the exclusively British alignment of the Large Prairie village suggested by the gun spalls may not be so straightforward. Also, the trade bead assemblage for MLe14 indicates that this village was occupied for most of the first half of the eighteenth century while MLe18 appears to have been abandoned twenty to thirty years earlier. This points to one of the challenges, and advantages, of Contact-period research. It is a period of rapid change, and two or three decades can be important in measuring that change.

However, the bulk of the artifacts from Chickasaw sites are derived from what local researchers call midden pits. These are broad shallow pits measuring two or three meters across and a meter or less in depth. They are likely to have been the source of the clay used in plastering the walls of the Chickasaw houses. Preliminary analysis of the contents from the midden pits assemblages in the Park Service collections indicates that they were filled with trash in a relatively short time after they were dug. So, although it is often not possible to reconstruct the proveniences from the notes with enough precision to allow levels within the midden pits to be understood, the basic unit of our analysis will be the pits themselves and we will be able to seriate them using the glass beads. The result will be a fine-scale chronology of the way in which the Chickasaws related to their neighbors and their economic partners.

The study of Contact-period lithic assemblages shows promise of contributing a great deal to anthropology. In the first place, a study of the distribution of lithic artifacts in time and space can yield insight into the social and economic adjustments of this dynamic period. Patterns of innovation and replacement can be proposed on the basis of the archaeological record and tested using the documents, then refined by returning to the archaeological record. As we bring together the work of the various specialists working on the Chickasaw project, including an ethnohistorian, we are beginning to be able to take advantage of the relationship between the various data sets and to derive a much clearer picture of the past.

ACKNOWLEDGMENTS

First, I would like to thank the National Endowment for the Humanities for providing the funding for this project. A number of people have contributed to the research, primary among them being my collaborators: Robbie Ethridge, John O'Hear, Keith Jacobi, and Susan Scott. We thank the people at the Southeast Archaeological Center in Tallahassee for taking such good care of the artifacts for all these years and for introducing us to the mysteries of the National Park Service cataloging system. The Chickasaw Nation has helped us in many ways. In particular I thank them for LaDonna Brown and Donna Rausch, two Chickasaw graduate students who counted most of the rocks that I report on in this paper.

5
Tools of Contact

A Functional Analysis of the Cameron Site Chipped-Stone Assemblage

Michael L. Carmody

The introduction of European materials into Native-American cultures during the Contact period had undeniable ramifications on traditional technological systems. From a functional perspective, the articulation between the new European materials, particularly metal, and stone tools is crucial to understanding how native cultures integrated European materials into their cultural systems. Our reconstructions of this integration must consider the potential for both functional and symbolic uses of the new European materials within the native cultural systems. This analysis focuses on the chipped-stone assemblage from the Cameron site, a Central New York Oneida Iroquois site dating to approximately A.D. 1590–1600. I conducted use-wear analysis on a sample of formal and informal tools from the collection to delineate the types of activities performed with chipped-stone tools on the site.

Projectile tools, which dominate the Cameron site assemblage, appear to indicate increasing external conflict during this time period. Traditionally, archaeologists attribute Iroquoian aggression during the Contact period as competition for beaver trapping grounds. This paper critically evaluates the cultural assumptions inherent in the "Beaver Wars" hypothesis and presents an alternate hypothesis for Iroquoian aggression during the early Contact period which fits within a traditional Iroquoian cultural framework.

TRADE ITEMS, PERCEPTION, AND LITHIC ANALYSIS

The introduction of trade items in the early Contact period brought several new classes of materials to the Native Americans. Prominent among these materials was metal. Twentieth-century Westerners generally consider base metal in terms of technological efficiency. However, even in our modern culture with our technologically oriented worldview, metal serves many symbolic functions such as decoration for jewelry, as well as mixed techno-symbolic purposes such as found with fine silver (Wells 1991:91). This dynamic interplay cannot be ignored. Hence, an analysis of new materials in cultural systems must address multiple potential meanings and uses (Bradley and Childs 1991; Miller and Hamell 1986).

Among the Iroquois, metal tools eventually replaced stone tools in many cases (Pratt 1976:122; Wray et al. 1991:322). While this did not necessarily occur immediately in all lithic categories, the introduction of knives, axes, and other metal tools was often directly responsible for the cessation of some stone tool production. This replacement implies a clear understanding of the functional utility of the metal object in the mind of the user. This might have been the case in some situations, but not all.

James Bradley and Terry Childs (1991) hypothesized that an awareness of native worldviews is essential in understanding how Iroquoians incorporated Europeans and their goods into their world. Bradley and Childs's analysis of the manufacturing techniques, the composition of the materials, and the distribution of the spiral and hoop copper artifacts found on sixteenth-century Iroquois and Susquehannock sites indicates that these items are actually of native manufacture, although the materials are of European origin. Previous theories postulated that these items were of European manufacture and were subsequently traded into the Northeast. Bradley and Childs (1991:16) believe that the native worldview reflected in reworked European objects created a situation in which the early European colonizers were viewed as "returning cultural heroes, otherworldly man-beings who rose up from beneath the World's rim on floating islands, bringing with them a wealth of Under(water) World substances." They argue that the copper obtained through trade was reshaped by the Iroquois in the form of hoops and spirals to represent the panther's tail. In Iroquois mythology, the Underwater Panther was the guardian of the underworld with dominant power in the underworld (Bradley and Childs 1991:16). Representations of the panther have been found on Iroquoian sites dating before European contact as far back as the Middle Woodland period. This interpretation presents a strong argument for a symbolic understanding of metal trade items in the early Contact period.

Christopher Miller and George Hamell (1986:314) have come to similar conclusions with regard to the symbolic importance of European trade items in the early Contact period: "both the historical and the archaeological record indicate that the impact of early European utilitarian trade goods on practical subsistence was negligible." This view led them to conclude that Native Americans did not view European trade goods as something new, but assimilated them into "traditional native ideological systems . . . as material components of great ritual significance" (Miller and Hamell 1986:315). One such situation on which Miller and Hamell elaborate is that of glass trade beads (Hamell 1983; Miller and Hamell 1986). They feel that, among the Iroquois, these items were equated with shell beads and crystals. It was through this association that trade beads entered into the Iroquois cultural system (Miller and Hamell 1986:316). Archaeological and ethnohistoric data regarding context and possible uses of trade beads supports this interpretation (Hammell 1983; Pratt 1983:217; Wray et al. 1991:119–121, 317–321).

Lithic use-wear analysis provides an avenue of inquiry into one traditional technological system—chipped-stone tool use. We can view the sorts of activities stone tools performed on a site and look at the potential for the functional incorporation of some of the trade items that were introduced. In this regard, we can identify the level of functional incorporation of trade items into the practical subsistence activities of the Native communities.

THE CAMERON SITE

Located in Oneida County, New York, the Cameron site is an early Contact-period Oneida Iroquois site (Figure 5.1). It is situated on a peninsula of land extending westerly into the Stockbridge Valley. The north and south sides of the site have steep slopes which extend down to small creeks, both flowing west into Oneida Creek (Figure 5.2). Due to its isolated geographical location, the Cameron site, unlike many sites in upstate New York, has not been disturbed by farming. It is approximately a quarter of a mile in length (402.25 m) and 75 feet wide (22.86 m) (Bennett 1981:2; Bennett and Clark 1978:1).

The slopes on both the northern and southern sides of the site are covered with very rich middens reaching approximately one-and-a-half feet (.5 m) in depth. Avocational archaeologists and pot hunters have excavated large portions of these middens over the years (Bennett 1981:2; Bennett and Clark 1978:2–3; Pratt 1976:121). The eastern edge of the site was heavily fortified with a double stockade, as is common with Iroquois sites of this time period. Archaeologists identified traces of a double stockade on the northern and southern edges of the site as well. Approximately 15 storage pits have been located to date, scattered across the living area of the site (Pratt 1976:121).

In the summer of 1991, Binghamton University conducted a field school at the Cameron site. The field school excavated on the upper portion of the site in a midden 75 feet (22.9 m) west of a longhouse. Twenty-two, 5 × 5 ft (1.5 × 1.5 m) units were excavated that summer. Twenty-one of these units were continuous and located within the midden. A single unit was excavated 30 feet (9.1 m) north of this area in an attempt to explore one of the hillside middens. The midden provenience of the recovered artifacts provides the basis for the assumption that a wide range of the domestic activities conducted on the site is represented in this collection.

Among the Oneida Iroquois, the earliest identified site with European goods

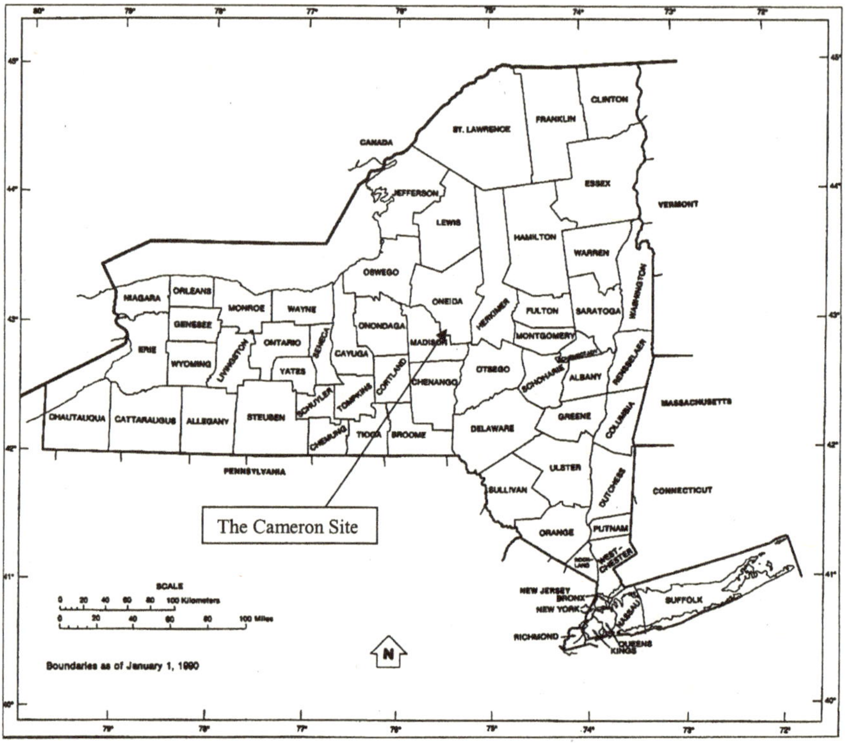

Fig. 5.1. Location of Cameron Site in New York State

is the Vaillancort site. Dating to the mid–sixteenth century, this site has only produced a large iron knife and small quantities of brass beads and buttons (Grumet 1995:378; Pratt 1976:117–118). Following the Vaillancort site in the Oneida sequence are the Bach and Diable sites, both with limited numbers of European items, most notably glass trade beads (Pratt 1976:118–120). Chronologically, the Cameron site is the next site in the Oneida sequence. This site has produced much higher quantities of European goods, including 15 wrought iron axes, an iron sword blade, at least 25 iron knives, a number of glass trade beads, a brass kettle, and numerous brass and copper scraps. Many of these copper scraps have been cut into triangular pieces, presumably for use as projectile points, but several have been rolled into tinklers and several animal effigies have been recovered, including bear and salamander shapes (Pratt 1976:122–123). The quantity of European goods found at the Cameron site clearly indicates increased trade between the Iroquois and Europeans at the close of the sixteenth century.

The degree of direct contact the Oneida Iroquois had with the Europeans

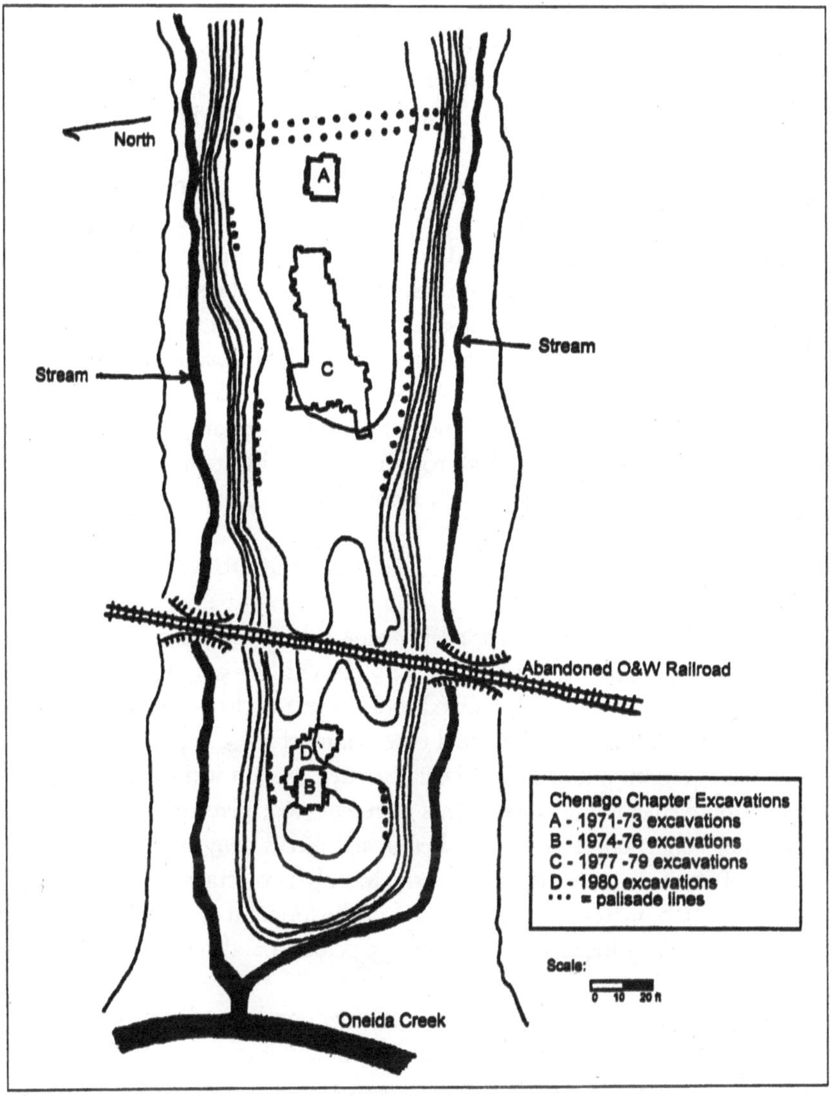

Fig. 5.2. Map of the Cameron Site. The 1991 Binghamton University excavations were situated 75 feet (22.9 m) west of area C (adapted from Bennett 1991)

this early in the Contact period is difficult to assess. The Oneida are located in the central portion of Iroquoia. While the Cameron site is the fourth site in the Oneida sequence on which trade items have been located, it is likely that other Native-American groups with greater exposure to the Europeans, such as the Mohawk, traded these items into Iroquoia. In this scenario, the individuals at the Cameron site would have had no actual physical contact with Europeans. The first recorded journey into the heart of Iroquoia was Harmen van den Bogart's 1634 (van den Bogart 1988) diplomatic journey into Mohawk and Oneida territory, occurring several decades after the proposed occupation of the Cameron site.

Pinpointing the exact source from which the Oneida obtained trade items is also difficult. The French maintained a presence in the Great Lakes region to the northwest. The Dutch colonized Long Island and surrounding areas to the east and southeast, while the English colonized areas to the south as well as the coastal northeast. All of these groups are potential origins of the items recovered at the Cameron site. The only item recovered from the Cameron site that has been traced to its origin is a sword blade. It bears the maker's mark of Hans Maum, an expert sword-maker working in Solingen, Germany, in the latter portion of the sixteenth century (Pratt 1976:123). But this item could have been obtained through any of the previously mentioned groups.

LITHIC ASSEMBLAGE AND METHODOLOGY

The tool assemblage from the 1991 Binghamton University excavations at the Cameron site is dominated by bifaces (43.5 percent, *N*=54). The bifacial tool category encompasses bifacially worked tool fragments that could not be positively identified as a more specific tool type. Many of these appeared to be projectile point margins but could not be categorized as such without the presence of a hafting element. Projectile points represent 36.3 percent (*N*=45) of the formal tool collection (Figure 5.3). Retouched pieces comprised 12.1 percent (*N*=15) of the tool assemblage. Interestingly, only two scrapers were identified in this collection, representing 1.6 percent of the formal tool assemblage. Other tool types identified include four burins (2.5 percent) and one graver (1.6 percent).

Use-wear analysis addresses issues of tool function beyond technological aspects of production. Wear patterns on the tool sample were analyzed and specific attributes, discussed below, were compared to assess the range of variation in the general types of wear-patterning present. A basic assumption of use-wear analysis, which has been validated by experimental tests, is that different tool functions and worked materials produce different wear patterns (Bamforth 1988; Bamforth et al 1990; Juel-Jensen 1994; Keeley 1980; Vaughan 1985). Tools from the Cameron site were placed into use-wear categories based on similar use-wear patterning. These categories represent tools that are assumed to have been used to work like materials in a similar manner.

One of the major criticisms of use-wear analysis is that it is an extremely time-consuming procedure (Odell 1975:230; Odell and Odell-Vereecken 1980). This is a valid critique, but it should not prevent lithic analysts from making use of such a valuable technique. To circumvent this problem, the tool assemblage from the Cameron Site was sampled, providing a representative group of tools for analysis. Because tool form is frequently associated with function, it was crucial that all of the defined tool types be included in the use-wear analysis in order to critically evaluate this assumption. Specimens were sampled within the defined tool types so that a minimum of 15 percent of each of the tool types was examined.

All of the tools selected for use-wear analysis were examined at low magnification (7×–30×) before being examined at high magnification (100×–500×). A Cambridge Instruments stereomicroscope was used for the low magnification analysis. Two wear attributes were recorded: edge damage and striations (Odell and Odell-Vereecken 1980). The dimensions of variation recorded to assess edge damage were type, amount, and location of scarring. The type of scar was recorded in relation to the negative impression of the flake termination. These categories were feathered, stepped, or hinged. The amount of scarring was recorded in subjective categories: absent, minimal, moderate, or extensive. Minimal damage referred to tools in which edge damage was present but limited to a small number of flake scars. Moderate edge damage referred to tools in which the original edge of the tool was still present in most areas of use, but more than just a few flake scars were present and/or edge rounding was present. Extensive edge damage referred to tools in which the original edge of the tool was no longer present in the area of use, a high number of flake scars were visible, and/or the edge of the tool was highly rounded.

The dimensions of variation recorded for the striations were amount and orientation to the edge. The amount of striations was recorded as absent, minimal, moderate, or high. The orientation of the striations was recorded in relation to the edge of the tool (e.g., parallel, perpendicular, diagonal, or multidirectional).

The low magnification analysis provides information on the hardness of the worked material and the motion of the tool. Harder worked materials, such as wood and bone, create more edge damage and produce more striations, while softer materials, such as plants, do less damage to the edge and leave fewer striations. The orientation of striations to the edge of the tool and the location of edge scarring are strong indicators of tool motion. For example, a tool with striations perpendicular to the edge of the tool and with edge scarring only on one surface is an indication of a tool used with a transverse motion relative to the used edge, commonly referred to as a scraping motion (Odell and Odell-Vereecken 1980:99; Vaughan 1995:20).

The high magnification analysis focused on characterizing micropolishes at 100×–500× magnification. An Olympus Metallurgical reflected-light microscope was used for this analysis. The dimensions of variation for polishes recorded

Fig. 5.3. Projectile points recovered from the Cameron Site

during this analysis were location, degree of intrusion, reflectivity, boundary type, component linkage, topography, texture, and directional features and their orientation (Juel-Jensen 1994; Vaughan 1985).

ANALYSIS

Use-wear analysis delineated seven different polish and wear pattern categories and one non-diagnostic category in the 35 tools analyzed (Figure 5.4). Tools displaying wear patterns consistent with use as projectiles represent 41 percent of the tool sample (*N*=14). This category included all of the morphologically defined projectile points, but it also included bifaces with wear patterns consistent with use as a projectile. All of the formal projectile points were of the triangular Madison type. Tools characterized as projectiles were further subdivided into heavily and lightly used projectiles. The lightly used projectiles show limited hafting wear at the implement's base and very little edge damage, particularly at the tip.

Hafting wear primarily consists of isolated polish bright on the interior surface of the tool near the basal end. These polish bright spots are frequently linear in nature or contain linear elements, such as striations in the surface of the polish. These linear elements appear to be related to the haft bind and are generally oriented perpendicular or nearly perpendicular to the lateral edge of the tool (Juel-Jensen 1994:250–251; Kay 1996:329–330). Occasionally, the basal edge exhibits damage in the form of abrasion, edge scarring, or both (Odell and Odell-Vereecken 1980:100). Of the 14 tools classified as projectiles, nine were lightly used.

Heavily used projectiles exhibit hafting wear and edge damage at the tip, including striations with multidirectional orientation and edge scarring (frequently in the form of step fractures) and a spotty generic weak polish development restricted to the higher areas around the tip. Only one of the 14 designated projectiles shows wear patterns indicative of secondary use as a cutting implement.

The production and use of projectile tools is likely associated with hunting and warfare activities. Due to the high frequency of projectile tools relative to other use categories, it must be concluded that these activities were of central importance to the Iroquois during this time period. However, that these activities occurred on the site proper is doubtful. No evidence of warfare at the Cameron Site exists, but the location of the site, a highly defensible position with fortification in the form of palisades, indicates that external conflict likely occurred during this time period. This conclusion is supported by the ethnohistoric record (Morgan 1851:8–9). Of the use-wear tool sample, 41.2 percent (*N*=14) were classified as projectile tools. Pratt identifies 99.1 percent (*N*=1416) of the chipped-stone tool assemblage taken from avocational excavations at the Cameron site as projectile points (Pratt 1976:253–255). The high frequency of both these tools and the wear patterns associated with projectile tools make it apparent that activities associated with projectiles, such as the preparation for hunting and warfare, were a significant focus of activity on the site. This preparation likely focused on the production of projectile points. A technological assessment of the debitage recovered from the 1991 Binghamton University excavations revealed that later stage biface production, such as

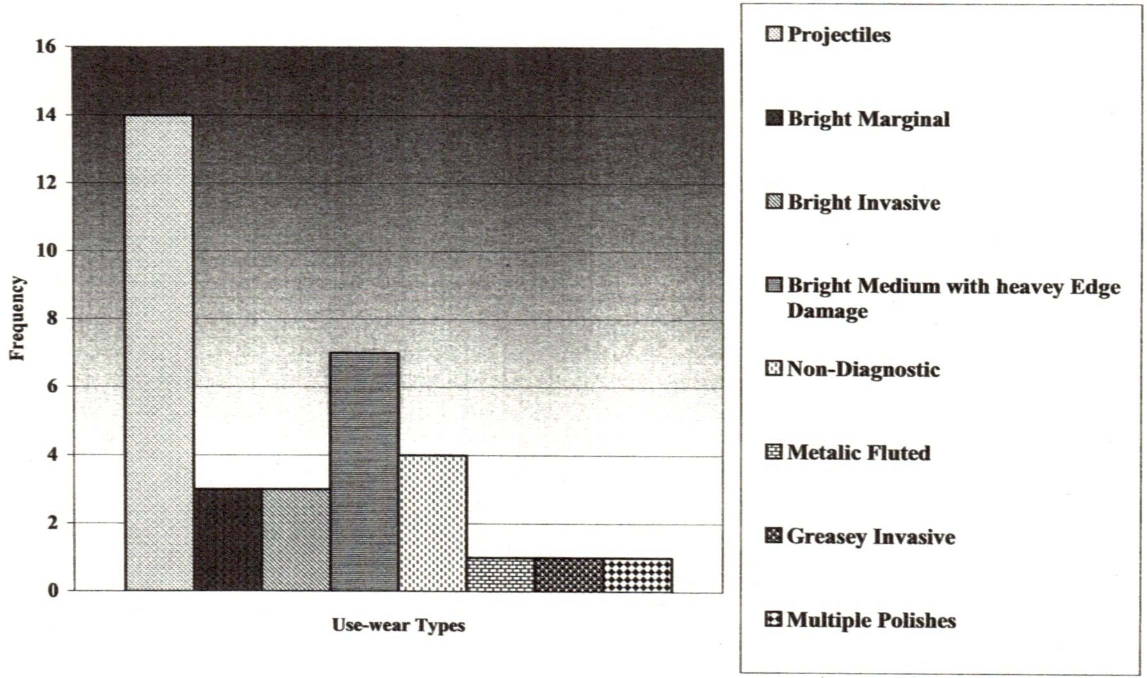

Fig. 5.4. Frequency of wear pattern types

projectile point production, was a focus of the chipped-stone technology at the Cameron site (Carmody 1999:69–71).

Tools characterized by moderately intrusive bright polishes with heavy edge damage are the second most frequently occurring tool type at 21 percent (*N*=7). Uniformity of edge damage was the most distinctive characteristic of this group. These tools exhibit large and small scalloped-shaped edge scars, typical of flakes that have a feathered termination, and edge scars with step fractures. Four of the seven tools in this group exhibit both types of edge scarring, while the other three exhibit extensive scalloped scarring. All but one of the tools exhibit linear features in the form of striations either in the surface of the rock or in the surface of the polish. Edge damage is accompanied by a bright moderately intrusive polish. The surface topography of this polish is a combination of domed and flat. This variation is likely the result of the duration of tool use, but could also indicate that this category of wear patterning includes several types of similar worked materials.

While a confident assessment of the specific activities that these use-wear patterns represent would require an experimental replication project, which was not conducted as part of this research, this type of use-wear patterning is consistent with cutting and scraping motions on relatively hard siliceous materials such as fresh wood or soaked antler or bone (Juel-Jensen 1994:231–232; Vaughan 1985:31–34). This likely represents activities such as making arrow shafts, carving decorative and ceremonial items, and longhouse maintenance. The frequency in which these use-wear patterns occur indicate that these activities occupied a less significant amount of time than the production of projectiles but were still an important aspect of stone tool activities.

Tools characterized by marginal to moderately intrusive bright polishes comprise slightly under 10 percent of the tool sample (*N*=3). The most distinctive characteristic of this tool group is the lack of edge damage. The polish on all of these tools was characterized as bright with a smooth texture. Both domed and flat polish topographies are present in this category.

This type of wear pattern is consistent with cutting soft siliceous materials such as plants (Juel-Jensen 1994; Vaughan 1985:35–36). These tools likely represent activities such as plant gathering and some food preparation. Marginal polishes are indicative of tools that do not penetrate deep into the material being worked, thus eliminating some types of food processing from this category. Also, nonplant food products, such as meat, produce very different types of use-wear patterns. The preparation of these types of food products must be excluded from this category of use-wear patterns.

The second use-wear pattern category occurring in slightly under 10 percent of the tool sample is characterized by intrusive bright polishes accompanied by a moderate damage (*N*=3). The combination of very intrusive polishes and edge damage, in the form of large scalar scars, are the distinctive attributes of this use-wear category. These types of use-wear patterns are consistent with cutting siliceous material of moderate hardness, such as fibrous plant material (Juel-Jensen 1994; Vaughan 1985:33–36). The invasive nature of the polish indicates that these tools penetrated relatively deep into the material they were working. These activities likely included food preparation and the production of some craft items such as basketry. Both of the last two use categories occurred in low frequencies. These activities, while present on the site, do not appear to have been the focus of stone tool activities on the site.

Two tools in the sample have a polish with a greasy reflection. One of these also exhibits a marginally intrusive bright polish along the opposite edge. The presence of two polish types indicates that this tool likely performed multiple functions. The second tool with a greasy polish exhibits a considerable amount of edge damage in the form of large and small scalar scars and step fractures. Striations oriented diagonally to the edge were also observed on the same edge. Polish bright spots, often associated with hafting, were located on the opposite edge of the tool. This edge also had some larger scalar edge scars, possibly resulting from a haft.

Greasy polishes are generally associated with animal butchering (Bamforth et al. 1990:420; Vaughan 1985:38). One of the two tools identified with a greasy polish also has other use-wear patterns consistent with animal butchering. The second tool has two edges with different use-wear patterns. One edge has characteristics similar to animal butchering use-wear patterning. However, this edge does not appear to have been extensively used. The low frequency in which tools with this type of use-wear occurs indicates that stone tools were not frequently utilized for animal butchering activities on this site.

The final use category was designated non-diagnostic and represents slightly over 10 percent of the tool sample (N=4). These tools have polishes in the initial phases of development. During this phase of polish development, the dimensions of variation that make polishes diagnostic have not yet developed. Several materials can produce polishes that never progress beyond this initial phase of development. Because the polish on these four tools all occurred on very limited areas of the tool edge, they have been interpreted as tools used for a very brief period of time, instead of being indicative of working materials that only produce weak polishes.

One tool in the sample exhibits a very different polish type found at the tip of the tool. This polish was characterized as metallic in reflectivity with a fluid topography. The surface of this polish has fluting or wave-like ripples, as well as striations oriented parallel to the edge of the tool. This type of polish is typical of a tool that was scraped hard against a piece of metal such as a screen, shovel, or trowel. As a result, this polish is not considered functionally related.

Use-wear evidence indicates a relatively limited range of activities represented in the chipped-stone tool assemblage from the Cameron site. Due to the dearth of Contact period use-wear studies, very little comparative data exists. Lithic assemblages from two early Contact-period Seneca sites, the Tram and Seneca Cameron sites, indicate that a slightly broader range of morphological tool types were recovered. Also, the projectile points were not identified in such high percentages relative to other tool types (Wray et al. 1991). This is an indication that stone tools likely performed a broader range of activities at these sites. While seven separate use categories were defined in the tool sample, only two of these occur in frequencies high enough to be considered foci of activity on the site. Projectiles are clearly a main focus of the Cameron site chipped-stone tool assemblage. These tools likely represent two separate activities—hunting and warfare. The other category abundant enough to indicate a focus of activity on the site were tools with moderately intrusive bright polishes and extensive edge damage, likely representing wood and bone working. The tools with bright marginal and bright intrusive polishes were likely used in activities that occurred with moderate frequency, probably plant processing. The other use-wear categories present in this sample occurred in less than 5 percent of the sample. This indicates that, although other activities occurred on the site, they were limited in scope or carried out with non-lithic tools.

DISCUSSION

The relatively limited range of tool functions identified through the functional analysis at the Cameron site is an indication that trade goods likely filled at least some functional roles in on-site activities. Cutting activities were primarily limited to plant processing, while animal butchering activities were represented in very low percentages. Throughout the years, excavations at the site have revealed at least 25 iron knives, tools that might well have served this function (Pratt 1976:123). Additionally, archaeologists have not recovered any stone axes from the site, while at least 15 iron axes have been located (Pratt 1976:123). These items likely filled functional roles very similar to those for which they were manufactured.

Copper and brass scraps are the most prevalent trade items found on the Cameron site, presumably cut from kettles traded into Iroquoia (Figure 5.5). Several of the early avocational excavations at the Cameron site revealed two compete brass kettles (Pratt 1976:275). While an exact number of copper and brass items recovered from the site throughout the years is difficult to ascertain, all site reports indicate a relatively high frequency of copper and brass items (Bennett 1981; Bennett and Bigford 1968; Bennett and Clark 1978). As mentioned earlier, these items were found in the form of triangular projectile points, as well as tinklers and effigy figures (Grumet 1995:378; Pratt 1976:279). This class of trade goods appears to have filled both symbolic and functional roles in the early Contact-period Oneida Iroquois context.

One class of stone tools is conspicuously absent from the Cameron site collection—scrapers. Reports of early avocational excavations report only five chipped-stone scrapers recovered on the site. No trade items recovered appear to have served in this capacity. The absence of scrapers is particularly striking because of the well-documented intensification of the fur trade throughout the Contact period (Campisi 1978; Odell chapter 3; Trigger 1978). The dearth of scrapers clearly indicates that the trapping and processing of beaver pelts, the fur type in highest demand among Europeans, was not a focus of activities among the individuals at the Cameron site. This conclusion has important ramifications for the interpretation of the uses behind the projectile points, so prevalent in the Cameron site assemblage.

The simultaneous production of copper projectile points and chipped-stone projectile points throughout the Contact period highlights the importance of projectile tools to Iroquoian groups during the late sixteenth and seventeenth centuries. The numerous projectile points recovered from the Cameron site has led Pratt to state, "the vast quantities of projectile points exceed those recovered at any Oneida village and attest to a preoccupation with warfare at this site" (Pratt 1976:122). Excavations at the Eaton site, a Contact-period Seneca site dating to approximately the same time period as the Cameron site, show similar patterns in projectile point production (William Englebrecht, personal communication 2000).

Evidence of external conflict—starting in the late prehistoric period with the first appearance of fortified villages located in easily defensible positions—continues into the Contact period with more heavily fortified villages and intensified production of projectile points. Increased warfare during the Contact period is frequently associated with the fur trade. The intensification of the fur trade throughout the Contact period is well established (Brandao 1997:86; Trigger 1978:354). Iroquoianists frequently interpret this intensification as a fundamental shift in the economic basis of the Iroquois (Campisi 1978:482; Trigger 1978:354). This shift changed the focus of the Iroquois economy from the seasonal round of farming and hunting to trapping beavers for their pelts and trading them to Europeans, mostly Dutch and French, in exchange for European goods. This model of the Iroquoian economy during the Contact period posits that as the Iroquois became more accustomed to European goods they became dependent on these items (Brandao 1997:51). This dependence led to the intensification of the fur trade. As beaver populations decreased due to overexploitation, the Iroquois had to travel greater distances to trap beaver for trade (Trigger 1978:353). Iroquoian warfare during this period is frequently regarded

Fig. 5.5. Copper artifacts recovered from the Cameron Site

as competition for prime beaver-trapping grounds. This model of conflict is referred to as the "Beaver Wars" (Campisi 1978:482; Trigger 1978:354).

Due to a lack of evidence for these economically driven wars, the "Beaver Wars" interpretation has recently been challenged on the grounds that this hypothesis is based on unsupported assumptions about Iroquoian culture (Brandao 1997; Richter 1992:50–74). Brandao (1997:9) feels that at the heart of the "Beaver Wars" interpretation are ethnocentric assumptions that the Iroquois culture was inferior to European culture and that the Iroquois would naturally value

European goods over their own. He sees the notion of economically driven warfare as alien to the Iroquois and baseless in their cultural system:

> Insofar as warfare was an expression of cultural, political, and military dictates, no goal of warring was as crucial to the Iroquois as the capture of people. Prisoners were central to nearly all the functions served by warfare. Without captives, warriors did not gain as much esteem, victims for torture were lacking, deaths could not be avenged, and grief could not be assuaged. More important, without prisoners to be adopted into Iroquois society to take the place of the deceased and to bolster Iroquois fighting strength, the Iroquois would wither away and die. The decline in population would lead to the fragmentation of their clan system and with it the social and political structures of their society (Brandao 1997:44).

With the high quantity of projectile points, the fortification of the site, and the location of the site in an easily defensible position, the Cameron site provides evidence for external conflict. Additionally, the lack of scrapers at this site seems to indicate that the trapping of beavers and processing of their furs was not likely a motivation behind this external conflict.

By the mid–seventeenth century, Iroquois League attacks on outside groups became so intense that they had completely decimated the Huron and Pentun, two native groups located in present-day Ontario (Brandao 1997:75). These groups were located near prime beaver-trapping grounds. This fact led to the interpretation of these attacks as economically motivated. However, the beaver pelts might only have been the spoils of victory. Also, attacking groups who were returning to their villages weighed down with beaver pelts might have been a strategy of procuring captives (Brandao 1997:51–54; Richter 1992:50–74).

Evidence indicating intensive warfare throughout the Contact period is overwhelming. The motivation behind these attacks is difficult to ascertain, but interpreting these attacks as economically driven does not coincide with contemporary understandings of traditional Iroquoian culture. The Iroquois had much to gain from obtaining beaver pelts, but it seems unlikely that control of hunting grounds was the impetus for these attacks, particularly in the early Contact period. The need to obtain captives to adopt into their groups remains a strong hypothesis for the motivation behind these wars (Brandao 1997:51–54; Richter 1992:50–74). Increased mortality rates due to disease is a potential reason for a rise in adoption during the early Contact period.

Adoption, a well-documented practice among the Iroquois, functioned to replace individuals who had died within a group (Brandao 1997:42–43; Campisi 1978:482; Englebrecht 1985:174; Morgan 1851:339–344; Richter 1992:32–38;

Snow 1994:73). Captives of war raids generally faced two fates: adoption, torture, or both. Frequently, an individual who showed particular resilience to the pain of torture was selected for adoption. Once adopted, an individual enjoyed all of the privileges of the position in Iroquoian society that the individuals they replaced had earned throughout their lives. The practice of adoption allowed the Iroquois to remain a powerful political force throughout the eighteenth century (Brandao 1997:41–43).

One political factor, the formation of the League of the Iroquois, and two social factors, increased site population density and increased population mobility, are nonbiological factors that could account for an increase in disease transmission during the late prehistoric and early Contact period. As discussed above, an increase in disease would likely trigger the need for adoptees to replace the dead. The time period at which the League of the Iroquois formed has been a topic of considerable debate among Iroquoianists. Snow (1994) argues that the League of the Iroquois could not have formed before 1500. This formation strengthened Iroquoian clans and concurrently decreased the emphasis on lineages in determining residential patterning. With the limited number of clans among the Iroquois, it would be easy for individuals, or groups of individuals, to find members of their particular clan elsewhere in the League, thus allowing for an increased degree of mobility (Englebrecht 1985:173–175; Tuck 1978).

Englebrecht's (1985) analysis of late prehistoric and protohistoric ceramics from Seneca and Oneida sites identified a trend of increasing heterogeneity in ceramic artifacts throughout this time period. The Cameron site, referred to as the Wayland-Smith site, is included in this analysis. Englebrecht attributes this heterogeneity to the increased mobility of women, who were frequently responsible for carrying provisions on journeys or who might have also been traveling on their own. He also suggests that tribal exogamy might have allowed increased movement of individuals during this time period (Englebrecht 1985:178–179).

Among the Mohawk, site population density increased from a level of 20 square meters per person, prior to 1500, to 12 square meters per person between 1500 and 1633 (Snow 1992:177). It is likely that similar population density changes occurred among the Oneida during this time period. Increased site population density would likely lead to crowded living quarters, as Snow (1992) identified. Additionally, the typical Iroquoian village had refuse dumps, containing considerable amounts of organic waste, scattered between the longhouses and around the perimeter of the site, as was the case at the Cameron site. These conditions would attract blood-feeding insects, like ticks and mosquitoes, as well as scavenging dogs and rodents, all of which would dramatically increase the chance of infectious disease epidemics. The potential formation of the League of the Iroquois during the late prehistoric or early protohistoric time period, as well as increased site population densities and increased mobility, should be considered important nonbiological factors aiding in the propagation of microorganisms which could lead to disease epidemics.

It is very possible that the external conflicts witnessed during the Contact period began as small warring parties focused on capturing potential adoptees during the late prehistoric period, cultivating an atmosphere of violence between the League and neighboring groups. As the aggression intensified, exposure to native diseases increased through conflict with the captives. As European diseases arrived in the sixteenth century, the practice of taking captives would serve to spread these deadly new diseases over a relatively wide area at a fairly rapid rate, potentially increasing the need for more warring parties and increased conflict.

The timing of the archaeological evidence for external conflict—placing it prior to European contact—highlights the need for a hypothesis that fits within a traditional Iroquoian cultural framework as the basis for this conflict. Traditionally, the need for individuals for adoption purposes was a central function of Iroquoian warring parties (Brandao 1997:42–43). The dominance of projectile points and tools classified by the functional analysis as projectile implements point to the importance of hunting and warfare during the early Contact period among the Oneida Iroquois. The simultaneous production of copper and chipped-stone projectile points in relatively high quantities is a clear indication that this tool category was functionally central to day-to-day life at the Cameron site. This fact, taken in tandem with the absence of scraping tools (normally used in the processing of beaver pelts) in the Cameron site assemblage makes motivations for conflict based on the production of beaver pelts seem unlikely.

CONCLUSION

The need to understand the functional context of traditional tools is essential in determining how trade items entered the existing material culture assemblages. The dearth of functional analysis on Contact-period sites makes it difficult to contextualize the results of this analysis on a broader scale. As Odell (chapter 3) notes, his analysis on the Wichita Lasley Vore site and Bamforth's (1993) work on the Chumash village of Helo' in southern California are possibly the only two functional analyses of Contact-period lithic assemblages sites in print. Clearly many trade items acted to replace traditional tools, such as appears to be the case with axes at the Cameron site, but other items might have followed very different trajectories as they became incorporated into the Native-American material culture assemblages, as Bradley and Childs (1991) and Miller and Hamell (1986) point out. The co-occurrence of copper and stone projectile points is an excellent example of how European materials mingled with the social reproduction of traditional cultural systems.

This analysis underscores the importance of a clear understanding of tool function and the ramifications this might have on the more broad-based reconstructions of economic interactions. However, the limitations of this analysis should be acknowledged. The collection used for the analysis was taken from a single midden on the site. It was assumed that a range of activities conducted on the site would be represented, but differential use areas scattered around the site might bias the collection. When possible, data from avocational excavations conducted on other portions of the site was consulted. Also, I did not conduct an experimental replication project that would be necessary to create solid links between use-wear patterning and tool use. While the literature is rife with use-wear data, experimental replication is still the best way to verify functional conclusions.

This research also highlights the analytical value of Contact-period lithic studies. While trade items contain an abundance of information, traditional technological systems continue to provide archaeologists a window into issues of production and labor that can prove valuable in reconstructing past social systems. Our understanding of trade items, particularly ones that come from our own cultural system, is undoubtedly influenced by preconceptions. While our understanding of traditional cultural systems is not free of preconceived ideas, the continuity of these systems in native cultures allows for the identification of meaningful patterns and trends.

ACKNOWLEDGMENTS

This chapter presents a portion of the research conducted for my M.A. thesis. During that time, Binghamton University provided equipment and lab space. In particular, I would like to thank Charles Cobb for his hard work in getting this volume off the ground, as well as for his editorial comments on the many iterations of this paper. His insightful perspective and continual encouragement proved invaluable. I am indebted to Melody Pope for the many hours she spent training me on the ins and outs of use-wear analysis. My thanks to Lynn Clark who provided a well-excavated lithic assemblage with which to work and to the Oneida Nation and the Oneida Indian National Youth Group for their assistance in the excavations. Finally, I would like to thank my wife Sharon for her unending support.

6
Lithic Artifacts in Seventeenth-Century Native New England

Michael S. Nassaney and Michael Volmar

When the seventeenth-century Narragansetts were told the biblical creation story involving Adam and Eve, they responded by offering their own account of human origins. They claimed "that Kautantowwit made one man and woman of a stone, which disliking, he broke them in pieces, and made another man and woman of a tree, which were the fountaines [*sic*] of all mankind" (Trumbull 1866:157–158). When Roger Williams recorded this account in the early–1640s, stone tools were still practical and important in everyday native life, and stone as a raw material held a symbolic significance. While we may never know why stone was an inappropriate raw material for the first human models, southeastern New England natives employed it for a variety of tools well into the seventeenth century. Perhaps the substitution of wood figures for stone in this account can serve as a metaphor for the widespread replacement of stone tools in post-Contact material assemblages.

Beginning in the early seventeenth century, the Dutch and English introduced trade goods such as metal axes and knives that began to replace their lithic counterparts. However, in some cases suitable replacements were lacking or considered unacceptable substitutes for traditional forms in certain contexts, as we show in this study. Furthermore, innovations in stone tool forms were developed, and these were assigned new meanings in the post-Contact world.

In this paper, we examine the stone tool technology of the Narragansetts and neighboring groups in southeastern New England immediately before and after contact (Figure 6.1). As in much of Native North America, metal was only used sparingly prior to the seventeenth century. Subsequent European trade relations involving metal tools had a profound impact on native lithic technology. Yet, in this complex process of intercultural exchange, native peoples were active agents in choosing the tools they made, acquired, and used in everyday life. Indeed, several classes of lithic artifacts persisted well into the seventeenth century, including pestles and pipes, and some new elaborated forms were made possible by European iron implements (e.g., Turnbaugh 1976, 1977). We also suggest that the retention and modification of stone pestle and smoking pipe technology were not merely by-products of European interaction or resistance to a foreign technology. Rather, pipes and pestles were employed in creating and reproducing new social roles that were being restructured in the turmoil brought about by European disease, land encroachment, and demands for commodity production (Nassaney 2002). Relationships along gender lines, in particular, were being redefined, and lithic artifacts, we argue, were actively implicated in reinforcing the new roles enacted by men and women.

THE GENDER-BASED DIVISION OF LABOR AND STONE TOOLS PRIOR TO CONTACT

Recent archaeological interest in social relations and ideology has led practitioners to reconceptualize lithic artifacts and stone tool technology as more than mere clues about economy. They are now seen as potential entry points into the organization of production, the gender-based division of labor, and the belief systems of ancient societies (Cassell, chapter 10; Cobb 2000; Cross 1990; Nassaney 1996; Silliman 2001:201–204, chapter 9; Thomas 2000). The most convincing interpretations of stone tool form, function, and meaning combine insights gained from archaeology, experimentation, oral traditions, and documentary sources, using each as a crosscheck against the other.

Ethnographic and ethnohistoric sources suggest that age and gender formed the basis for the division of labor among the natives of southeastern New England, not unlike most other North American Indian groups (Bragdon 1996a, 1996b; Shoemaker 1995; Simmons 1978; Williams and Bendremer 1997). Native women in southeastern New England planted, cultivated, and harvested the crops and gathered wild plant foods. These tasks would have required the use of stone, shell, or bone (deer scapula) hoes (see Hoffman [1991], Wilbur [1978], and Willoughby [1973] for illustrations of stone hoes and other lithic artifacts). The women also produced a variety of domestic objects including pottery, baskets, clothing, and textiles and were responsible for cooking, serving meals, and childcare. Bifacial knives, expedient flake tools, scrapers, and drills were common cutting and piercing implements used in processing food and raw materials for clothing, whereas mortars (often wooden) and stone pestles were essential for food preparation. The well-known soapstone bowls of the Late Archaic and Early Woodland periods had been abandoned long before Contact and replaced by the low-fired earthenware vessels that women crafted (Johnson 2000; but see

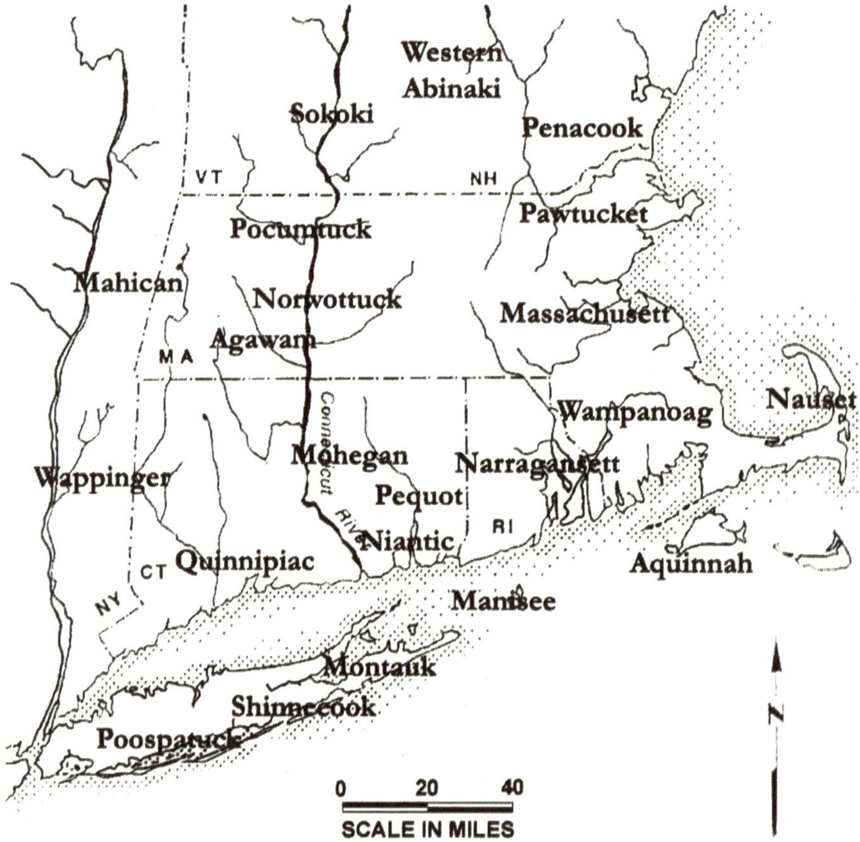

Fig. 6.1. Map of southern New England showing the locations of major tribal groups in the early seventeenth century

Sassaman [1999] for an alternative view on the chronological relationship of soapstone bowls and ceramic vessels in the Northeast). Presumably, women made many of the tools that they regularly needed to complete daily tasks.

Male contributions to agriculture were confined to clearing the fields and cultivating tobacco. Men typically cut the poles that framed their dwellings, although women literally made and kept house (Williams 1973). Wigwams were covered by large sheets of bark that were harvested in late spring and early summer, often by men and women working in communal groups. The large sheets of bark used on some wigwams represent substantial physical activity to fell the trees and peel the bark. Heavy woodworking activities such as this required stone adzes, axes, celts, and other related tools (e.g., wedges). Men contributed to subsistence through hunting and fishing, though the latter was sometimes a communal activity. Simple notched stones served as net sinkers to facilitate the capture of fish and other aquatic animals. Stone projectile points obviously were hunting implements used to tip darts, arrows, and spears or harpoons for fishing. The same weapons that were designed to capture game could be used in warfare, an activity nearly dominated by men, who were also involved in political decision-making and creating alliances. Men were also responsible for producing wooden implements such as bowls, bows, and handles for various objects, for which they used light woodworking tools such as small adzes, knives, and scrapers. They also employed a lapidary industry that involved the production of smoking pipes (Turnbaugh 1977) and other ornaments.

Decorative objects such as neck and ear pendants were ground and carved out of stone, though Willoughby (1973:180) claimed that most personal ornaments were probably made of perishable materials. Algonquian peoples from eastern Canada to New Jersey believed that spirits inhabited not only animals and humans but also effigies crafted from stone, metal, and wood. "There are few young men among the Savages, who have not some stone, or other thing, which they keep as a token of dependence upon the Demon, in order to be happy in the hunt, or in play, or in war; it is either given them by some sorcerer, or they dream that they will find it in some place, or their imagination makes them believe that the Manitou presents to them what they encounter" (Jesuit Relations 1898:31:191). According to this system of beliefs, objects (or even tattoos) with animals or human forms would necessarily have been charged with spiritual power. Both men and women wore these items, often in the forms of "birds, beasts, and fishes" (William Wood, cited in Willoughby 1973:180).

Gender-based identities were recognized within a hereditary matrilineal-based kinship system in which groups identified themselves as members of local communities that were occasionally integrated into larger confederacies that formed for purposes of alliance (Johnson 1999). In matrilineal societies, descent is reckoned through the female line, whereas the allocation of authority appears to have been vested in males. While both men and women are known to have held positions of leadership in the seventeenth century, men held most of these positions. There were also a number of religious specialists in Native societies who could seek spiritual power through visions and encounters with otherworldly beings (Simmons 1986:41–64). These included powwows that exhibited many shamanic traits, as well as herbalists and a range of other religious practitioners. Their roles were generally to ensure the physical, social, and spiritual well-being of the community. Both men and women participated in ritual life, though they apparently derived their power in different ways. According to a contemporary Mohegan account, "Native women are born with natural connections to the earth and the universe. Although lacking this connection, men are born with a strength to create a connection of ritual and ceremony that balances the natural power of women and helps to protect and ensure the continuation of the community" (Aganstata 1988:39). One way in which men established this connection was through the ritual use of tobacco, an important element of shamanic practice (see Nassaney 2000, 2001; Turnbaugh 1992).

In sum, native men and women in southeastern New England had complementary roles in a complex division of labor aimed to ensure the physical survival and spiritual well-being of the group. Individuals employed various raw materials from the natural world to achieve these ends, not the least of which was stone suitable for chipping and grinding. Most of these lithic resources were available in the local environment including chert, argillite, jasper, steatite (soapstone), dolomite, and a range of other igneous, metamorphic, and sedimentary rocks. These materials could be obtained either directly from source areas or from intermediaries through exchange. Many of the artifact forms discussed above were also actively implicated in creating and reproducing gender roles since men and women seldom performed the same activities. Yet, as the social, economic, and political conditions surrounding Native societies began to change in the seventeenth century, there were corresponding changes in the types and forms of stones that men and women used and the meanings that they imposed on them.

THE CONSEQUENCES OF EUROPEAN CONTACT ON STONE TOOL PRODUCTION AND USE

The establishment of European settlements along the southern New England coast and into the interior in the seventeenth century had a profound impact on native societies. A sizable and continually expanding literature documents the processes and consequences of European discovery, exploration, and settlement in the region (e.g., Brenner 1988; Johnson 1993, 2000; Nassaney 1989, 2002; Robinson 1990; Rubertone 2001; Salisbury 1982). While the nuances are continually being debated, the general tenor of the arguments now recognize that native peoples were not merely the passive victims of an inevitable process that would make them obscure and invisible. Despite the fact that native peoples did not disappear from the landscape and become the vanishing race predicted by Manifest Destiny, most categories of native material culture were replaced by European goods, lithic technologies notwithstanding (Bragdon 1988; McMullen 1995). Whereas ornamental objects (e.g., rolled brass beads, tinkling cones) were among those first obtained by native peoples, more "utilitarian" items soon entered their material culture inventories supplanting indigenous stone equivalents. This replacement is documented through both the inventories of trade goods and the archaeological record where objects were often deposited to accompany the dead into the afterlife. Our inferences are heavily dependent on the mortuary record; seventeenth-century habitation sites have been notoriously difficult to identify (Thorbahn 1988; see also Hasenstab 1999). The extent to which natives continued to employ traditional stone implements in daily, domestic activities throughout the seventeenth century remains subject to empirical investigation contingent upon further excavation.

In a sample of over a dozen Contact-period sites in southeastern New England, the prevalence of iron axes and hatchets (*N*=19) indicate that they had almost completely replaced stone axes and stone celts (*N*=2) (Tuma 1985). Iron-edged tools were technologically superior, as recent experimentation by Volmar in 1999–2000 has clearly indicated. In his study, Volmar used stone axes to cut down a 36" diameter white pine tree to craft into a dugout canoe. Ethnohistoric accounts suggest that Indians used fire and chopping, perhaps combined with other techniques, to fell the tree (Williams 1973). The stone axes used in this experiment required frequent resharpening during the 30 hours it took to chop down the tree. Also, burning and chopping were deemed counterproductive during the felling of the tree, as the fire hardened the wood. Further, live trees contain too much moisture to be effectively burnt down, making chopping the best solution to felling a live tree. Chopping and burning techniques were effectively combined during the hollowing out phase of canoe production. There is no doubt that stone axes are less efficient than metal axes in this type of activity. If stone tools persisted while superior metal alternatives were present, there must have been a nontechnological (social or ideological) reason for their persistence (see Cobb and Ruggiero, chapter 2). Volmar's work suggests that the time and effort to produce and use a stone axe would be difficult to justify after iron tools became readily available. Odell (2001:180–183) has recently developed and applied a generalized replacement model elsewhere in North America that supports this argument.

Iron hoes, knives, and awls must have been adopted because of the ease they brought to chopping, cutting, piercing, and drilling (Trigger and Swagerty 1996:377–378). Stone-tipped arrows and bows were not immediately replaced by guns, which were slower to diffuse into Native societies for obvious reasons related to European trade. It was initially unlawful to trade English guns to the Indians. When a group did acquire them, the guns probably provided a slight (if any) military advantage vis-à-vis their neighbors, given the warfare tactics that were prevalent at the time (see Malone 1991). However, small, triangular-shaped pieces of iron and brass, sometimes perforated near their bases and often cut out of used-up kettles, made effective arrow points and are plentiful in the archaeological record (Hoffman 1991:114–115). Iron awls, metal drills, and nails were employed to drill shell beads at a rate that far exceeded the earlier techniques. This technological innovation, along with a growing demand for shell beads, led to standardized forms and provided an economic incentive to substantially increase wampum production by the mid–seventeenth century. These technological changes had important ramifications for the organization of labor as women were drawn into commodity production that could be intensified in a way that maize agriculture could not (Nassaney 2002).

The mortuary and documentary records suggest that many classes of metal tools were adopted by native peoples and became common in native tool kits throughout the region, functionally substituting for their lithic counterparts (see Brenner 1988; Tuma 1985). For example, Ceci (1989:64, 1990:50) argued that the proliferation of true wampum production was a seventeenth-century phenomenon made possible by the introduction of Dutch and English metal drills and awls. This may partly explain why stone micro-drills are rare in the New England Late Woodland archaeological record, compared to their presence in roughly contemporaneous Mississippian sites in the Mississippi and Ohio river valleys where shell beads were more common (Morse and Morse 1983:222–224, 250–251; Yerkes 1983). One stone drill used to produce wampum that was made of European flint was excavated at RI-118, a seventeenth-century palisaded village dating from 1636–1676 on Block Island, Rhode Island (Volmar 1998:94). Native manufactured wampum was drilled using two holes, one from each end that met in the middle of the bead. For this task, metal drills were probably preferred because they were more durable than their stone counterparts. Mary Rowlandson reported that Weetamo, the Squaw-sachem of the Pocaset Wampanoag "ma[de] girdles of wampum and beads" (Rowlandson [1682] 1953:54). Shell bead manufacture would have also required grinding stones or specialized abrading tools to create cylindrical forms from roughly chipped shell blanks. Interestingly, these types of stone artifacts occur frequently in Contact-period cemeteries where they are generally associated with men (Brenner 1988; Tuma 1985; Nassaney 2002).

Stone drills and abrading tools were not the only indigenous technologies that persisted, however, as indicated by archaeological evidence of a lapidary industry that was used to produce smoking pipes and pestles well into the seventeenth century. These artifact classes were made and used after contact and exhibited some important formal changes that inform about shifts in gender roles and ideology instigated by the European presence. Several recent studies have used archaeological data to demonstrate that ritual acts and ideologically charged objects were significant elements in native responses to the changing social and political climate of the seventeenth century (e.g., Nassaney 1989; Robinson 1990; Robinson et al. 1985; Turnbaugh 1993; Volmar 1992; Zymroz 1997). It is in this context that we argue that smoking pipes (male objects) and pestles (female objects) were directly implicated.

Smoking Pipes in Native New England

The use of pipes for smoking tobacco (often mixed with other substances) has considerable antiquity in New England. The presence of platform pipes (Willoughby 1973:Figure 107e) suggests that the practice was at least two-thousand years old, based on the prevalence of this pipe style in well-dated Middle Woodland contexts (ca. 200 B.C.–A.D. 200) in the Midwest (Otto 1992). These pipes were typically made of stone-like steatite (soapstone) that was relatively soft when initially quarried. The ceramic elbow form became more common later and was observed in use during the Contact period throughout the region (Hoffman 1991:95–97; MacNeish 1952:50; Willoughby 1973).

Ethnohistorical accounts suggest that the cultivation of tobacco was a male ritual activity throughout much of North America, and this seems to have been the case in southern New England, particularly among the Narragansetts (see e.g., McGuire 1899:417, cited in Turnbaugh 1975:63; von Gernet 2000:70). For example, Spinden (1950:66) noted "that in the past Indians did not smoke for pleasure." He also described the use of wild tobacco by the Thompson Indians of the Interior Plateau at the end of the nineteenth century: "there was a special ceremony for gathering the herb and in the old days only men smoked, or such women as had shamanistic power. Later smoking became general and mostly for pleasure." Tobacco was similarly confined to male use among the Huron and the Hidatsa. Edward Winslow (cited in Simmons 1986:47) "informs us that the men smoked much tobacco, but it was inappropriate for younger boys to do so" in southeastern New England. This implies that its use was indeed restricted. Though seldom explicitly stated, men, tobacco, and ritual were often associated among North America Indians prior to European contact; whether Narragansett men used it exclusively is suggested, but difficult to demonstrate. What is likely is that smoking became more widespread in native society by the mid–seventeenth century and was participated in by men, women, and children (Nassaney 2000:424; Turnbaugh 1980:21).

Turnbaugh (1975, 1980, 1992) was among the first to suggest that tobacco use and pipe smoking became less restricted among Algonquian groups after contact. He argued that the practice was facilitated by the introduction of widely available European-manufactured white clay pipes, which quickly became disseminated among women and children. This shift also accompanied the introduction of a new species of tobacco from the Caribbean (*Nicotiana tabacum*) that substituted for *Nicotiana rustica* (Turnbaugh 1975:66). *N. rustica* apparently has a higher nicotine content than *N. tabacum* (Winter 2000a:99). Men continued to cultivate *N. rustica* and to smoke it in ritual contexts using stone pipes long after women and children began consuming imported *N. tabacum* in white clay pipes (see Nassaney 2001).

English and Dutch pipes are ubiquitous in the archaeological record of sites that post-date the third quarter of the seventeenth century, indicating that casual tobacco use was prevalent among the English and Indians as well. In a sample of nearly 20 native mortuary sites from the region, white clay pipes are found with men, women, and children and occur three times as frequently as stone pipes (Nassaney 2002). If tobacco use had previously been a male activity confined to ritual contexts, smoking it for pleasure would have led to social tensions between men and women by undermining an activity that had once served to reproduce gender relations and ideologies. As Turnbaugh (1980:21) states, "the traditional employment of the tobacco pipe as a socially significant male-only activity was losing ground." While the use of tobacco, as inferred from pipe availability and oral accounts, was more widespread in native society by the mid–seventeenth century, the reasons for the expansion of the practice were more complex than mere emulation of European usage (Nassaney 2001) or addiction, as discussed further below.

The more widespread use of tobacco during the Contact period may be related to spiritual beliefs. Among the Huron, as well as other groups in the Northeast such as the Mohegan, smoking was believed to bring people into contact with the spiritual realm: "My brothers, said he, these two tobacco-pipes are yours. We must in the future have only one breath and a single respiration, since we have only one and the same soul" (Jesuit Relations 1899:40:207). The use of tobacco beyond adult males may be related to the society at large seeking some way to re-establish spiritual and physical well-being in the face of imbalances and tensions brought about by European technologies and disease that forever altered native life.

When women began to employ European clay pipes, they challenged traditional tenets of male authority and means of communicating with the supernatural. While most women were unable to acquire stone pipes or ascertain ritual knowledge, the use of tobacco and potential access to its experientially derived spiritual power was no longer confined to men. Women and children sought to use tobacco in a more personal and less institutional manner. According to Turnbaugh (1975:67), one possible male response to the wider dissemination of the practice was to idealize native pipes, embellish them with effigy forms, and reemphasize smoking as a ritual activity. Two unfinished stone pipes, one an elaborate human effigy, were recovered from a seventeenth-century Indian grave in southern Rhode Island (Figure 6.2). An iron file was found in association with the effigy pipe and both pipes show clear signs of having been manufactured with metal tools. According to Turnbaugh (1977:3):

> These 2 pipes and the accompanying iron file indicate some of the techniques of pipe-making shortly after European contact. It is notable that the

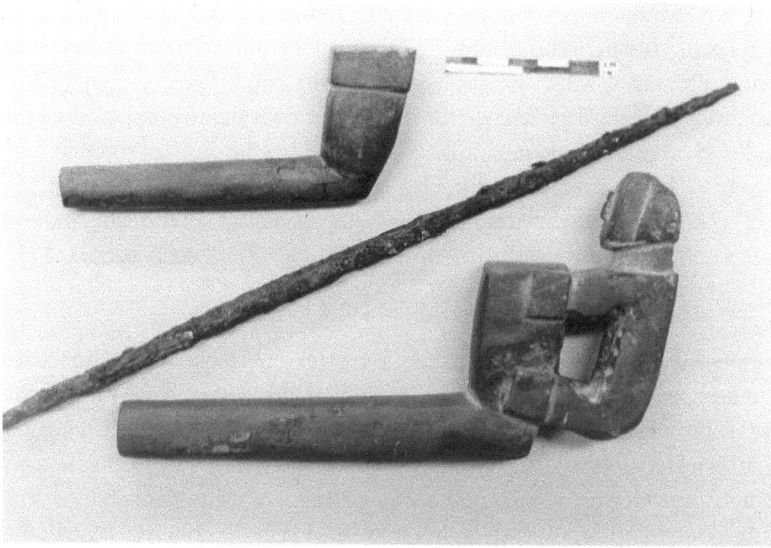

Fig. 6.2. Two unfinished stone pipes and an iron file from a seventeenth-century Indian grave in southern Rhode Island (courtesy of William Turnbaugh)

pipes are of aboriginal workmanship, even though steel tools were employed in the process. Few other native-made items occurred at this site, a situation that generally prevailed in late Narragansett culture as the products of European trade quickly supplanted nearly all of those of indigenous manufacture (Simmons 1970). The pipes, then, stand nearly alone as an exception to this trend.

In 1634, William Wood (1977:80) observed that the Narragansetts employed European metal tools to manufacture "their great stone pipes, which will hold a quarter of an ounce of tobacco." While these pipes might have been produced prior to sustained European contact, they seem to have experienced a renaissance or revitalization in the seventeenth century (Turnbaugh 1976, 1977, 1992). Some of these pipes were traded to groups hundreds of miles from the Narragansett homeland (Turnbaugh 1992:119). A number of stone pipes have been recovered from Contact-period cemeteries in southern New England (Gibson 1980; Tuma 1985; Turnbaugh 1984; Willoughby 1973:181–190). Others might have been curated or purposefully hidden to assure that no one other than their makers/owners would use the pipes (see Nassaney 2000:422–427). The preference for pipes of native manufacture for ritual purposes has been documented elsewhere on the frontier of eastern North America in the eighteenth and early nineteenth centuries, as in the example of the extensive use of catlinite and other red pipestones for the calumet ceremony (Gundersen et al. 2002). This suggests that indigenous stone pipes were not confined to southeastern New England after the Contact period (see Trubowitz 1992; Wagner, chapter 8). By maintaining a decided preference for using their own pipes as opposed to those introduced by trade, some men might have sought to limit ritual tobacco use for themselves. This may support the idea that "native pipes filled with native tobacco" (*Nicotiana rustica*) were necessary to effect the appropriate ritual outcome in communicating with the supernatural (see Turnbaugh 1980:21).

Pestles in Native New England

Stone pestles constitute another artifact type that has frequently been recovered in the archaeological record of native New England. Pestles have a long history of use in New England, having been found in Late Archaic (ca. 4000 B.P.) cremation cemeteries in eastern Massachusetts (Dincauze 1968). Usually associated with mortars in ethnographic use, pestles are cylindrical-shaped stones used to pound corn and other grains into meal prior to cooking. Many pestles were laboriously pecked into a near perfect roller shape. Both ends are generally rounded; one end has characteristic concentric striations from pounding and grinding. Much of their surface areas typically exhibit pecking, grinding, and polishing marks from their manufacture.

Some pestles exhibit sculpted representations on one end. The sculpted ends of these so-called effigy pestles can assume a variety of different shapes or representations including zoomorphic, anthropomorphic, and ambiguous forms (Figure 6.3). Recent study of a sample of over 60 effigy pestles suggests that they date to the Contact period (Volmar 1992).

A sample of these artifacts was compared with a sample of non-effigy pestles to determine if there are any significant differences between the two groups (Volmar 1992). While they are similar in length, effigy pestles are slightly wider than non-effigy pestles. The two groups also exhibit different frequencies of use wear. Whereas 80 percent of the non-effigy pestles exhibit use wear, only 17 percent of the effigy pestles have use wear. This supports the contention that effigy pestles were not domestic artifacts. Another important observation is that there is a significant difference in breakage patterns. Twenty-two percent of the effigy pestles are broken, compared to only 2 percent of the non-effigy pestles. These results strongly support the argument that effigy pestles are not functionally similar to pestles—they are not merely fancy utilitarian pestles.

Their contexts of discovery indicate that effigy pestles are usually associated in mortuary context with women or (mainly female) children; they are almost never found with men. Pestles are also linked to women in folktales (e.g., Simmons 1986). Finally, the animals depicted by the effigies (e.g., bears, snakes) are often the forms taken by supernatural beings as they appear to humans in visions.

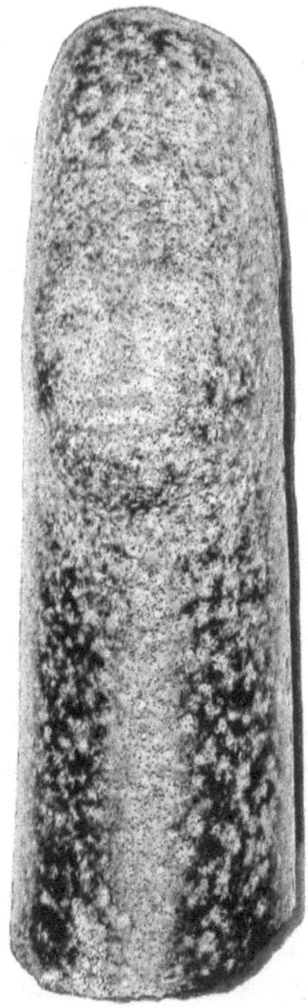

Fig. 6.3. Anthropomorphic effigy pestle from southern New England (Haffenreffer Museum of Anthropology, Brown University)

Thus, it can be argued that effigy pestles were introduced in the seventeenth century as symbols of female power that evoke mythological beings to reify women's social position in Algonquian society (Volmar 1992:22).

The principle deity who appeared to humans in apparitions and dreams was Hobbamock, whose name is related to the color black, the words for death, the deceased, dead man, and the cold northeast (Simmons 1986:39; Volmar 1992:25). A great celebration was held if a person had a vision in which Hobbamock appeared in the form of a snake. Spiritual power was conferred upon those who dreamt of Hobbamock. Inanimate objects, particularly snake-shaped objects with representations of human and animal forms like effigy pestles, could be charged with spiritual power derived from Hobbamock through a dream or vision.

In the onslaught of a crumbling social order that challenged the predictability of roles and relations, individuals developed new ways to make contact with otherworldly forces and beings as a means to rectify an unstable situation represented through mortuary ritual and effigy pestles. Pestles were not the only items of material culture meant to make contact with the supernatural or designed to signify changes in social relations along gender lines. For example, Mohegan pots made in southeastern Connecticut exhibit stylized references to women's bodies (namely, their genitalia) and women as mothers and nurturers (see Handsman 1988:31; McMullen 1986; Nassaney 2002; see also Wonderley 2002). These served to remind everyone of the need to reproduce biologically and socially and to infuse native culture with a new vitality. Some of the same symbolism extended to mortars, thus implicating pestles as female tools that helped to assure sustenance for the physical and spiritual well-being of the group.

These new artifact forms constitute some of the ways in which Native women both countered colonization and simultaneously employed colonization to contest male-controlled spheres of activity. They also suggest how individual agents attempted to rationalize the demographic, social, and political upheavals that their communities were experiencing (e.g., Handsman 1988; Volmar 1992; Zymroz 1997). Effigy pestles, pipes, and changing mortuary patterns are physical embodiments of efforts to ameliorate the imbalances that Europeans created in native society. This was expressed in the use of symbolically charged objects in mortuary rituals at supernaturally strategic locations on the landscape in an effort "to secure and increase their individual and social physical and spiritual well-being" (Zymroz 1997:246). The concentration of certain classes of spiritually powerful grave goods with children, especially young females, underscores their importance in social reproduction and the biological survival of the group. This pattern occurs at a number of Contact-period cemeteries in southeastern New England including Long Pond in Connecticut (Kevin McBride, personal communication, 2000), RI 1000 (Robinson 1990; Turnbaugh 1984), and Titicut in Massachusetts (Zymroz 1997). Likewise, women fashioned effigy pestles—objects long associated with female domestic tasks—to symbolize new means of strengthening ties with the supernatural. They also adopted tobacco smoking, not for pleasure or in imitation of their European neighbors but in an attempt to connect with the cosmological forces that could help restore balance in an increasingly unintelligible world of conflict, animosity, and death. They might have tried to employ male tactics of smoking if they felt that their own innate natural connections to the earth and universe were fallible or becoming ineffective. In the maelstrom of change, ritual was becoming less institutional and more personal as earlier religious practices were questioned or they failed to deliver the desired outcome (Nassaney 2001). Von Gernet (2000:78, 80) arrived at a similar interpretation which he referred to as "democratized shamanism" in which all members had the potential to acquire spiritual power for themselves and their community. The practice became popular among those who circumvented the hegemony of the shaman and sought their own direct communication with spirit beings.

CONCLUSION

From the previous discussion it should be apparent that stone persisted as a raw material after contact in native New England. Pipes, pestles, and other lithic objects continued to be made and used by native peoples, despite the availability of metal and ceramic objects, some of which were functional equivalents of traditional stone implements. Some lithic artifacts became more prevalent after contact as a result of new economic, social, and ideological needs. For example, abrading and grinding stones used to produce wampum might have actually increased in the seventeenth century, based on the numerous specimens found in tool kits associated with the graves of, initially, male and later also female wampum makers (Brenner 1988; Nassaney 2002; Turnbaugh 1984). Native peoples also cast buttons, small ornaments, pipes, and musket balls in homemade molds cut from slate and soapstone after they developed metallurgical skills in the seventeenth century (Wilbur 1978:89; Willoughby 1973). Pewter and lead were often employed for such purposes as they had relatively low melting points, though brass was also used. Both open-faced designs and two-piece stone molds have been recovered archaeologically (Wilbur 1978:89). Roger Williams (1973) commented on the ease with which the Narragansetts adopted black smithing skills to make horseshoes, to repair guns, and to replenish ammunition by using stone molds to produce lead shot (see Wilbur 1978:89).

But perhaps more significant for this study are the stone pipes and pestles that were used and elaborated upon by men and women respectively in response to the changes societies were confronting in the seventeenth century. Both artifact classes had a long history of use in the region, but each was significantly modified after contact. Pipes were produced in a variety of different raw materials prior to contact, but stone became the material of choice for male ritual smoking after iron files became available and inexpensive European clay pipes diffused widely throughout the region (Nassaney 2000; Turnbaugh 1977, 1980). That they were produced in increasingly complex forms after iron files were introduced is no surprise, but their revitalization is also an attempt for men to re-appropriate the power of tobacco consumption for ritual use. This tension may be part of a larger process whereby native society was becoming transformed from matrilineal to patrilineal organization (Burton and Lowenthal 1974; McMullen 1986, 1995:5).

Changes in artifact forms, raw materials, and their contexts of use clearly point to struggles not only between natives and Europeans but also between native men and women. As infant mortality and juvenile death rates increased (Robinson et al. 1985), social solidarity was challenged due to war, land loss, and economic erosion. Women sought to re-establish social and political stability and employed the conditions of colonialism to secure a new place in a rapidly changing society. They sought to connect to supernatural life forces in new and potentially more effective ways. Taking up the pipe (albeit European ones), employing new ceramic iconography, and reinventing utilitarian pestles formally and symbolically, native women countered and accommodated to colonialism. Effigy pestles were nonutilitarian artifacts that were not used as typical grinding pestles, yet they remind the viewer of several common motifs in Algonquian worldview. Their general shape is reminiscent of the pestle, evoking the idea that women produce much of the food that is consumed daily and traded periodically. Such reminders underscore women's importance as producers of commodities as well as consumers and distributors of desirable European goods obtained through trade. Simultaneously, effigy pestles are objects imbued with spiritual power; they are material representations of otherworldly forces such as Hobbamock that often took the forms of bears or snakes, a popular effigy depiction (Volmar 1992). These objects would have marked a woman as important to her community's relationship with the spiritual world. Such a woman could have used the effigy pestle to heal the sick, divine the future, or threaten (and possibly attack) those whom she perceived as dangerous. In "The Tale of Chahnameed," a beautiful young girl protects herself and perhaps metaphorically preserves her way of life by using her mortar and pestle to impede the efforts of her pursuing husband whom she reluctantly married (Simmons 1986:274–276). Finally, these women were interred in death with their effigy pestles, which were personal possessions for use in the afterworld.

Similarly, stone pipes were (and continue to be) seen as powerful male symbols. Those who controlled such powerful symbols exhibited special personal attributes both in this world and in the next. For example, in the oral account of "The Silver Pipe" a woman desires to smoke from her husband's pipe after his death (Nassaney 2000; Simmons 1986:124). Despite repeated attempts, she is unable to grasp the pipe as it moves away from her. Eventually, she is able to hold the pipe once she promises to return it to her husband's grave.

What is it about stone as a raw material that lent itself to being selected for the complex meanings and symbolic associations discussed above? Certainly, lithic raw materials were more difficult to control than most European commodities. In the early nineteenth century, Shawnee Prophet beckoned his followers to turn away from European goods and return to the resources of mother earth (Edmunds 1983; see also Wagner, chapter 8). Indeed, stone is a natural resource that natives could obtain independent of Europeans, much like shell, wood, and organic materials used for basketry. Many of these raw materials also persist in so-called traditional material culture or have come to represent traditional culture and to retain their symbolic values. We must not judge a culture's authenticity by the objects its members select to create and recreate their material world without recognizing that humans bestow meanings on objects in culturally distinctive and historically contingent ways. By decoding these meanings from variation in artifact form and archaeological context, we can gain valuable insights into the roles and relationships that men and women entered into in the process of creating and recreating their culture through daily practice.

ACKNOWLEDGMENTS

We would like to thank Charlie Cobb for inviting us to contribute a chapter to this volume. Paul Robinson and Rob Mann were helpful in locating source materials pertaining to the Narragansetts' origin story and the Shawnee Prophet, respectively. Tim Bober, Dan Lynch, Yolanda Rico, Paul Robinson, Steve Silliman, Bill Turnbaugh, and two anonymous reviewers read an earlier draft of this chapter and offered useful commentary that we have tried to incorporate into our thinking on this topic. Discussions and correspondence with John Brown, Dena Dincauze, Eric Johnson, Ann McMullen, Ramona Peters, Paul Robinson, and William Simmons have also been influential. Nassaney's research for this chapter began with his fellowship at the John Nicholas Brown Center for the Study of American Civilization at Brown University and was also supported by funds from the Faculty Research and Creative Activities Support Fund, Western Michigan University.

7
Stone Adze Economies in Post-Contact Hawai'i

James M. Bayman

Identifying and interpreting stone adze economies in Hawai'i offers valuable insights on the technological consequences of contact between non-Western societies and Europeans. Western contact occurred relatively late in the Hawaiian archipelago (Figure 7.1) compared to much of the Old and New Worlds (e.g., Cobb and Ruggiero, chapter 2; Odell, chapter 3), and indigenous metal working did not develop until after the arrival of Europeans in A.D. 1778. After European contact and colonization, a reorganization of indigenous Hawaiian stone adze technology ensued, along with a wide array of profound economic and sociopolitical changes.

Adzes were an integral component of traditional Hawaiian society and served a variety of functions (Figure 7.2). These stone tools were used for felling trees, making canoes and building houses, carving religious images, and perhaps to display mana or rank (see Leach 1993:39). Use-wear analyses of Hawaiian adzes indicate that perhaps they were also used to till soil for the preparation and maintenance of agricultural plots (Dockall 2000). Pre-contact adzes were made with a variety of materials including hardwood, coconut husk, and marine shell, although stone adzes (*ko'i pōhaku*) are most commonly preserved in the archaeological record. Because of their durability and relative abundance in the archaeological record of the Hawaiian islands, stone adzes have been used by archaeologists to construct culture-historical sequences (e.g., Emory 1968; Kirch 1972; cf. Cleghorn 1992), to examine technology and craft specialization (e.g., Cleghorn 1986; Lass 1994), and to identify patterns of interaction and exchange (e.g., Cleghorn et al. 1985; Weisler and Sinton 1997).

Although archaeologists have long acknowledged the value of stone adzes to early Polynesian societies (e.g., Brigham 1902; Buck et al. 1930; Cleghorn 1986; Duff 1959; Emory 1968), they rarely study the use of stone tools in post-

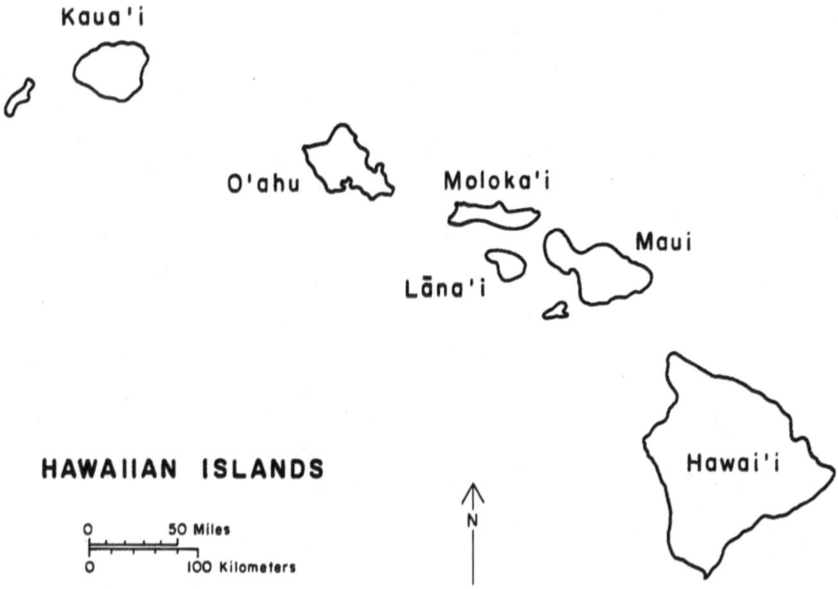

Fig. 7.1. Major islands of the Hawaiian archipelago (drawn by Ronald Beckwith)

Contact Hawaiʻi (see Kirch 1992 for an exception). This trend contrasts notably with other areas in the Pacific, like New Guinea and Australia, where anthropologists have explicitly examined the consequences of European metal on indigenous stone technologies (e.g. Salisbury 1962; Sharp 1952; Townsend 1969). The tendency to overlook evidence for the persistence of stone adze economies in the Hawaiian islands may reflect the view of some archaeologists (e.g., McCoy 1990:92–93) that stone adzes were quickly replaced by metal adzes after European contact.

This article reviews published archaeological and documentary evidence that stone adze use persisted in Hawaiʻi for nearly a century after European contact. The protracted demise of stone adzes illustrates that an array of factors governed the selective adoption of European technologies by indigenous Hawaiians. Although the performance capability of stone adzes actually favored their continued use by canoe craftsmen, other economic and political factors also encouraged their persistence. Chiefly monopolization of European imports, which began in the late–1700s, constrained commoners' access to metal adzes and other foreign trade goods. Communities located near major seaports (i.e., Honolulu and Lahaina) were better situated to acquire and utilize European goods (e.g., metal adzes). During this time, residents of outlying rural districts were unable

Fig. 7.2. Hafted adzes from Hawai'i: left, a stone adze; right, a stone swivel adze, used for working the interior of canoes. Both adzes were acquired by Joseph S. Emerson in the 1880s (photo courtesy of the Bernice P. Bishop Museum)

to participate fully in the post-Contact market economy because of their geographic isolation.

EARLY CONTACT HAWAI'I

Contact between Hawai'i and Europeans first took place on January 18 in 1778, when the British naval captain James Cook encountered the island of Kaua'i as he sailed to the Pacific Northwest (Cook 1967). At first contact, Hawai'i had the most complex hierarchical organization and largest scale of economic production found among Polynesian societies (Kirch 2000:300). The eight major islands of the archipelago were divided into four major polities that have been described as complex chiefdoms or "archaic" states (Hommon 1986:55; Kirch 2000:300). The organization of early Contact-period Hawaiian polities was pyramidal: it centered on paramount chiefs (*kaukau aliʻi*) and administrators (*konohiki*) of local territorial communities (*ahupuaʻa*) (Hommon 1986: 57; Malo 1951). Commoners (*makaʻāinana*) were the economic and social foundation of traditional Hawaiian society; they worked the land and paid chiefly tribute (Kamakau 1964; Malo 1951). Ethnohistorical and archaeological examinations (e.g., Earle 1978) reveal that each island was divided into several large districts comprised of multiple *ahupuaʻa* after A.D. 1400 (Hommon 1986:65).

It was the local territorial communities, or *ahupuaʻa*, that formed the essence of Hawaiian zonal economic organization. Hawaiian *ahupuaʻa* were relatively narrow, wedge-shaped territorial communities that cross-cut larger ecological zones between the coastal lowlands and the interior uplands. The Hawaiians practiced a varied subsistence economy that included cultivation of root, tuber, and tree crops, fishing and aquaculture, and animal husbandry with pigs and dogs. Although *ahupuaʻa* varied greatly in size and population, many of them contained the economic resources (e.g., fish, salt, wood, fiber, potable water, and arable land) necessary to be self-sufficient (Earle 1978; Hommon 1986:65).

European contact in 1778 lay behind the catastrophic loss of indigenous population in Hawaiʻi through disease epidemics over the next few decades (see Stannard 1989; cf. Dye and Komori 1992). Hawaiʻi also witnessed the conquest and political unification of the entire archipelago in 1810 by the paramount Hawaiian leader, King Kamehameha I. Shortly thereafter, in 1819, traditional Hawaiian religious practices were outlawed by royal Hawaiian decree. Missionaries later began a sustained effort to convert indigenous Hawaiians to the Christian religion.

The period between 1812 to 1830 is frequently called the "Sandalwood Era" (Sahlins 1992:55), a time when the economy of the Hawaiian Kingdom was heavily driven by its export of sandalwood to China (Kuykendall 1938). This trade activity eventually waned and international whaling dominated Hawaiʻi's economy during the "Whaling Period" from 1830 to 1860. The net effect of both economies (i.e., sandalwood export and whaling) was to strengthen Hawaiʻi's participation in an expanding world system (see Sahlins 1992). Aside from disease and the demise of the traditional religion, few events transformed Hawaiian life as much as the division and privatization of land ownership during the *Māhele* (land reform) of 1846–55 (Chinen 1958).

These political and economic events accelerated the pace of technological change in the Hawaiian islands, including the introduction of metal adzes by

Europeans. To provide a context for considering the use of stone adzes after contact, I summarize their design and technology.

HAWAIIAN ADZE ECONOMIES

Stone adzes in Hawai'i were generally made with flakes that were modified by percussion, ground, and hafted on wood handles (Weisler 1990:38–41) (Figure 7.2). The cutting-edge of a Hawaiian adze blade is transverse to its hafting element (Figures 7.2 and 7.3), unlike an axe blade which has a cutting-edge that is parallel to its hafting element. Adzes often have a contracting "tang" behind the so-called shoulder to facilitate hafting (Figure 7.3). Moreover, their cutting-edges are typically beveled, and adzes were frequently ground and polished.

Because the Hawaiian archipelago was formed through volcanic eruptions, stone tool technology in this region relied on basalt. The Hawaiian islands are derived from oceanic crust, which, unlike continental crust, is comprised almost entirely of basalt with scattered crystals of black mineral pyroxene, pale gray plagioclase feldspar, and apple-green olivine (Macdonald et al. 1983:124). Basalt that was potentially useful for making adzes was relatively widespread across the islands, and yet material from certain geologic locales was evidently preferred for its specific properties.

Indeed, stone adze production was most concentrated at twelve known quarries scattered across the archipelago (Sinton and Sinoto 1997:198). The largest and most studied adze quarry in the Pacific is located on the mountain of Mauna Kea, on the island of Hawai'i (e.g., Cleghorn 1986; McCoy 1990). Smaller quarries beyond Mauna Kea, including Pololû, Haleakalâ, and Kapohaku, have also been examined by archaeologists (e.g., Lass 1994; Powers 1939; Weisler 1990). Some researchers (e.g., McCoy 1990:92–93) have concluded that stone adzes were quickly replaced by metal adzes after contact, and that large quarries like Mauna Kea were abandoned. Documentary evidence exists, however, that Hawaiians used stone adzes for nearly a century after European contact.

Ethnohistoric Perspectives

Nineteenth-century accounts by native Hawaiians like Samual Kamakau and David Malo offer valuable clues on stone adze production (Kamakou 1964; Malo 1951; also see Lass 1998:24–38). Both men wrote their accounts during portions of a span of time (ca. 1830 to 1870) when indigenous Hawaiians still retained many elements of their traditional (i.e., pre-Contact) culture.

Kamakau's (1964) and Malo's (1951) observations that adzes were made from stone (in this case, basalt) having particular properties imply that Hawaiians obtained raw materials selectively and from a limited number of quarries (probably

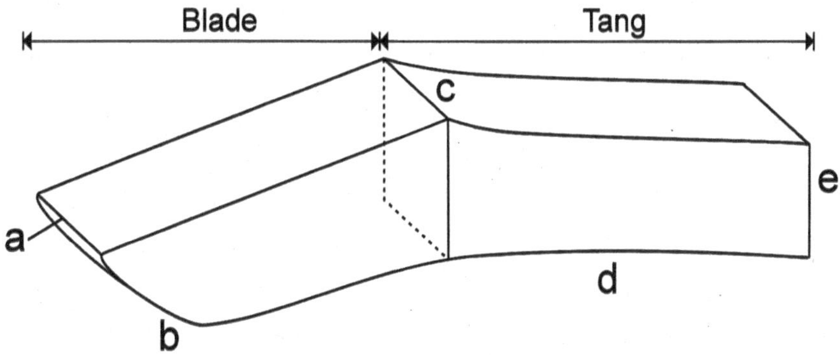

Fig. 7.3. Parts of an adze: a) cutting edge, b) bevel and chin, c) shoulder, d) base, e) poll (derived from Buck et al. 1930; drawn by Brad Evans)

the twelve locales reported by Sinton and Sinoto [1997:198]). A description of stone adze production by Joseph Emerson, a mid–nineteenth century resident of Hawaiʻi (Summers 1999:55), illustrates that it was a time-consuming endeavor which took several days. Mary Kawena Pukui (1939:15) noted that: "Making a stone adz was a laborious task. [There was] the chipping, the grinding, the lashing, and so forth." Furthermore, Malo's (1951) claim that adze-makers were a "greatly esteemed class" also impies that adze production was practiced by craft specialists.

Documentary sources also provide tantalizing insights on the introduction of metal adzes from Europe to Hawaiian society. Following Captain Cook's arrival to the island of Kauaʻi in 1778, Hawaiians were eager to acquire nails and bits of iron, which Cook traded for pigs, chickens, potatoes, plantains, taro, and potable water (Cook 1967:264). Cook even had his own armorers fashion iron into the native dagger (*pāhoa*) and adze (*koʻi*) (Linnekin 1990:159). When Cook and his men stopped at Kauaʻi to fill their casks with water in March of 1779, one Hawaiian demanded a metal adze for every barrel of liquid (King 1967:586–587). The chiefs were particularly interested in acquiring iron guns and ammunition from the Europeans (Linnekin 1990:159).

The lateness and intensity of European contact in Hawaiʻi may explain why some historic sources (e.g., like Cook's journals) emphasize the rapid adoption of iron by Contact-era Hawaiians. Yet other sources, like Cheever (1851), note that metal tools were far from abundant among commoners until the mid–nineteenth century. In fact, Brigham (1902:409–410) witnessed the use of both metal and stone adzes to fashion wood canoes: "In watching the shaping of a canoe I have seen the old canoe-maker use for the rough shaping and excavating an ordinary foreign steel adze, but for the finishing touches he dropped the foreign tool and returned to the adze of his ancestors, and the blunt looking stone cut off a delicate shaving from the very hard koa wood and never seemed to take too much as the foreign adze was apt to do." Brigham (1902:408, 415) claimed also that while the production of stone adzes terminated shortly after the introduction of metal, their use continued at least as late as 1864, and probably longer—almost a century after contact.

Hawaiians continued to use adzes made of stone, and perhaps also wood, until the latter part of the nineteenth century. According to Joseph Emerson, adzes made with soft wood, rather than stone, were used for delicately trimming the outrigger float (*wilwiwili*) of canoes (Summers 1999:60). Thus, many types of adzes, made with a variety of materials, were used for building canoes. Indeed, no fewer than 30 Hawaiian language words are used to denote adzes with different functions (Holmes 1981:26–27). Documentary accounts also suggest that adzes made with stone and wood were preferred over metal adzes for certain canoe building activities.

In fact, the introduction of iron adzes and disease epidemics in post-Contact Hawai'i is associated with a decrease in the quality of canoe craftsmanship. Freycinet (1829:614) reported that canoe construction became increasingly shoddy as iron tools became increasingly available (Haddon and Hornell 1975: 20) and as skilled craftsmen were lost to various diseases. This observation was corroborated in a 1900 report by John Cobb: "the older ones [canoes] are very handsome in design and workmanship, the old-time native boat builders having been especially expert in their manufacture. The present generation has sadly deteriorated, however, and the canoes made now (late–1800's) by natives rarely show very much skill in design and workmanship . . . " (quoted in Holmes 1981:42).

Although iron adzes apparently contributed to a decline in the quality of canoe craftsmanship, some areas of the islands acquired them more quickly than others in the first half of the nineteenth century. The observation of George Byron that stone adzes were "becoming rare" in Honolulu by 1825 (Byron 1826: 137) is not surprising since Honolulu was already a major port in the islands. More rural districts, however, remained isolated from the market economy until the middle of the nineteenth century (Linnekin 1990:173). In the settlement of Waimea, located in the interior of the Island of Hawai'i, Hawaiians were still using stone adzes (*ko'i*) at least as late as 1847 (Lorenzo Lyons, in Doyle 1953:145). Stone adzes were likely used in other remote districts, especially on the islands without major seaports (e.g., Moloka'i).

Indications also exist that iron was differentially distributed between chiefly elites (*ali'i*) and commoners (*maka'āinana*), since elites monopolized trade with Europeans (see Sahlins 1981). Chiefs used their traditional prerogatives to confiscate commoners' possessions and practiced the right to use the sumptuary taboo (*kapu*) on the use of foreign goods by commoners (Linnekin 1990:161). In the late–1700s, Portlock (1789) witnessed a chief demand bits of iron from a commoner who had bartered for them from foreigners (Linnekin 1990:162). Not surprisingly, chiefs had "more Iron than they knew what to do with" by 1793 (Bell 1929:30:1:63), although commoners still sought the material, especially nails and scissors.

A more careful reading of ethnohistoric accounts suggests that archaeological evidence of post-Contact stone adze economies in Hawai'i may well exist, particularly in outlying areas away from the seaports where Europeans and their goods arrived in the islands. Finding such evidence is challenging, however, since Contact-period archaeological sites are difficult to identify in Hawai'i, particularly in sites that lack substantial amounts of European artifacts and other foreign materials. Yet identifying such areas—and such continuity in traditional technology in the face of rapid economic and political transformation—is integral to interpreting the Contact period of the Hawaiian archipelago. Archaeology also offers the promise to address questions about post-Contact stone adze economies that are unresolved by documentary accounts.

Archaeological Perspectives

No attempt has yet been made to produce a comprehensive inventory of archaeological evidence for post-Contact stone adze economies in Hawai'i, and such an undertaking is beyond the scope of this study. Instead, I briefly examine several instances where archaeologists have either reported such evidence, or where such evidence might be present but was overlooked. For several reasons, identifying early post-Contact occupations is a daunting problem in Hawaiian archaeology.

Perhaps most importantly, it is particularly difficult to use radiocarbon age-estimations from archaeological sites since contact between Hawai'i and Europe took place less than 250 years ago. Intervals for radiocarbon dates from samples frequently include the "present" (i.e., 1950) when they are reported at one or two standard deviations. Although hydration rind dating of volcanic glass artifacts was once a popular technique for estimating the age of archaeological sites in Hawai'i (e.g., Barrera and Kirch 1973; Cordy 1981), serious problems with this approach remain unresolved (Olson 1983).

Consequently, the best method for identifying post-Contact sites is an approach that Kirch (1992:166) used during his research in Anahulu Valley on the island of O'ahu (Figure 7.4). Kirch (1992) used the presence of European artifacts, archival sources, and radiocarbon dating to identify post-Contact-period sites. Many Contact-era sites (particularly nonelite habitations in rural areas), however, are not likely to contain Western artifacts, since access to imported goods was restricted by chiefs.

Despite these problems, Kirch (1992) conclusively identified eight Contact-

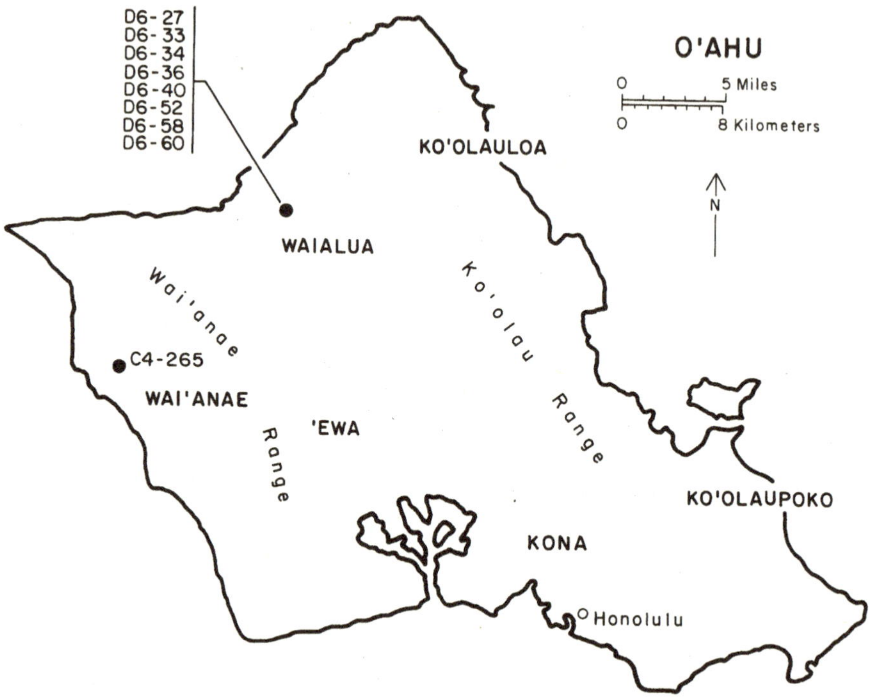

Fig. 7.4. Selected archaeological sites with stone adzes on the island of O'ahu (drawn by Ronald Beckwith)

period sites with stone adzes in their assemblages: four house sites and four rockshelters (Table 7.1, Figure 7.4). The upper levels of the rockshelter sites date to the so-called Sandalwood Era (1812–1830) that began about three decades after European contact. Not surprisingly, the diversity of foreign artifact types is relatively low at these rural locales (Kirch 1992:180–181). Moreover, as Kirch (1992:181) notes, the rockshelter occupants were still using many traditional Hawaiian items, including adzes, hammerstones, abraders, and poi pounders. Low numbers of European artifacts in these sites may reflect, in part, the specialized economic functions of these sites, such as upland resource procurement.

The house sites were first occupied in 1804 when a large force of Hawaiian warriors occupied O'ahu (Kirch 1992:49–53), nine years after Kamehameha I conquered the island of O'ahu in 1795. The house sites were also occupied into the succeeding "Whaling Period" (1830–1860), after the rockshelter sites were abandoned. To some extent, a greater number of foreign artifacts in the house sites may reflect their residential functions. However, foreign artifacts are also certainly indicative of intensified mercantilism during this later era, as well as the fact that oxcart routes from Anahulu Valley to Honolulu had been constructed

Table 7.1 Selected Archaeological Sites in the Hawaiian Islands with Reported Post-Contact Occupations and Stone Adzes

Island	Site No.	Site Type	Adze artifacts	Foreign artifacts	Occupation Span	References
O'ahu	C4-265	House	Adze flakes (numerous), grinding stone fragment	China, metal, glass	Pre-1850 to late 19th century	Riconda 1972:14–20
	D6-36	Rockshelter	1 adze frag., 15 adze flakes	Glass, metal, gunflints	A.D. 1650 to after Contact	Kirch 1992:36, 39–40; 47:Fig. 2.11
	D6-52	Rockshelter	1 adze and 29 adze flakes	Glass, metal, gunflints	A.D. 1500 to after Contact	Kirch 1992:33–35, 36; 47:Fig. 2.11
	D6-58	Rockshelter	1 adze and 39 adze flakes	Glass, metal, ceramics	A.D. 1325 to after Contact	Kirch 1992:37–39, 36; 47:Fig. 2.11
	D6-60	Rockshelter	1 adze preform, 1 adze frag., 29 adze flakes	Glass, metal, ceramics, gunflints	A.D. 1450 to after Contact	Kirch 1992:35–37, 36; 47:Fig. 2.11
	D6-27	House	6 polished flakes (adze flakes)	Iron, glass, flint flake	A.D. 1804–1815 and A.D. 1845–1880	Kirch 1992:86; 166:Fig. 5.1
	D6-33	House	Adze frag., 2 adze flakes	Glass, metal, ceramic, flint, slate	A.D. 1804–1825	Kirch 1992:76; 166:Fig. 5.1
	D6-34	House	Adze, adze flakes, hammerstone	Glass and flint	A.D. 1804–1885	Kirch 1992:71–72; 166: Fig. 5.1
	D6-40	House	Adze, 3 adze flakes	None	A.D. 1804–1815	Kirch 1992:64; 166:Fig. 5.1
Hawai'i	7702	Not reported	adze	Not reported	Post-A.D. 1800 (portions)	Hay et al. 1986; Lass 1994:72
	T-1	Not reported	adze	Not reported	Post-A.D. 1800	Bath and Rosendahl 1984; Lass 1994:72

Table 7.1 *Continued*

Island	Site No.	Site Type	Adze artifacts	Foreign artifacts	Occupation Span	References
	H2	Not reported	adze	Not reported	Post-A.D. 1800	Emory and Sinoto 1969; Lass 1994:72
	2732	House	2 adzes, 8 adze flakes, 4 hammerstones, 24 basalt flakes	Metal, chert flake, plaster	Post-A.D. 1800	Clark and Kirch 1983; Lass 1983:72
	2776	House	165 adze flakes, 317 basalt flakes	None	Post-A.D. 1800	Clark and Kirch 1983; Lass 1994:72
	8824	House	1 adze, 5 adze flakes, 2 hammerstones, 24 basalt flakes	None	Post-A.D. 1800	Clark and Kirch 1983; Lass 1994:72
	303	Not reported	adze	Not reported	Post-A.D. 1800	Barrera 1971; Lass 1994:72
	73	Not reported	adze	Not reported	Post-A.D. 1800	Spear 1987

by this time (Kirch 1992:179–180). Both mercantilism and transportation routes accelerated the penetration of Western material culture into rural life, although Hawaiians evidently continued to use traditional artifacts like stone adzes (Kirch 1992:180).

Additional post-Contact sites with stone adzes have also possibly been identified on the island of Hawai'i, the largest island in the archipelago (Table 7.1) (Lass 1994). Most of these sites are located in the vicinity of Waimea, in the island interior (Figure 7.5). As noted previously, stone adzes were still used at Waimea in 1847 (Lyons, in Doyle 1953:145). However, less confidence can be placed on these particular archaeological sites since their dating depended heavily on chronometric techniques (i.e., radiocarbon and obsidian hydration) rather than the presence of historic artifacts. That said, the dearth of historic artifacts at these sites could simply be a function of their rural isolation.

Other early historic sites (Ki'ilae village) on the island of Hawai'i (Figure 7.5) have also yielded stone adzes (Ladd 1986). Whether or not these adzes were actually contemporaneous with the historic occupation of the village is uncertain. For example, it is conceivable that pre-Contact stone adzes were already present when the historic village was established. Alternatively, perhaps they were discovered elsewhere on the island and brought to Ki'ilae as "curios," or recycled for some other purpose besides woodworking. In either case, it is possible that stone adzes were used at this locale, but it remains to be conclusively demonstrated.

In short, Anahulu Valley contains the strongest evidence of stone adze use in the post-Contact period. What remains unanswered, however, is whether stone adzes were actually manufactured after Contact. With few exceptions (e.g., Bayman et al. 2001; McCoy 1990), stone adze quarries have not been well dated in Hawai'i. Some radiocarbon dates from Mauna Kea, the largest quarry in the Pacific region, have intervals that include the "present" (i.e., 1950) (Bayman et al. 2001; McCoy 1990). These dates may (albeit arguably) reflect post-Contact quarry activity. Because Mauna Kea is an extremely remote, high-elevation quarry, the lack of European artifacts should not be surprising. However, without such artifacts, post-Contact adze production cannot be conclusively substantiated at this locale. Although further research on this problem is needed, evidence for post-Contact use (if not the production) of stone adzes is well documented by archaeological and documentary materials in the Hawaiian islands.

CONCLUSION

Stone adze technology in the Hawaiian islands was markedly affected by the changing political and economic milieu of the early post-Contact era. The intensified production of canoes and the export of sandalwood were only two of

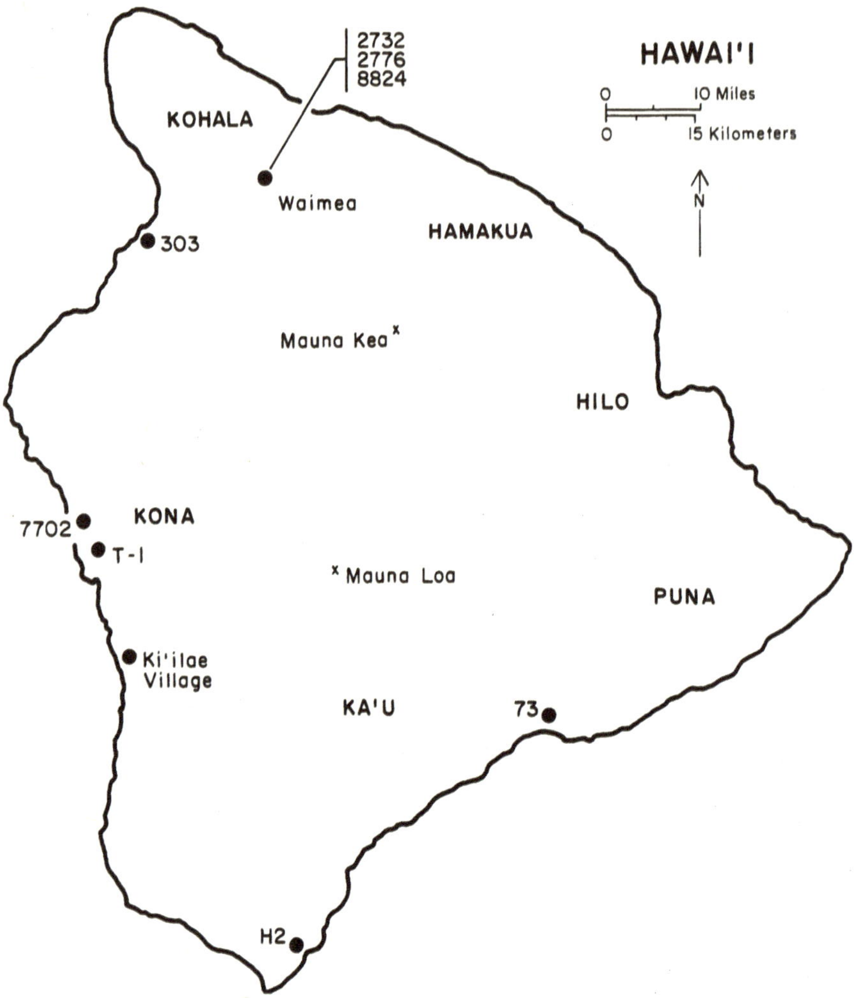

Fig. 7.5. Selected archaeological sites with stone adzes on the island of Hawai'i (drawn by Ronald Beckwith)

many economic activities in which adzes were used in the first half of the nineteenth century. However, the introduction of metal adzes and other Western tools did not alter indigenous Hawaiian technology in the fashion implied by conventional models of European contact and colonialism.

In conventional models, the assumption is typically made that craft materials (e.g., metal) and technologies introduced by Western societies are technically more efficient in comparison to indigenous (i.e., non-Western) tools and technologies (Cobb, chapter 1). Consequently, it is expected that indigenous societies will quickly abandon their traditional technologies in favor of Western-introduced technologies as they are drawn into an ever-expanding world system of market economies and capitalism.

In the Hawaiian case study, powerful chiefs initially constrained the ability of their commoners to obtain metal adzes and other European goods in the Hawaiian islands. Communities located in rural settings (like Waimea, on the island of Hawai'i) away from major seaports were also, in some instances, too isolated to acquire metal adzes. To understand this pattern more fully, future archaeological investigations of stone adze economies in post-Contact Hawai'i should focus on islands (like Moloka'i and Kaua'i) that did not have major seaports. Geographic constraints on the adoption of metal has been documented in southeastern North America (e.g., Johnson 1997, chapter 4), and it certainly played a role in the Hawaiian islands.

Together, these factors initially reinforced, rather than diminished, stone adze use in post-Contact Hawai'i, despite some superior performance characteristics of metal over stone. Experimental archaeology outside the Pacific confirms that metal axes are indeed more "efficient" than stone axes in the amount of wood they can process per unit of time (e.g., Mathieu and Meyer 1997; Saraydar and Shimada 1971). Such findings would almost certainly apply to Hawaiian stone and metal adzes. However, economic and productive "efficiency" were not always paramount in crafting a traditional Hawaiian canoe.

As Brigham (1902) noted, Hawaiian craftsmen preferred stone adzes over metal adzes for certain steps of canoe building. Hawaiian canoe craftsmen apparently practiced a "technological style" that compelled them to use stone adzes in some instances, even if they were less "efficient" in terms of productive output. Changes in this aesthetic might have originated from the increasing pressure to pay increased volumes of tribute (in the form of canoes) to their ruling chiefs. Larger payments of tribute would have precluded the skilled, careful craftsmanship that traditional canoe-making with stone adzes once entailed.

A decline in the quality of canoe craftsmanship by 1829 (see Haddon and Hornell 1975:20) is attributed to a diminishing availability of stone adzes, since their large-scale production apparently ceased shortly after Contact (Brigham 1902:408). For reasons as yet unknown, indigenous Hawaiians did not manufacture stone adzes after the middle of the nineteenth century. Perhaps stone adze makers left their skilled profession to work in emerging industries such as commercial whaling. In either case, many stone adze craftsmen died from disease epidemics that entered the islands after European contact, and their technical knowledge could no longer be transmitted through word-of-mouth communication or apprenticeship. Consequently, the production of new stone adzes must have waned, even if the use of older stone adzes continued. The use-life of stone adzes is poorly documented in Hawai'i, and yet they would certainly require replacement after long-term resharpening. The declining availability of stone adzes eventually compelled canoe craftsmen to only use metal adzes, whether they desired to do so or not. By this time, powerful Hawaiian chiefs were obliged to allow their constituents access to metal adzes and other Western technologies since it strengthened their ability to mobilize tribute.

Conventional models of European contact have long emphasized the relatively high productive efficiency of Western technology, compared to the technologies of indigenous societies. The Hawaiian case study confirms that a rich variety of political, economic, and geographic factors governed the persistence of stone adzes after the introduction of metal tools. Archaeological research elsewhere in the world should also strive to identify the contexts that favored the persistence of stone technology. In doing so, general interpretations of European contact and colonialism will achieve a greater degree of historical integrity.

ACKNOWLEDGMENTS

This paper was conceptualized during the University of Hawai'i Archaeological Field School at Pôhakuloa in 1998 and 1997. I am grateful to the many students who contributed their energy and enthusiasm to the field school. Kanani Paraso and Tim Rieth were especially valuable in this regard, and their contributions are sincerely appreciated. Other colleagues who provided support and encouragement for the field school include Dan Brown, Michael Graves, Bion Griffin, Elliott Lax, Peter Mills, Jadelyn Moniz Nakamura, Craig Severance, and Miriam Stark. Thanks, too, to Charlie Cobb for his invitation to contribute to this volume.

8

In All the Solemnity of Profound Smoking

Tobacco Smoking and Pipe Manufacture and Use among the Potawatomi of Illinois

Mark J. Wagner

Tobacco smoking played a pivotal role in the religious, social, and political lives of Native-American peoples throughout eastern North America (West 1934; Winter 2000d). In Illinois, stone smoking pipes first appear during the Late Archaic period (Koldehoff and Seidel 1990:11–13; Winters 1969) although the earliest tobacco-seed remains in the state (and indeed all of eastern North America) date to the much later Middle Woodland period at ca. 100 B.C.–A.D. 250 (Wagner 2000:190). Some researchers, however, suggest that the tobacco species *Nicotiana rustica* might have reached the Mississippi Valley by 1000–2000 B.C. if not earlier (Winter 2000c:324), a date range that agrees with the appearance of stone smoking pipes in the archaeological record. The recovery of smoking pipes and tobacco from Middle Woodland, Late Woodland, and Mississippian contexts attests to the continued ritual importance of tobacco smoking throughout prehistory (Emerson 1982; Jensen 1963). During the early (post-1673) historic period, tobacco smoking in stone pipes (as part of the calumet ceremony) played an important role in avoiding conflicts between unfamiliar and possibly antagonistic peoples. Groups such as the Illini "sang" the calumet with members of other Native-American groups—as well as French and English explorers, soldiers, and officials—as a means of establishing peaceful relationships (White 1991:22–24).

The recovery by archaeologists over the years of small numbers of stone pipes from sites associated with groups such as the Sauk, Kickapoo, and the Kaskaskia has revealed that Native-American peoples in Illinois continued to use stone pipes into the late eighteenth and early nineteenth centuries (Berkson 1992: 107–205; Good 1972:70; Jensen 1963). These pipes often were recovered from contexts, however, that provided little or no information about their manufacture or use. This situation persisted until the mid–1990s when limited excavations at the former location of Little Rock or Rock Village—an early-nineteenth-century Potawatomi settlement now known as the Windrose site (11Ka336)—recovered both stone pipe preforms and broken finished pipes from a sheet midden in association with discarded early-nineteenth-century fur trade-related artifacts and faunal remains (Wagner 2001). This recovery context made it possible to investigate the manner in which members of one particular Native-American group continued to manufacture, use, and discard stone smoking pipes at a time when the independent Native-American occupation of Illinois was drawing to a close. Additionally, the identification of the Windrose site as the remains of a specific Potawatomi settlement made it possible to examine the cultural and social factors behind the continued manufacture and use of stone pipes by the Kankakee River Valley Potawatomi during a time period in which functionally equivalent European-manufactured metal and clay smoking pipes were readily available to them.

The persistence of stone tobacco-pipe manufacture and use by the early-nineteenth-century Potawatomi must be viewed within the context of the social and political relationships that existed between the Potawatomi and the American government officials, missionaries, and settlers of the time. I have elsewhere argued (Wagner 1998) that the Kankakee River Valley Potawatomi actively responded to American acculturation pressures through a policy of selective change. European-manufactured items compatible with early-nineteenth-century Potawatomi lifeways including seasonal village movement, exploitation of fur-bearing mammals, and subsistence agriculture were accepted. Items and behaviors associated with forced acculturation—including the wearing of American-style clothing, the raising of domesticated food animals such as cows and pigs, the adoption of American farming techniques, and the use of refined earthenware dishes and cutlery—were recognized and rejected (Wagner 1998:430–456).

I interpreted the continued manufacture and use of stone pipes by the Potawatomi as an indicator of a continuity of traditional lines of Potawatomi authority, belief systems, and ideology into the early nineteenth century (Wagner 2000:170). While I still believe this to be the case, I argue in this study that such technological persistence in the creation of stone objects with ritual and political associations by Algonquian peoples also should be viewed within the larger historic context of the nativistic revitalization movements that occurred among many of the Native-American groups of eastern North America during the late eighteenth century and throughout the nineteenth century (Dowd 1992; Wallace 1969; White 1991:503). The most significant of these resistance movements against American hegemony that developed during the early nineteenth century—led by the Shawnee Prophet Tenskwatawa and his brother Tecumseh—deeply influenced the Kankakee River Valley Potawatomi.

In this chapter I first use historic research to examine the social, ritual, and political contexts of tobacco smoking and smoking pipe use among the nineteenth- and early-twentieth-century Potawatomi. I then present the historic background for the study with particular emphasis on the rise of nativistic religious movements and prophets as Native-American societies in the mid–continent attempted to cope with widespread spiritual and physical demoralization engendered by their losses in the unequal struggle with the dominant American culture of the early nineteenth century. Primary records, including travelers' accounts, government documents, and maps, as well as a variety of secondary sources, are used to examine the role of the Kankakee River Valley Potawatomi in the nativistic movement led by the Shawnee Prophet during the first two decades of the nineteenth century. The archaeological data from the Windrose site are then used to examine the types, raw materials, method of manufacture, and context of use of stone smoking pipes among the early-nineteenth-century Kankakee River Valley Potawatomi. When viewed within the context of early-nineteenth-century Indian-white relationships within eastern North America, I argue that these and other archaeological data from the Windrose site are indicative of Potawatomi resistance to American attempts at domination through the strengthening or revitalization of traditional practices in which tobacco-smoking in stone pipes acted as a facilitator.

THE POTAWATOMI

The Potawatomi are an Algonquian group that lived in the area of Lake Huron in the 1600s. Starting in the mid–1600s the Potawatomi began migrating westward as the result of pressure from the Iroquois. By the early-1800s, at least several thousand Potawatomi occupied villages located around the Great Lakes in southern Wisconsin and Michigan, northeastern and central Illinois, and northwestern Indiana (Wheeler-Voegelin 1974:11–122). Approximately 2,000 Potawatomi occupying at least 26 separate villages are estimated to have been present in northeastern Illinois in the late–1820s (Tanner 1987:138; Wagner 1998:436). Approximately 100 to 120 "Potawatomies, Ottawas, and Chipways" reportedly lived on the "Rock Bank" of the Kankakee River in the general location of the Windrose site in the early-1830s (Chicago Historical Society 1833).

The early-nineteenth-century Potawatomi followed a pattern of seasonal movement between large summer agricultural villages and smaller winter villages. For six months of the year the Potawatomi raised corn and other crops with at least part of the village going off on a summer hunt. As soon as the crops were harvested in the fall, the Potawatomi dispersed to occupy small winter hunting camps where economic activities centered around the acquisition of fur-bearing mammals for trade and food. By the early nineteenth century, participation in the fur trade had been part of the Potawatomi economic system for almost 200 years. Traders associated with the American Fur Company visited the Potawatomi during the early part of the winter to buy pelts and re-supply the Potawatomi with ammunition and other goods (Wagner 1998:436–437).

POTAWATOMI TOBACCO-USE AND PIPE-SMOKING

Historic accounts and ethnographies indicate that tobacco-smoking formed an integral part of Potawatomi life from at least the early nineteenth to mid–twentieth centuries (Landes 1970; McCoy 1840; Ritzenthaler 1953; Skinner 1926). As with other Great Lakes Algonquian groups, tobacco smoking had symbolic significance, serving as a means of communication between individuals, groups, and Native Americans and the supernatural world (Trubowitz 1992, 1994:11–12). Many Algonquian groups, such as the Kickapoo, considered tobacco to be a manitou or powerful spirit. Tobacco offerings were made to other manitou (such as fire and Grandmother Earth) by throwing tobacco into a fire or burying it in the earth, respectively. Tobacco offerings to various manitou also formed an integral part of adoption, deer hunting, new house, and rain ceremonies, among others (Winter 2000b:19). Skinner (1926:269) noted that among the early-twentieth-century Prairie Potawatomi of Kansas "no ceremony could be conducted without tobacco." Individual Potawatomi kept tobacco in their houses to safeguard their families, sent it with invitations as part of a greeting ceremony, offered tobacco to the fire manitou before moving into a newly built house, and made tobacco offerings before going on deer or bear hunts (Skinner 1926:269, 271, 286–287). Tobacco offerings also formed part of naming, adoption, and other ceremonies into the 1930s (Landes 1970:121, 208). Ritzenthaler (1953:152) similarly noted that invitation by tobacco and tobacco offerings to spirits formed part of all religious ceremonials of the mid–twentieth-century Potawatomi of Wisconsin.

Historic accounts indicate that the widespread ritual use of tobacco by the Potawatomi recorded by twentieth-century ethnographers extends back into time at least into the early nineteenth century. Early-nineteenth-century Potawatomi leaders offered or smoked tobacco during religious ceremonies, at meetings with American military officers, during visits by American missionaries, and at treaty negotiations with government officials. In 1821 missionary Isaac McCoy participated in a greeting ceremony with Potawatomi leaders in Indiana in which he noted that, as "is usual on these occasions, business was opened by my throwing my tobacco in a heap on the ground, in the midst of the company, followed by a round of smoking. Next came our *talk*." (McCoy 1840:102, emphasis in original). American Army captain Samuel Levering, who was sent on a potentially dangerous mission to a Potawatomi village in central Illinois to arrange the surrender of three Potawatomi killers of American settlers, similarly participated in a greeting ceremony that involved tobacco-smoking before the start of the negotiations. Levering was struck by how the men of the village, instead of being hostile as he had feared, "generally left their sleeping places, [and] squatted around two fires in the center of the building, 'in all the solemnity of profound smoking.' This appears, says Capt. Levering, to be an etiquette due to strangers" (Edwards 1870:5). Isaac McCoy in Indiana in 1825 and traveler Colbee Benton in Wisconsin in 1833 also recorded the use of tobacco-offerings as part of ceremonies that appear to have preceded the start of animal hunts (Benton 1957:107; McCoy 1840:272–273). McCoy (1840:132) also described ritual tobacco smoking at Potawatomi funerals in the 1830s as well as the interment of tobacco and smoking pipes with the deceased, practices that continued well into the twentieth century among the Potawatomi of Kansas (Ritzenthaler 1953:144–150).

Potawatomi men also smoked for pleasure. As traveler Colbee Benton simply noted in 1833, Potawatomi men "played cards most all the time and smoked *all* the time" (Benton 1957:83; emphasis in original). Drawings and paintings made in Indiana by artist George Winters in 1837 similarly depict Potawatomi men as smoking while playing games or lounging around in camp. Interestingly, of the 10 pipes illustrated by Winters, two are clearly metal "tomahawk" pipes and four are kaolin. The remaining four pipes have long wooden stems similar to tomahawk pipes but the bowl type cannot be identified (Feest and Edmunds 1993:44, 47, 63, 74, 75, 84, 85, 94, 95). The absence of stone smoking pipes in Winter's illustrations, given their presence at the Windrose site (Wagner 2001), raises the possibility that such pipes might have been reserved for religious ceremonials.

The Potawatomi used two types of tobacco: *Nicotaina rustica* and *N. tabacum*. The first of these (*N. rustica*) is presumed on the basis of historic-period distribution to have been the species cultivated prehistorically in eastern North America (Wagner 2000:185). This strong-tasting dark tobacco was cultivated in small patches, used in religious ceremonies, and considered a sacred plant by Native-American groups throughout eastern North America. *N. tabacum*, a lighter tobacco with a milder taste that is used in the manufacture of modern-day cigarettes and pipe tobacco, was commercially introduced by Europeans into eastern North America from Brazil in the early seventeenth century. Many Native-American groups reserved *N. rustica* for use in religious and other ceremonies while using the commercially obtained *N. tabacum* for recreational smoking. Commercial tobacco supplied by fur traders and government officials also was used in pipe-smoking ceremonies that preceded the opening of treaty negotiations held between the Potawatomi and the American government in the 1830s (Feest and Edmunds 1993:6). The Kansas Potawatomi continued to plant "native tobacco" in small plots in the woods at least until the 1930s. These plots apparently were considered to be places of power and had to be avoided by passersby (Skinner 1926:286–287). Native tobacco maintained its ritual role among the Potawatomi at least into the 1930s when ethnographer Ruth Landes recorded its use during her naming ceremony. The Potawatomi shaman conducting the ceremony explained to Landes that at such a "feast, only *Indian* tobacco should be used, because it is a gift straight from the Great Spirit; plug tobacco [which is a white man's artifact] should be used only at Religion Dance [which is a modern, Christianized rite . . . rejecting pagan mysticism] (Landes 1970:207, 209, bracketed material and italics in original).

This distinction in usage between the native-grown *N. rustica* and the commercially obtained *N. tabacum* appears to extend back in time at least into the early nineteenth century (Benton 1957; Feest and Edmunds 1993; McCoy 1840). One of the clearest accounts of this distinction comes from Colbee Benton's account of his visit to a Potawatomi village led by Ontac (or Autuckee), a well-respected early-nineteenth-century Potawatomi leader. Benton distributed "figs" or plugs of commercial tobacco to Ontac and the other Potawatomi, which they smoked and gambled with during a day of feasting, foot races, card games, and ball playing. At the close of the day, however, Benton inadvertently stumbled on a private ceremony in a wigwam that involved the ritual use of tobacco and pipe-smoking. According to Benton, "Ontac cut up some tobacco and rubbed it until it was perfectly dry. Then he commenced . . . a speech or blessing, all the time the rest [of the Potawatomi men] were perfectly silent and did not move. After the blessing they all approached the Chief and filled their pipes with the tobacco he had prepared and lighted them by the fire on the ground in the centre of the wigwam" (Benton 1957:104–107). Although Benton did not identify the tobacco used in this ceremony as "native tobacco" or *N. rustica*, the reverential attitude of the Potawatomi toward its use suggests that it almost certainly could not have been the commercial tobacco supplied by Benton which the Potawatomi men apparently regarded so lightly that they felt comfortable in gambling it away earlier in the day.

NATIVE-AMERICAN REVITALIZATION MOVEMENTS

The last decades of the eighteenth century and first decade of the early nineteenth century were a period of intense stress and demoralization for the Algonquian groups of Indiana, Ohio, and Illinois. The almost continuous warfare during this time with the American soldiers and settlers who were pouring into the Old Northwest had resulted in the disastrous loss of most of the Ohio country and the crowding of Native-American refugees into northwestern Ohio and northern Indiana (Edmunds 1983:4–6). Although the Potawatomi retained control of their lands, Potawatomi warriors had participated in many of the conflicts and the Potawatomi as a people were not unaffected. Traditional lines of authority were disrupted as war leaders rose to prominence and usurped much of the traditional role of the village headman or okama. Intermarriage of Potawatomi women with American, British, and French fur traders also had resulted in a very large mixed-blood population and the consequent disruption of the web of interpersonal relationships and kinship networks that held Potawatomi society together (Wagner 2001:9). Alcoholism and violence within the Potawatomi villages also increased as fur traders provided raw frontier whiskey to hunters and their families in return for furs.

Prophets and visionaries, many of whom advocated a return to traditional values, arose among the various demoralized Native-American groups as they sought an answer to their problems (Dowd 1992; Wallace 1969; White 1991: 502–510). The most famous of the early-nineteenth-century prophets was the "Shawnee Prophet" Tenskwatawa or, as he is known in English, the Open Door. A former alcoholic, the Shawnee Prophet experienced a set of dramatic series of visions in 1805 in which he was told that the source of the problem lay in the falling away of Algonquian peoples from their traditional way of life. Tenskwatawa urged his followers to give up the ways of the whites and to return to the food, implements, and dress of their ancestors (Sugden 2000:235–236). Cattle, pigs, and sheep were unclean and were not to be eaten; people were to dress in leather animal skins and discard their American and European clothing; women were to discard their metal pots and return to making ones of clay; metal tools and implements were to be replaced with stone and wooden ones; and warriors were to hunt animals with "stone-tipped spears and arrows," using guns only for defense (Edmunds 1983:37; 1984:77–78).

The Prophet's teachings found a receptive audience among the Kankakee River Valley Potawatomi. As word of the Prophet spread to Illinois in 1807, large parties of Potawatomi warriors began traveling to Ohio to see him in person (Edmunds 1983:50; Sugden 1997:143). Among these was the leader of the Kankakee River Valley Potawatomi, the feared war leader and shaman known as Main Poc or the Withered Hand. Main Poc, although disdainful of some of the Prophet's teachings including his ban on the use of alcohol, invited him to move his village to lands claimed by the Potawatomi at the junction of the Tippecanoe and Wabash Rivers in Indiana. The Prophet accepted and in 1808 established the pan–Native American settlement of Prophetstown on Potawatomi land (Edmunds 1983:63–68, 1984:108–110). Prophetstown quickly became the center of Native-American resistance to American settlement as Potawatomi, Chippewa, Ottawa, Wyandot, Winnebago, Sac, Fox, Kickapoo, and Iowa warriors and their families traveled there to listen to the Prophet. In 1810, two years after its founding, Main Poc and a large number of Illinois Potawatomi also moved to Prophetstown (Edmunds 1983:86; 1984:125). Main Poc and the Kankakee River Valley Potawatomi were to remain the strongest supporters of the Prophet and his brother Tecumseh over the next several years (Sugden 1997:175).

The revitalization and resistance movement led by the Prophet collapsed almost as quickly as it had arose. Severely discredited following his defeat and the burning of Prophetstown by the Americans in 1811, the Prophet lost virtually all of his followers after the death of Tecumseh and the defeat of the British and Indian forces at the Battle of the Thames in 1813. Nevertheless, for almost a decade his message of resistance to Euro-American culture and a return to a more traditional way of life had resonated strongly with many Great Lakes Algonquian groups, foremost among whom were the Kankakee River Valley Potawatomi of Illinois. Thus, we should see clear indications of this nativistic movement at sites occupied during this time period by Native-American groups that were receptive to the Prophet's message. Such indicators may include the continued use of traditional objects, avoidance of some types of available European technologies, and a reliance upon traditional foodways.

WINDROSE SITE

The mid–1990s excavation of the Windrose site (11Ka336) in northeastern Illinois provided detailed information regarding the material culture of the early-nineteenth-century Potawatomi during and slightly after the time of the Prophet's revitalization movement. Located in dense woods along the Kankakee River in what is now Kankakee River State Park, the Windrose site represents a very small part of an extensive early-nineteenth-century Potawatomi summer village once known as Little Rock Village. More significantly, an 1815 map identifies this same village as that of Main Poc, the Prophet's strongest supporter among the Potawatomi and an inveterate enemy of the Euro-Americans (Tucker 1942:Plate XL). A notation contained on a second map of northeastern Illinois believed to date from 1811 further states that "Mainpocks [*sic*] band [is located] 7 leagues [or 21 miles] up this [the Kankakee] river" which again closely agrees with the location of the Windrose site (Tucker 1942:Plate XXXV). Main Poc's name also appears on a list of "Bad Chiefs" written on the back of the map with the additional warning that he is "worst [*sic*] than [Shawnee] prophet . . . do not go to See him" (Temple 1975:11–12).

The Windrose site excavations were limited in scope and primarily were restricted to investigating a portion of the site disturbed by an artifact collector. Nevertheless, excavation of a 30 sq m area of the site, including portions of two contemporaneous sheet middens believed to be flanking a traditional structure, recovered an extensive array of faunal remains, European manufactures, and Native American–made items. The Euro-American artifact assemblage was composed almost entirely of items associated with the Great Lakes fur trade including gun parts, kettle fragments, silver ornaments, iron tools, and other items. The recovery of temporally diagnostic artifacts such as a patchbox to an early-nineteenth-century Pennsylvania rifle, a buttplate to a pre-1825 Northwest Trade gun, and a U.S. Corps of Artillery button issued between 1815 and 1821 dated the Potawatomi occupation of the Windrose site to ca. 1800 to 1836 (Wagner 2001).

Chipped- and ground-stone artifacts including lithic debitage, retouched flakes, utilized flakes, a triangular arrowpoint, and ground stone pipe fragments were intermixed with the historic period artifacts. The Potawatomi midden, however, intergraded with and was underlain by prehistoric Archaic to Woodland period midden that contained a similar range of chert artifacts and debitage. As such, all of the chipped-stone artifacts (with the exception of a native-made gunflint and several reworked French and British gunflints) were interpreted as prehistoric artifacts. Ground-stone artifacts of any type, however, were not present within the prehistoric midden, leading to the interpretation of the ground-stone pipe fragments and preforms as early-nineteenth-century Potawatomi artifacts (Wagner 2001:56–71).

Ground Stone

Twenty-two ground-stone artifacts were recovered from the Windrose site. These consisted of 15 fragments representing the remains of nine separate smoking pipes, four dolomite objects interpreted as broken and discarded preforms, and three unidentifiable fragments.

Raw Materials

Raw materials for these artifacts included dolomite (*N*=19), igneous/metamorphic rock (*N*=1), and sandstone (*N*=2). Dolomite outcrops at many locations along the Kankakee River and also occurs in rubble bars within the river itself. An extensive dolomite outcrop that in all likelihood was the source for many if not all of the dolomite pipe fragments and preforms found at the Windrose site is located at the mouth of Rock Creek less than 30 m west of the two sheet middens from which these artifacts were recovered (Wagner 2001:43). Igneous/metamorphic rock also occurs within the immediate site area in the form of glacial till within glacial moraines, as erratics on the landscape, and as redeposited till within the rubble bars of the Kankakee River (Frankie 1997:22–24). Sandstone, in contrast, is a nonlocal lithic material. Although the source of the Windrose sandstone pipe fragments is unknown, the most likely source lies 80 to 100 km to the west in the upper Illinois River Valley near Starved Rock. This area, which contains extensive sandstone bedrock and bluff formations (Worthen 1883:39–40), formed part of the Potawatomi heartland within Illinois during the late eighteenth and early nineteenth centuries (Clifton 1977).

Pipe Manufacture

Five broken dolomite objects, at least four of which appear to be fragments of partially finished pipes that broke during various stages of manufacture, provide information regarding stone pipe-making techniques at the site. In combination, these fragments suggest that dolomite pipes were initially chipped or roughly ground into shape, further reduced and shaped using metal tools including iron files, then ground smooth to remove the metal tool scars. Smoking pipe researcher George West (1934:351) dismissed the idea that iron files were used in historic-period stone-pipe manufacture, noting that in his own experiments "no striations on the stone resulted . . . each time the file passed over the stone . . . [but rather it left] its tract perfectly smooth. In fact, how could it do otherwise?" He instead argued that the striations identified as "alleged file marks" were "identical to those which could be produced by the use of a piece of gritty sandstone." West appears, however, to have used a flat file in which the sides and faces meet at a right angle in his experiment. Use of such a file does indeed leave a smooth surface with no striations. I was, however, able to consistently produce sets of parallel striations on dolomite collected from the mouth of Rock Creek that were identical to those on the Windrose site dolomite pipe preforms by using a round file. Round files are used in woodworking for shaping curves (Blackburn 1974:48), a characteristic that also would have been useful in stone pipe manufacture. Native American–style stone pipes that appear to have been manufactured using drills, knives, and files also have been recovered from an eighteenth-century context at Ft. Michilimackinac, although it is unclear if these pipes were being made by Native Americans or Europeans (Trubowitz 1992:106). Further support for interpreting the striations on the Windrose pipe preforms as having been created by metal rather than sandstone tools is the almost total absence of sandstone at the site. Sandstone represented an insignificant part of the lithic assemblage, comprising far less than one-tenth of one percent of all unmodified rock recovered from the site (Wagner 2001:63). Sandstone simply was not readily available to the Potawatomi of the Kankakee River Valley for use for expedient grinding purposes.

The most intact of the Windrose site specimens consists of the lower section of a large-diameter (40.6 mm), flat-bottomed cylindrical preform for a straight-walled, flat-bottomed pipe (Figure 8.1a). The flat base and sides of this 10.5 to 24 cm long object were roughly flaked and partially ground into shape before the upper portion broke off and the item was discarded. A second, much smaller flat-bottomed ground dolomite object interpreted as a preform for a square pipe discarded during the initial stage of manufacture was recovered from the site surface (Figure 8.1b). Three sides of this object have been lightly ground, as has been the base. A series of very fine striations extend from the base upwards

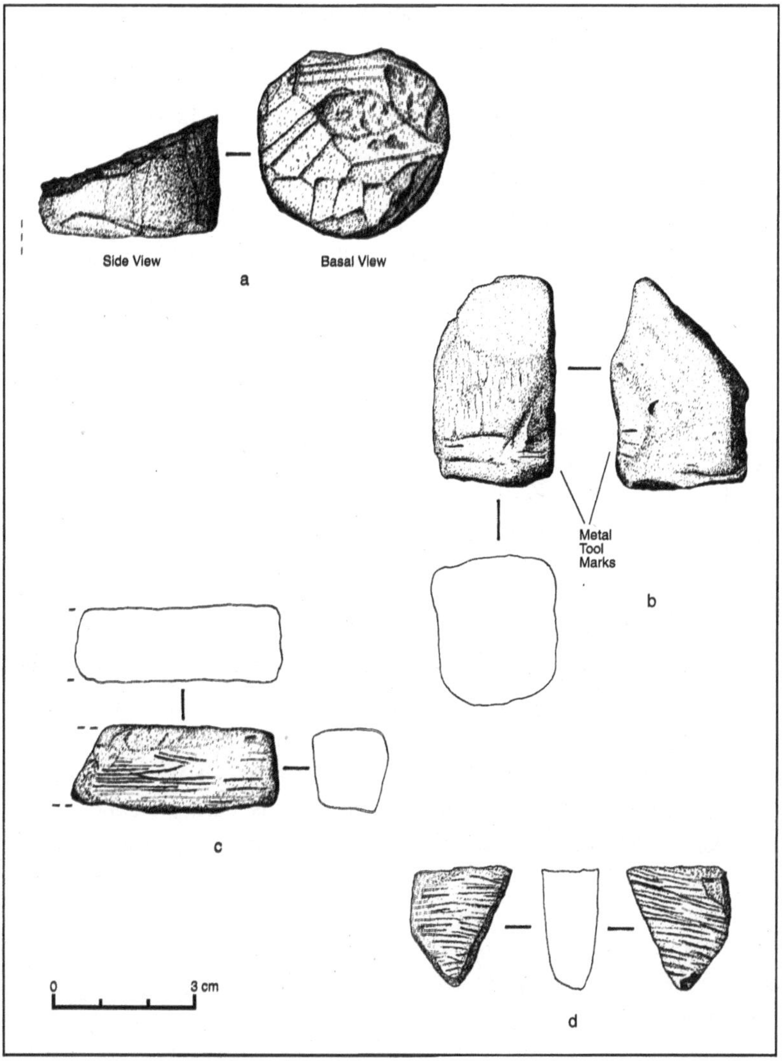

Fig. 8.1. Stone pipe preform fragments, Windrose site

on the most complete side of the artifact. In addition, a group of one to three horizontal incised grooves that possibly represent part of an unfinished design encircling the base are present on three sides extending upward from the base for approximately 10 mm. These narrow (1–3 mm), sharply defined grooves are v-shaped in cross section, a shape that could have been created by using a triangular iron file or the edge of a flat file.

Metal tool marks also are present on three other ground stone fragments, two of which at least appear to be sections of nearly complete pipe preforms that broke and were discarded. The first consists of an apparent undrilled, ground rectangular stem fragment with one unmodified and three ground sides (Figure 8.1c). Very fine parallel striations are present on two of the three ground sides and the proximal end of the stem. The absence of metal tool scars on one of the ground sides and their minimal representation on another suggest that shaping of the preform by filing and subsequent grinding of the surface to remove the striations were two separate stages in dolomite pipe manufacture at the site. Presumably all of the file marks would have been ground off if this pipe had not broken during manufacture.

The second heavily filed possible preform section consists of an approximate 10 to 12 mm thick triangular-shaped fragment with two broken edges and one slightly ground and filed edge (Figure 8.1d). The two faces of this object are covered with a series of tightly spaced, very fine metal file marks oriented obliquely to the unbroken edge. This combination of heavily filed surfaces and unmodified edge again suggests that this object might have been in the initial stage of manufacture when it broke.

Pipe Styles

Four pipe styles—vasiform, globular, micmac, and elbow—are represented in the Windrose assemblage. The single vasiform pipe consists of three fragments of a sandstone pipe comprising approximately one-third of the upper body of a vase-shaped pipe with a squared plain rim (not shown; see Wagner 2001:Figure 7.19C for a photograph of this pipe). A borehole is located on the side of the pipe approximately 30 mm below the rim. A charred botanical residue, unidentifiable as to genus, was still present within the pipe interior. Stemless pipes appear to represent a minority pipe style during the late historic period in the Great Lakes region. Miniature stemless vasiform pipes made of catlinite and limestone were associated with the late-seventeenth-/early-eighteenth-century Potawatomi to late-eighteenth-century components at the Rock Island site in Michigan (Mason 1986:159, 162). Stemless pipes also occur as a minority type at the eighteenth- to early-nineteenth-century Kaskaskia-occupied Guebert site in southwestern Illinois (Good 1972:70) and at an early-nineteenth-century Sauk site in northwestern Illinois (Jensen 1963:113).

The micmac pipe form is represented at the Windrose site by three fragments comprising parts of two pipes. A unique set of morphological characteristics including a bulbous bowl, constricted neck, keel-shaped base, and in some cases a basal plate distinguish this pipe type from other stemless pipe forms (West 1934). Micmac pipes were extensively used throughout the Great Lakes region from the late seventeenth to early twentieth centuries (Quimby 1966:157). The first Windrose site example consists of virtually the entire base, constricted neck, and bowl base of this distinctive pipe form (Figure 8.2a). A single raised line encircles the broken bowl base of the specimen. The sides of the base are decorated with two parallel incised horizontal lines while the ends are decorated with two parallel incised vertical lines. Two broken projections beneath the base are all that remain of a missing basal plate that would have contained one to two holes through which a string worn around the smoker's neck would have been inserted. The decoration on the pipe base is identical to that of a micmac pipe associated with the late-seventeenth- to early-eighteenth-century Potawatomi and Ottawa occupations at the Rock Island site in Lake Michigan (Mason 1986:161). A micmac pipe with a rectangular base decorated with two incised parallel lines also was recovered from the early-nineteenth-century Sauk-occupied Crawford Farm site in northwestern Illinois (Jensen 1963:Figure 48c). Unless it is broken off and not visible in the photograph, however, the Crawford Farm specimen lacks the basal plate found on the Rock Island and Windrose site specimens. The second Windrose site example of this pipe form is very fragmentary, consisting only of a portion of the stem, bowl, and basal plate (Figure 8.2b). Identification of this fragment as a micmac pipe is based on the distinctive basal plate located beneath the bowl. The pipe stem ends in a rounded, blunt-ended projection located anterior to the bowl. An attempt to drill a suspension hole through the tapered basal plate from both sides was never completed, suggesting that this pipe might have broken during manufacture and been discarded before being used. The stem and bowl borehole ends are visible within the broken bowl, however, suggesting that drilling of those sections of the pipe necessary for it to be smoked was completed.

The elbow pipe form is represented by two heavily ground contiguous fragments of a large dolomite pipe stem broken at both ends (Figure 8.2c). This very finely made stem has an oval cross-section with a diameter that varies from 21 to 30 mm. A slightly raised area at the distal end of the broken stem represents the very edge of the bowl, which was oriented at a right angle to and extended upward from the stem. The very base of the vertical borehole for the pipe bowl also is visible along the broken edge of the stem. The high quality of this pipe fragment clearly sets it apart from the majority of the other Windrose site smoking pipes and it is possible that it once formed part of a calumet pipe similar to those used in sacred ceremonies by various Native-American groups. Although typically made of catlinite, calumet pipes made of limestone, sandstone, and chlorite are known from the Great Lakes region and the Plains (Trubowitz 1992:101, 104; West 1934:231–278, 832–833, 847–848).

The single globular pipe consists of four heavily eroded fragments comprising the upper two-thirds of a stemless dolomite pipe bowl with a flattened rim and slightly extruded lip (Figure 8.2d). The stem borehole is located on the side of the bowl along the broken lower edge of the bowl. A square or rectangular recessed panel on one face of the pipe was created by removing approximately .5 mm of the pipe surface, the interior of which was then decorated with punctations and

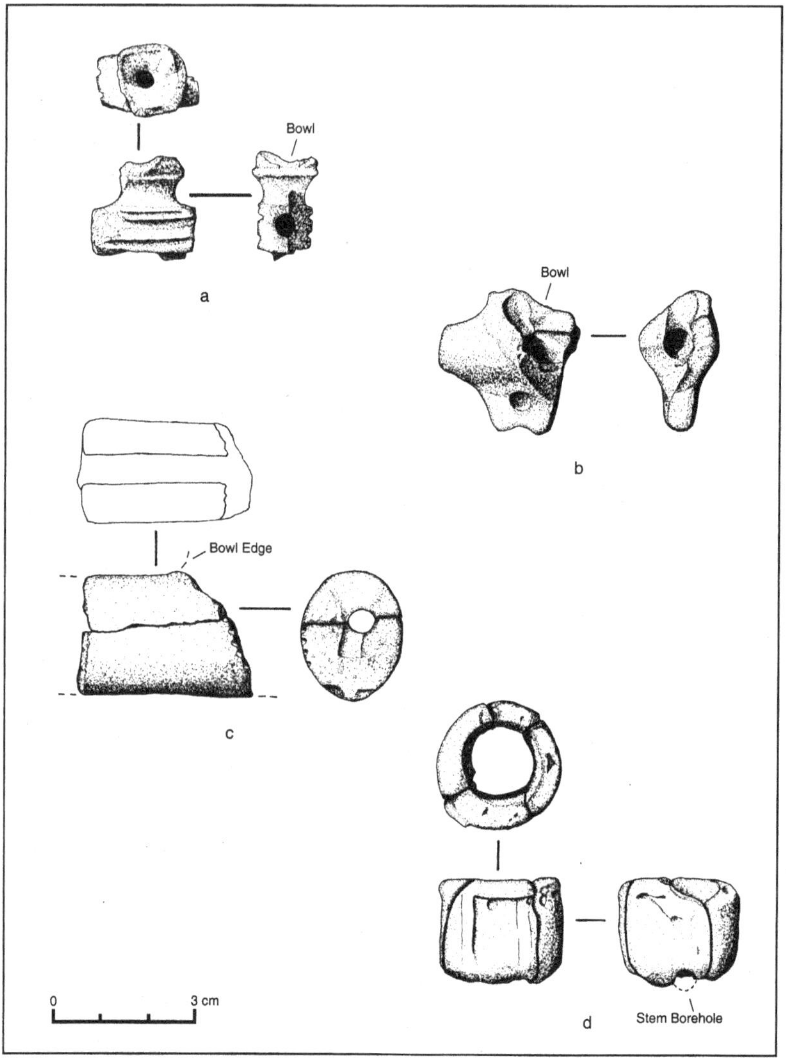

Fig. 8.2. Stone smoking pipe fragments, Windrose site

vertically oriented incised lines, only three of which now remain. The wall of the pipe angles in slightly at 19 mm below the lip to form the now-missing pipe base. It also is possible that this pipe, rather than being globular, represents the bowl section to a micmac pipe variant in which the borehole is located in the side of the bowl rather than the stem, similar to an example illustrated by West (1934:Plate 172, Figure 2).

Four pipe fragments were unidentifiable as to type. Three are dolomite pipe bowl fragments (Figure 8.3a-c), two of which exhibit a series of vertically oriented

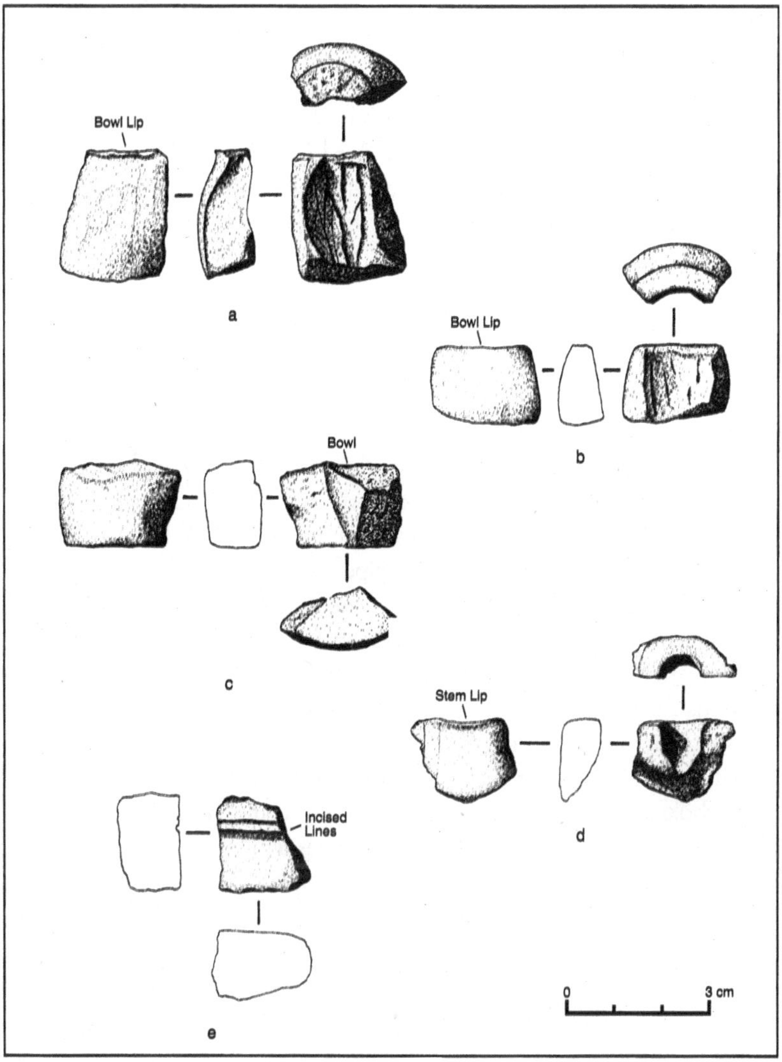

Fig. 8.3. Stone pipe and other ground stone fragments, Windrose site

narrow striations on the bowl interior that appear to have been incised with a sharp metal tool such as an awl or knife blade (Figure 8.2a-b). Although these could be associated with the manufacture of the pipe bowl, it is equally possible that they are pipe bowl cleaning scars. The single igneous/metamorphic pipe section (Figure 8.3d) recovered from the site consisted of a fragmentary hexagonal-shaped stem with a flange similar to those found on a number of catlinite pipe forms (Mason 1986:162–163) attached to one side.

Finally, three broken ground-stone objects were simply too incomplete to absolutely identify as smoking pipe fragments although I believe that is what they are. The first consists of a heavily ground dolomite fragment decorated with two parallel incised lines (Figure 8.3e) similar to those seen on many micmac pipe bases (West 1934:821, 825); the second (not illustrated) is a piece of sandstone with one heavily ground surface; and the third is a very small, thin, water-worn, broken piece of dolomite that contains five small shallow dimples on one surface. These dimples are very similar to a set of small drilled circular depressions used to decorate a stone pipe recovered from a late-eighteenth-century Wea village in Indiana (Trubowitz 1992:104).

CONCLUSION

The Windrose site data indicate that by the early nineteenth century the once vibrant Potawatomi ground-stone tool manufacturing industry of the early eighteenth century (Mason 1986:156–164) had diminished to the production of a single type of item: stone smoking pipes. The presence of filed and ground dolomite fragments indicate that dolomite pipes were being manufactured at the site while pipes made of nonlocal stone were transported to the site in a finished form. Broken stone pipes were discarded with other village debris rather than being afforded any special treatment, suggesting that any ritual or symbolic associations held by these items ceased when they were no longer functional. The absence of complete stone pipes at Windrose is notable, suggesting that such items either were curated or that they passed out of the material culture assemblage as whole items through interment with the dead. The Kankakee River Valley Potawatomi continued to inter smoking pipes with the dead into the 1830s, although it is unknown if these were native-made or European-manufactured items (Bloom 1883:8).

There are two significant features to the Windrose site stone pipe assemblage. The first is that the Kankakee River Valley Potawatomi clearly had access to and were using Euro-American smoking pipes at the same time they were making stone pipes. European- and American-manufactured pipes at the site included 53 kaolin stem and bowl fragments as well as two reworked blade sections to iron tomahawk smoking pipes (Wagner 2001:87, 112–117). The presence of these items indicates that the continued manufacture of stone pipes by the early-nineteenth-century Potawatomi was a matter of choice, not necessity. The second significant feature of the Windrose site is that metal tools, most notably round files, were used in the shaping of the stone pipes, suggesting that early Contact-period methods of grinding and drilling stone (see Mason 1986:156–164 for examples) had passed from knowledge by the early nineteenth century. The use of metal tools to create stone pipes also may indicate that the early-nineteenth-century manufacture of stone pipes by the Potawatomi represents more a revival of an earlier stone pipe making industry than a smooth continuation. The need for stone smoking pipes might have increased during the early nineteenth century as traditional practices in which native tobacco acted as facilitator were strengthened or revived in response to the Prophet's message. Kaolin and metal tomahawk pipes, although suitable for recreational smoking, might not have been acceptable for use in religious and other ceremonies that served as expressions of Native-American identity (Trubowitz 1992:107). In this sense, it should be noted that stone calumet pipes made from catlinite continued to form part of the material culture of the Prairie Band Potawatomi of Kansas into the 1920s, many of whom were descended from the Kankakee River Potawatomi. At that time the Potawatomi distinguished between six different types of pipe—catlinite pipe, chief's pipe, brave's pipe, bundle pipe, council pipe, and a pipe used to make peace for murderers—a distinction which suggests that different types of pipes were used for these various types of activities (Skinner 1926:287, 305). A pipe used for recreational smoking almost certainly must have been of a different form and raw material than one used in a serious ritual such as to make peace for murderers, although Skinner (1926) provides no information on the appearance of these various pipe types.

The Windrose ground-stone data are admittedly small, consisting only of 22 fragments representing a minimum of nine pipes, and my inferences regarding the symbolic meaning and use of these pipes may be incorrect. The argument that they are associated with a strengthening or maintenance of traditional values, however, is supported by other archaeological data from the site. The most convincing are: the almost total absence of pig and sheep remains in the faunal assemblage (only six fragments out of over 8,000 specimens); virtual absence of Euro-American clothing items (only two examples); and very low representation of refined earthenware ceramics (only one fragment) (Wagner 1998:445–446). In combination with the presence of stone smoking pipes, these data correlate strongly with the Prophet's admonition that Native-American peoples avoid the use of cattle, pigs, and sheep; put aside their American clothing; and return to ancestral practices, including the manufacture of stone tools and other objects (Edmunds 1983:37).

The Windrose site continued to be occupied after the collapse of the Prophet's movement, with final abandonment of the site probably occurring in the early-1830s shortly before the Potawatomi were forcibly removed west of the Mississippi River (Wagner 2001:33). That the data from this site, which might have been occupied for twenty years after the Prophet's downfall, correlate so strongly with his message suggest that his and other early-nineteenth-century Native-American nativistic movements drew upon well-developed religious traditions and sentiments regarding the negative effects of many aspects of Euro-American culture rather than originating these ideas (Dowd 1992:xix-xx, 193).

In the case of the Kankakee River Valley Potawatomi, a group bitterly opposed to American settlement and expropriation of their lands, the Prophet's message might have been so well-received simply because the Potawatomi already were adhering to a conservative way of life that incorporated many of his teachings, including a reliance upon wild game, subsistence agriculture focused on Native-American plants, and the maintenance of traditional political, social, and religious activities in which tobacco use and smoking acted as a facilitator and as an expression of Native-American identity. Indeed, as noted above, the use of native tobacco stone smoking pipes continued to form an important part of the religious practices of the descendents of the Kankakee River Valley Potawatomi in Kansas and elsewhere well into the twentieth century (Landes 1970; Ritzenthaler 1953; Skinner 1926).

ACKNOWLEDGMENTS

Archaeological investigations at the Windrose site were funded by the Illinois Department of Natural Resources (IDNR), which administers the state park containing the site. I would like to thank the personnel of that agency, most particularly cultural resources coordinator Hal Hassen, for their assistance and encouragement during the course of the archaeological investigations at the site. I also wish to acknowledge Brian Butler, Director of the Center for Archaeological Investigations at Southern Illinois University, Carbondale, and co-principal investigator for the Windrose site investigations. Without Brian's continued support and interest, this further investigation into the material culture and lifeways of the nineteenth-century Potawatomi who once lived at the Windrose site would not have been possible. Finally, I wish to thank Brian Del Costello (SIUC) who drew the illustrations of the Windrose site smoking pipes and preforms that accompany this article.

9
Using a Rock in a Hard Place
Native-American Lithic Practices in Colonial California

Stephen Silliman

There is a frequent assumption among the general public that contact with Europeans and their material technologies prompted all Native Americans to abandon stone tool technology rather quickly. Archaeologists have done a poor job of changing that misperception, but it would be difficult to dispel a myth that many archaeologists hold as part of their own academic worldview. One does not have to look far to see archaeologists writing about how impressed or awed Native-American people must have been at European technological prowess. The underlying premise is that technological choices are related only to functional efficiency, that our notions of functionality were shared by social actors in the past and that rocks must give way to metal. This paper will reveal how problematic such a premise is when it is assumed rather than tested empirically.

Despite the often implicit assumption among many archaeologists that lithic tools were replaced by supposedly superior colonial tools or remained behind as mere vestiges of an indigenous lifeway, several archaeologists have started to overturn these assumptions with more careful studies. The archaeological recovery and analysis of lithic artifacts in Contact-period and historical assemblages have vastly improved the study of colonialism and culture contact in the Americas (Bamforth 1993; Cobb and Ruggiero, chapter 2; Fox 1979; Hester 1977, 1989:219–223; Hudson 1993; Johnson 1997, chapter 4; Nassaney and Volmar, chapter 6; Odell, chapter 3; Whittaker and Fratt 1984). If nothing else, they have given due attention to the indigenous side of colonial interactions and have helped extract Native Americans and others from an assumed role of passivity. Even in cases where chipped-stone tools rapidly disappear, archaeological studies have revealed the material and social complexity of these colonial encounters and the diversity of lithic practices that may or may not continue into post-Contact periods. This volume offers many such cases. Most archaeologists have explored the functional side of lithic technology in Contact-period or colonial sites, arguing that stone tool use can be seen as an economic response to scarce supplies of metal (Hester 1989:235; Whittaker and Fratt 1984:16–17). Others have interpreted lithic tools as part of material symbolism (Hudson 1993:266; Nassaney and Volmar, chapter 6) or daily politics and identity (Silliman 2001), propelling discussions of lithic practices into explicitly social realms. Some archaeologists have certainly highlighted a shift in perspective to the social context of stone tool use (Gero 1991, Rosen 1996), but few archaeologists working on the historical periods of North America have taken sufficient notice.

In this chapter, I contribute to the growing archaeological literature that contextualizes lithic practices within social relations. My focus is a site in nineteenth-century Northern California associated with the Rancho Petaluma, a large land grant owned by a prominent Mexican-Californian military leader. The archaeological site contains a living area for Native-American people who worked on this Mexican rancho in the 1830s and 1840s. The case offers a unique glimpse of lithic practices in a distinctly colonial setting rather than in a separate "Contact-period" village or community. This means that the site records intense, sustained, daily interactions between Native-American and colonial individuals that hinged predominantly on relations of labor. This also means that many of the indigenous people involved in these contexts endured difficult and oppressive situations. For this reason, lithic technology and stone tools—"using rocks"—represent a salient material and social practice for Native-American people embroiled in a difficult colonial world (see also Cassell, chapter 10). Lithic technology was a practice of political consequence in everyday life (Silliman 2001). My emphasis here is on chipped-stone technology and raw material and the ways that these can be investigated in the context of technology, sourcing studies, and the availability of colonial mass-produced goods. This combination allows a clearer view of how lithic practices were used in colonial settings and how such a perspective might benefit other Contact-period studies.

WESTERN NORTH AMERICA, STONE TOOLS, AND SOCIAL ARCHAEOLOGY

Hunter-gatherer societies of Western North America provide unique opportunities for sorting out issues in Contact-period and post-Contact lithic technology. California is a particularly rich area for addressing this topic because of the diversity of lithic materials in site assemblages and the prevalence of frequently datable and sourceable obsidian raw material across much of the region. Numerous Contact-period sites with lithic artifacts have been recorded and studied, but only a few have been investigated in detail and widely published (e.g., Bamforth 1993; Schiff 1997). Archaeologists have also excavated several eighteenth- and nineteenth-century colonial sites that revealed lithic artifacts in Native-

American living areas. These include Spanish missions (Allen 1998:77–83; Deetz 1963; Hoover and Costello 1985:77–92), Spanish and Mexican ranchos (Frierman 1982:75–84; Silliman 2000a:191–262; Wallace and Wallace 1958), and Russian fur-trade colonies (Lightfoot and Silliman 1997; Schiff 1997). These cases are clear examples of Native-American people continuing to make and use stone tools in the face of other options and often burdensome colonial worlds. This is not a ubiquitous response across North America or even the West Coast any more than is the presumed abandonment of all lithic technology, but it is a phenomenon worthy of contextual study. Given that full colonization of California did not begin until 1769 with the arrival of the Spanish, the California cases are also intriguing as very late colonial encounters in the Americas.

By studying lithic practices in colonial and Contact-period settings, archaeologists are poised to consider issues of social agency. Rather than enter the debates over agency here (see Dobres and Robb 2000), I use the term simply to mean a focus on individuals living in a socially constituted world, acting with particular projects in mind, and carrying on their daily activities at varying levels of consciousness in a world of practice. My notions draw on the works of Giddens (1984) and Bourdieu (1977, 1990) and archaeologists who follow their lead (e.g., Dobres 2000; Dobres and Hoffman 1994; Johnson 1989; Lightfoot et al. 1998). In particular, I find the discussions of social theory and technology to be particularly relevant for studying colonial-period lithic practices since "technological choices and the organization of production activities are materially grounded but intrinsically social phenomena" (Dobres and Hoffman 1994:247). One may argue that the "contact" experience commonly intensifies or disrupts these social practices, making it a strong candidate for sorting out some theoretical issues (Silliman 2001). Because lithic technology is simultaneously wrapped up in social practices and individual strategies, this theoretical perspective envisions continuity or discontinuity in lithic technology as more than an adaptive interface or a functional concern. For example, instead of seeing artifact replacement and continuity in Contact-period settings as the result of natural selection working on functional traits in an expanded human phenotype (e.g., Ramenofsky 1998), I see them as involved in the production, reproduction, and contestation of daily life. These material practices of daily life are what individuals use to make sense of and to alter their worlds. Similarly, stone tool production and use are often constituted as gendered activities. As Dobres has cogently argued, studying past technology requires paying close attention to social relations and to people (Dobres 2000).

In Contact-period settings, the absence of stone tool technology should not be read simply as functional replacement by metal or other implements, just as the presence of lithic practices should not be construed as straightforward examples of cultural continuity. The ways that Native-American individuals continued to practice lithic technology, opted to transform or alter it, or sought to replace stone raw material and finished products with other material items should be studied on a contextual basis (Cobb, chapter 1). These otherwise very physical and material aspects make sense only in their broader social context. For instance, material continuity may belie major shifts in social or political relations surrounding the use and production of items that once had different or more neutral political connotations. As I have demonstrated elsewhere, this appears to be the case in nineteenth-century Northern California at the Rancho Petaluma (Silliman 2001).

LITHIC PRACTICES AT THE NINETEENTH-CENTURY RANCHO PETALUMA

The archaeological site of interest lies within the Petaluma Adobe State Historic Park in Northern California, and it is protected as part of the cultural heritage of a nineteenth-century Mexican-California rancho (Figure 9.1). The Rancho Petaluma was a large Mexican land grant, sizing in around 270 km^2, offered to Mariano G. Vallejo in 1834 as material and symbolic compensation for his service to the provincial colonial government in California during this time (Hoopes 1965). At its inception, the rancho served to block Russian colonial expansion inland from their few settlements on the coast, to obtain land previously controlled by a nearby Franciscan mission for secular use, and to secure the Northern Frontier of Alta California for further colonial settlement (Tays 1937). Much like its contemporaries, the Rancho Petaluma rode on the heels of the dismantled Spanish mission system. Vallejo owned the Rancho Petaluma land into the 1850s, but the operation had diminished rapidly following the American takeover of California between 1846–1850 (Silliman 2000a:65). Throughout its 15 to 20 years of full-scale operation, the rancho was a major center of economic production focused on goods manufacture, agriculture, and livestock, with the latter directed toward the lucrative hide-and-tallow trade (Hoopes 1965; Silliman 2000a).

Like many ranchos across California, the Rancho Petaluma operated by the hard labor of Native-American people (Greenwood 1989; Silliman 1998). At this rancho, hundreds, if not thousands, of Native people served as laborers in and around the large adobe-brick building known as the Petaluma Adobe and out on the large rancho. The 3600 m^2 of the Petaluma Adobe served as the administrative and residential center. Native people worked as household servants who cooked and served food, artisans who made goods for general distribution and trade, field hands who planted and harvested crops, and vaqueros who herded and butchered livestock. Native-American workers found themselves on

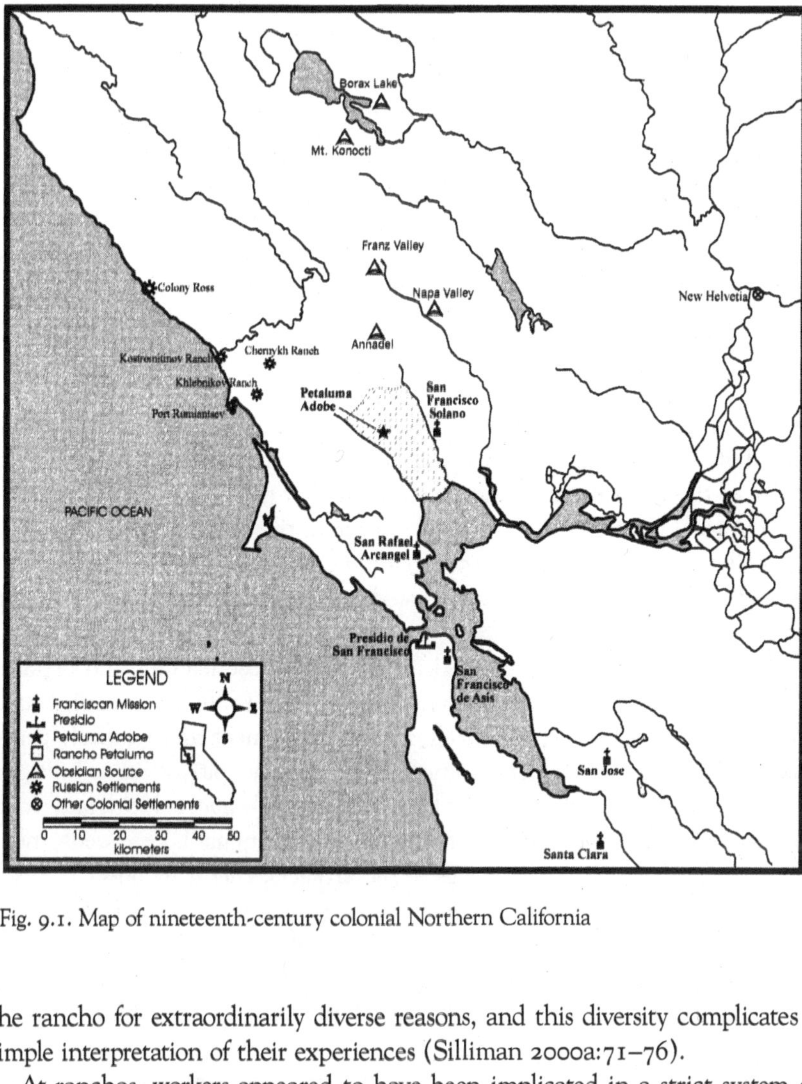

Fig. 9.1. Map of nineteenth-century colonial Northern California

the rancho for extraordinarily diverse reasons, and this diversity complicates a simple interpretation of their experiences (Silliman 2000a:71–76).

At ranchos, workers appeared to have been implicated in a strict system of indebted peonage rather than wage earning (Bancroft 1888:347; Cook 1943: 48–51; Rawls 1984:21). Some transferred to the Rancho Petaluma at the demise of the two nearby Franciscan missions in 1834, a type of community that some of them might have lived in for up to 20 years. Other individuals from nonmissionized hunter-gatherer groups joined the rancho to cement political and military alliances between Vallejo and nearby native leaders (Davis 1929: 135–136) or to include it on a seasonal round for access to goods and food (Silliman 2000a:76). Although livestock and settlers had infiltrated various regions of Northern California, some indigenous groups had managed to escape all but military excursions into their homelands. Still others were dragged to nearby ranchos as prisoners after Mexican-Californian settlers ransacked their villages to punish reputed horse-thieves or field-burners (Cook 1941:9; Davis 1929:63; Lothrop 1932:181, 194).

The study of California Indian people on ranchos is a relatively new phenomenon, although their artifacts have been found intermittently on rancho excavations across California since the late–1950s (Frierman 1982; Greenwood 1989; Wallace and Wallace 1958; see Silliman 2000a:44–52 for summary). A recent archaeological project at the Rancho Petaluma has begun to expand the study of ranchos and colonialism (Silliman 1998, 2000a, 2001). Archival data for the Rancho Petaluma are not rich, but they sketch general outlines of Native-American life in and around the rancho (Silliman 2000a:66–71, 88–100). This includes the likelihood that most, if not all, indigenous laborers lived outside of the main Petaluma Adobe structure. For this reason, the majority of archaeological research focused on loci away from the colonial structure. Across the nearby stream and less than 150 m east of the Petaluma Adobe, a major site, designated CA-Son-2294/H, was located, mapped, and excavated (Silliman 2000a:106–147).

Excavation at the site uncovered an array of refuse features and deposits that are markedly residential and Native in character (Silliman 2000a). Found amidst the removal of approximately 23 m^3 of sediment and relatively dense residential midden were several cultural features: three pits of burned artifactual, floral, and faunal material; two basins of thermally affected rock and wood charcoal; and one large, extensive refuse pile full of animal bones, seeds, shellfish, glass beads, glass, groundstones, lithic artifacts, thermally affected rocks, and other materials. A distinct midden area a few meters toward the stream contained these same kinds of materials—faunal remains, burned seeds and other plant parts, shellfish, rocks, chipped-stone and groundstone artifacts, glass beads, glass, ceramics, nails, and other metal artifacts—in much higher quantities and densities. No residential structures of any sort were discovered; however, the occupants of the missing structures undoubtedly dumped much of their debris into the areas excavated. These materials provide unique insights into the daily lives of California Indian people implicated in the rancho labor regime.

STONE TOOLS ON THE RANCHO: AN ANALYTICAL APPROACH

For the remainder of this chapter, I focus on the ubiquitous lithic artifacts and their relationships with other material and social practices. The lithic artifacts provide solid evidence of distinctly indigenous practices in this colonial world and the high quantities of chipped-stone artifacts warrant full attention here. I do *not* mean to imply that colonial settlers of Hispanic heritage, especially those with antecedent ties to Mexico, did not practice various forms of lithic manufacture—the evidence is clear that some did (e.g., Moore 1992). However, there is presently no evidence that Vallejo, his family, or his non-Indian employees ever engaged in such a practice.

I consider the lithic assemblage as a whole rather than by site locus, but I have documented intrasite spatial differences elsewhere (Silliman 2000a:230–234). This site-level coarseness is justified here since all loci represent refuse deposits of one form or another and since there is currently no way to separate the artifacts per household or other similar analytical unit. Similarly, I do not summarize all of the finer details of lithic analysis from the Rancho Petaluma site. The details on technological analysis, lithic sourcing and dating, and presentation can be found elsewhere (Silliman 2000a:192–262).

I draw on obsidian sourcing and dating information, but I will not elaborate on the methods and results (Silliman 2000a:216–224, 2002). Suffice it to say that the obsidian-hydration analysis revealed some pre-Contact obsidian artifacts in the assemblage, but I can currently offer no temporal comparison (or separation) since unequivocal pre-Contact artifacts are recognized by only 33 artifacts out of 111 viable obsidian-hydration samples. Non-viable obsidian-hydration readings mean that they revealed no visible hydration. Given their prevalence in this collection, these specimens may well reflect nineteenth-century use since the lack of hydration band may indicate a very young age. If true, this addition would drive the artifacts into a smaller percentage of the total and make the assemblage even more strongly contemporaneous. There is also minor evidence for individuals recycling and reusing "prehistoric" tools in the 1800s (Silliman 2000a:224). Yet, I could detect no significant differences in lithic types present in the small pre-Contact obsidian collection versus the entire site subassemblage, with the exception of formal tools occupying a higher proportion of the "prehistoric" (42.4 percent) than "historical" (20.5 percent) artifacts (Silliman 2002). Most importantly, virtually all obsidian artifacts were directly associated with colonial mass-produced artifacts such as glass bottle fragments, glass beads, and metal. Excavation also revealed not a single pre-Contact feature or unambiguous deposit. For these reasons, I consider all lithic material as contemporaneous and as nineteenth century in date in the following discussion.

To structure my lithic analysis, I primarily followed guidelines suggested by Andrefsky (1998) with some attention to the diversity of recommendations and caveats provided by Shott (1994), Morrow (1997), and the contributors to Amick and Mauldin (1989). This methodology established a minimum set of analytical attributes and a hierarchical classification of debitage and tools. In my version of an appropriate analytical strategy, I focused on formal and flake tools, cores, and debitage with the latter divided into technological products such as complete flakes, proximal flakes, flake shatter, and angular shatter. No debitage was identified as to its presumed function (e.g., biface thinning flake) or production method (e.g., percussion versus pressure) due to the ambiguities surrounding such identifications. Instead, following recommendations in Andrefsky (1998), I recorded the following replicable attributes for debitage: a) size, monitored by ordinal rankings for all debitage and ratio measurements for complete flakes; b) flake termination, classified as feather, step, or hinge; c) platform type, divided into flat, complex (meaning multiple facets), cortex, and abraded; d) dorsal cortex, recorded in a four-rank ordinal scale of percentage; e) dorsal flake scars, noted as none, one, two, or multiple; and f) thermal alteration, indicated by potlids, differential luster, crazing, or a combination (Silliman 2000a:196–200). Weight was not recorded, although it might have offered further resolution of the patterns. With the exception of thermal alteration, the other attributes should give some indication, when juxtaposed with each other, of lithic reduction strategies. Any one of these attributes may not clearly distinguish lithic production stages or types, given the controversies raging among archaeologists over how to analyze and interpret debitage. Therefore, I combined many attributes to generate more robust interpretations.

RESULTS

The following raw materials exist in the Rancho Petaluma lithic assemblage: obsidian; chert, chalcedony, and other microcrystalline silicates (referred to as chert for the remainder of the chapter); felsite and other igneous materials; quartz; petrified wood; and others such as schist, basalt, and sedimentary rock (Table 9.1). The list reflects order of abundance in the assemblage. Obsidian and chert together occupy 82.7 percent of the total of 3,009 lithic artifacts. Obsidian (43.3 percent) outnumbers chert (39.4 percent) artifacts only slightly, but their relative position shifts depending on the particular site locus. Of the total assemblage, igneous/felsite and quartz hold less than 10 percent each, petrified wood slightly over 2 percent, schist only .4 percent, and basalt and sedimentary stones barely .1 percent. For this analysis, I restrict my discussion to the numerically dominant obsidian and chert artifacts, which, despite some overlap in form and use, individuals at the Rancho Petaluma put to quite different uses.

Obsidian

Obsidian artifacts number 1,303 (see Table 9.2). Although predominantly debitage, the collection includes 9 (.7 percent) cores, 5 (.4 percent) unmodified nodules, and 64 (4.9 percent) formal tools including bifaces, projectile points, and

Table 9.1 Frequency, Percentage, and Density of Chipped-stone Lithics

Raw Material	N	Percentage	Density (N/M^3)
Obsidian	1,303	43.3	53.6
Chert, Chalcedony, Other Silicates	1,187	39.4	50.1
Igneous/Felsite	266	8.8	11.4
Quartz	165	5.5	6.8
Petrified wood	71	2.4	3.0
Basalt	2	0.1	0.09
Sedimentary	3	0.1	0.13
Schist	12	0.4	0.5
Total	3,009	100	125.62

their fragments. Obsidian materials record the full spectrum of lithic production from cores to finished tools. Obsidian cores are primarily multidirectional and small, but some examples of unidirectional working and bipolar reduction are present. All nodules excavated from the site are similarly small. In contrast to the primary cortex evident on some of the actual cores (meaning quarried specimens with weathering), the unmodified nodules display characteristic secondary cortex from fluvial transport and weathering.

Unhafted bifaces (N=46) occur predominantly as small fragments of larger tools (Figure 9.2). In most cases, these bifaces are in early or middle stages of bifacial thinning, as defined by Whittaker (1994) and Callahan (1979), with width/thickness ratios for all reliably measured bifaces ranging from 1.9 to 3.8. It is currently unclear how many of these bifaces might have served as preforms or as final tools, but both functions seem likely. At least seven bifaces show macroscopic signs of use damage on one or more margins, but breakage patterns include a combination of bending, perverse, and radial fractures. These seem to suggest at least some manufacturing failures. Included in this biface category is the only drill fragment (Figure 9.2b). The use of the term, drill, reflects the long, narrow shape of the bifacial implement rather than any microscopic examination of use-wear. These bifacial tools date to both Contact and pre-Contact periods based on the obsidian-hydration analysis.

The excavations produced 18 projectile points and point fragments (Figure 9.3). Unlike the biface collection, some projectile points (N=7, 38.9 percent) are complete or nearly complete artifacts, but the collection is still rather fragmented. Other than three indeterminate point forms, all projectile points with enough of the tool remaining to identify are corner-notch points (Figure 9.3b-h, j, 1-n). These are common in late pre-Contact sequences in the region (Fredrickson 1984). Several examples show unworked margins or faces, incomplete

Table 9.2 Frequency and Percentage of Obsidian and Chert Lithic Types

	Lithic Types														
Raw Material	Nodule	%	Core	%	Formal Tools	%	Ang Shatter	%	Flake	%	Proximal Flake	%	Flake Shatter	%	Total
Obsidian	5	0.4	9	0.7	64	4.9	216	16.5	543	41.7	34	2.6	432	33.2	1,303
Chert	5	0.4	25	2.1	1	0.1	598	50.4	289	24.4	7	0.6	262	22.1	1,187

Fig. 9.2. Obsidian unhafted bifaces and biface fragments

thinning, and unformed point sections. Therefore, point fragmentation might have been at least partly the result of manufacturing complications on the not-yet-finished tools. The archaeofaunal and archaeobotanical remains indicate substantial hunting and gathering by Native people on the rancho, despite the abundance of evidence for cultigens and livestock in the site's deposits. Presumably, individuals made these points for hunting, given the variety of wild fauna such as black-tailed deer in the associated faunal debris (Silliman 2000a:286), but it is possible that individuals designed these arrowheads for conflict on the colonial frontier.

Obsidian debitage falls into the broad categories of angular shatter, complete flake, proximal flake, and flake shatter (see Table 9.2). At a gross level, the entire obsidian assemblage (*N*=1,303) can be summarized as 16.5 percent angular shatter, 41.7 percent complete flake, 2.6 percent proximal flake, and 33.2 percent flake shatter. The tools, cores, and unmodified nodules comprise the other 6.0 percent. I reserve discussion of debitage size, dorsal cortex, and dorsal flake scars

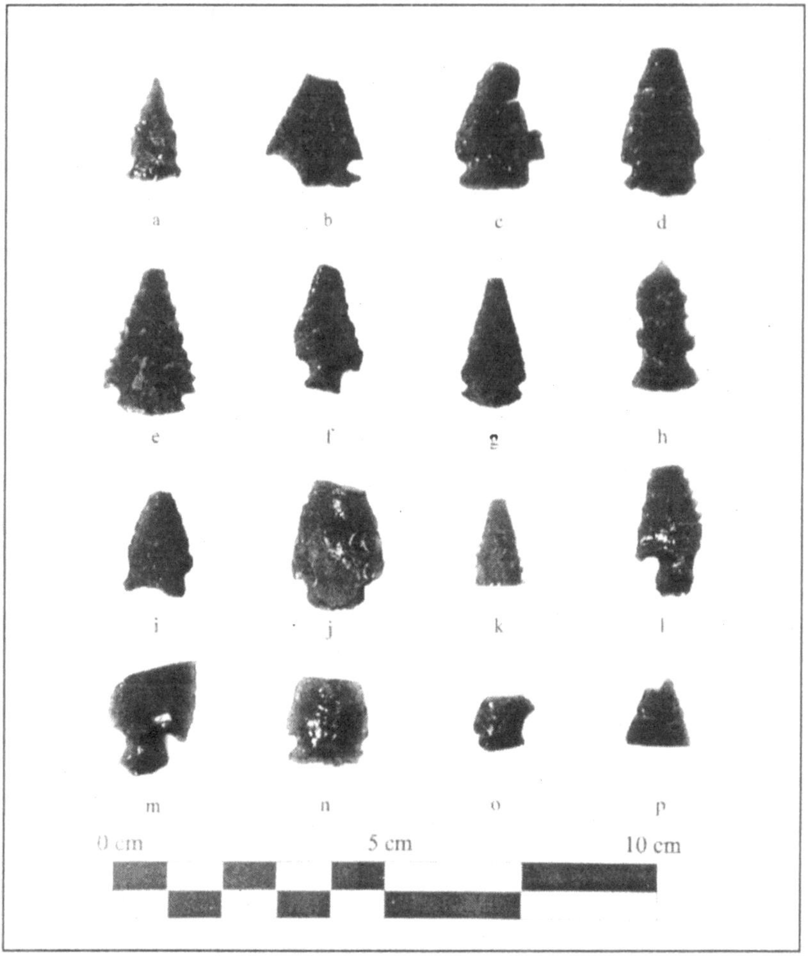

Fig. 9.3. Obsidian projectile point and point fragments

for a comparison of obsidian and chert debitage in a later section. Flake tools (i.e., debitage with retouch or use damage) are 9.9 percent (*N*=128) of the obsidian debitage.

Chert and Related Silicates

Chert artifacts number 1,187 across all site loci (see Table 9.2). The assemblage differs notably from the obsidian in its almost complete lack of formal tools, more angular shatter, and more abundant cores. Only 2.6 percent of the entire subassemblage are anything other than debitage. This proportion includes 25 (2.1 percent) cores, 5 (.4 percent) nodules, and only 1 (.1 percent) formal tool, a rough biface.

The 25 cores and 5 unworked nodules range in size, but they are much larger than those in the obsidian subassemblage. Several of these cores appear to be exhausted (five are less than 30 mm in maximum dimension), whereas others are large cobbles with minimal reduction. Reduction trajectories are exclusively multidirectional. Four cores have evidence of thermal alteration with potlids or differential luster. Only one chert artifact qualifies for inclusion as a formal biface tool, and it is in very early stages of manufacture based on short flake scars and no significant thinning.

As with obsidian, I classified the chert debitage into angular shatter, complete flake, proximal flake, and flake shatter (see Table 9.2). Other than the 2.6 percent as nondebitage discussed above, summary percentages for the site as a whole reveal the remaining 1,156 artifacts to be 50.4 percent angular shatter, 24.4 percent complete flake, .6 percent proximal flake, and 22.1 percent flake shatter of the total 1,187 artifacts. It is noteworthy that the chert subassemblage displays a significant percentage (15.9 percent) of artifacts with thermal alteration. Differential luster accounts for 6.8 percent, potlids for 4.5 percent, crazing for 1.0 percent, and a combination of two or more of these for 3.5 percent. Whether or not this thermal alteration on chert is from controlled heating, accidental exposure to fire, or purposeful refuse burning is currently unclear, although I suspect at least some of it relates to heat treatment. The lack of unambiguous burning on the obsidian artifacts lends further credibility to this interpretation.

Comparison of Obsidian and Chert Artifacts

Lithic reduction and use for the obsidian and chert raw material differ significantly. Initial stages of reduction are present in both raw materials with flakes at 100 percent dorsal cortex, cores, and unmodified nodules. However, evidence points to individuals focusing on obsidian for the full range of production from cores to formal tools while using chert primarily for early-stage reduction of cores. At the terminal end of the sequence, the presence of numerous broken obsidian bifaces and projectile points confirms the production of formal tools, but only one rough chert biface exists. So, were obsidian bifaces traded in or manufactured on-site, and were chert bifaces manufactured on-site and traded out?

Some obsidian bifaces might have been manufactured elsewhere, but the debitage size, number of dorsal flake scars, and platform preparation suggests that, in contrast to chert, on-site obsidian reduction was devoted in large part to later stages of reduction and biface production. For one, obsidian debitage is consistently smaller than chert debitage (Figure 9.4). This pattern also relates strongly to a smaller hypothesized size of original nuclei (discussed below), so I offer it only hesitantly. In addition, percentages of dorsal flake scar counts reveal that obsidian flakes possess far greater dorsal flake scarring (Figure 9.5). I made no attempt to determine scar complexity or the number of flake scar directions. Perhaps most importantly, the complexity of platform preparation in obsidian

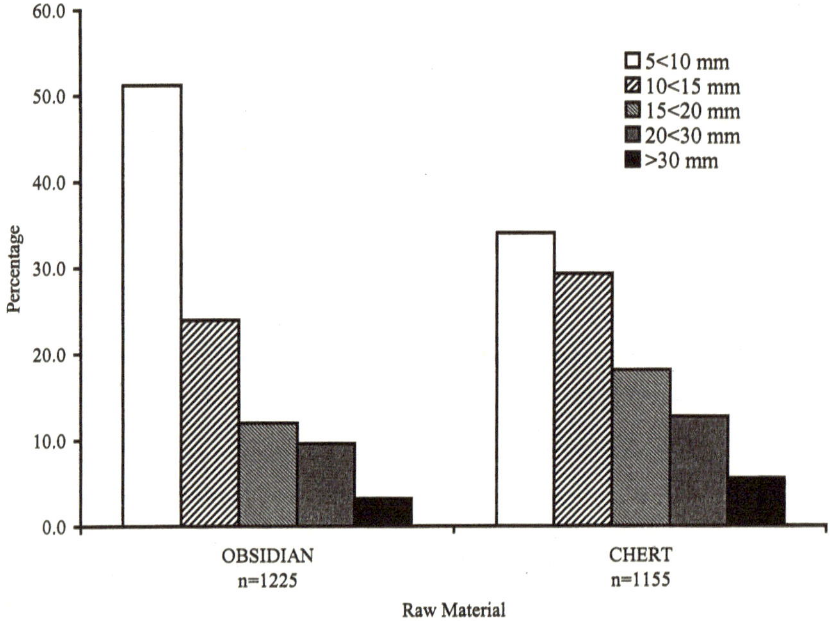

Fig. 9.4. Percentage of debitage size for obsidian and chert

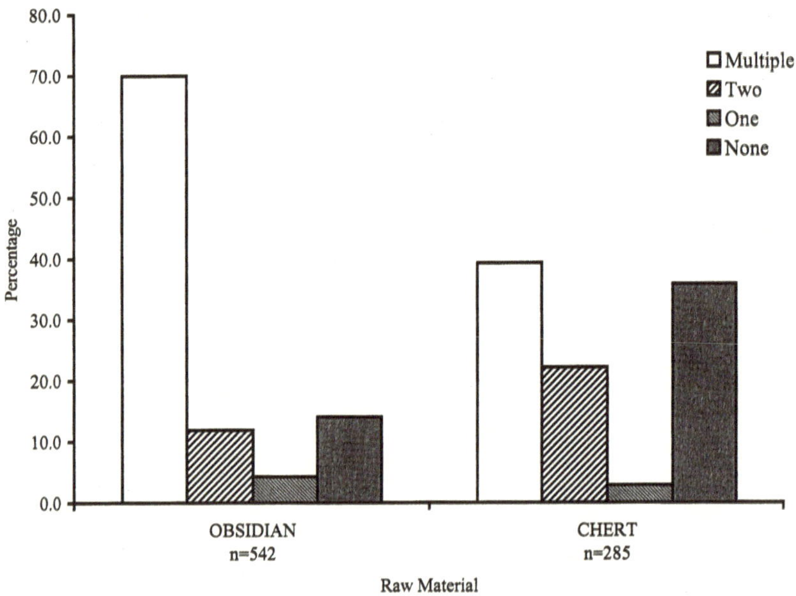

Fig. 9.5. Percentage of dorsal flake scars for complete obsidian and chert flakes

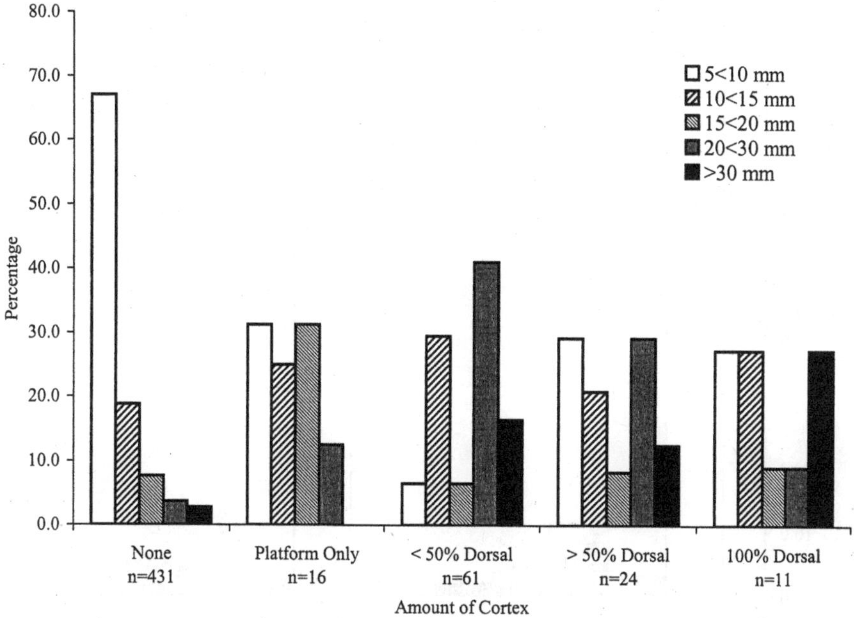

Fig. 9.6. Combined percentage of dorsal cortex and size for complete obsidian flakes

Table 9.3 Platform Frequency and Percentage for Obsidian and Chert Complete and Proximal Flakes

Material	Flat	%	Cortex	%	Complex	%	Abraded	%	Indet	Total
Obsidian	323	56.9	61	10.7	180	31.7	4	0.7	9	577
Chert	221	75.7	35	12.0	36	12.3	0	0.0	3	295

far exceeds that in chert (Table 9.3). Obsidian possesses 31.7 percent of complete and proximal flakes with complex platforms, and chert possesses only 12.3 percent. Similarly, only 56.9 percent of obsidian flakes have simple flat platforms, but 75.7 percent of chert flakes have them. Obsidian flakes show an additional 10.7 percent cortex-bearing platforms; chert has a similar proportion of 12.0 percent (Silliman 2000a:Table 6.8, 6.10). Finally, Figure 9.6 yields support to the interpretation of obsidian formal tool production and the relative lack thereof in chert. Almost 70 percent of all obsidian flakes having no dorsal cortex are in the smallest size category, but less than 30 percent of chert flakes with no cortex are of such small size. In total, these data suggest that chert and obsidian underwent different production sequences.

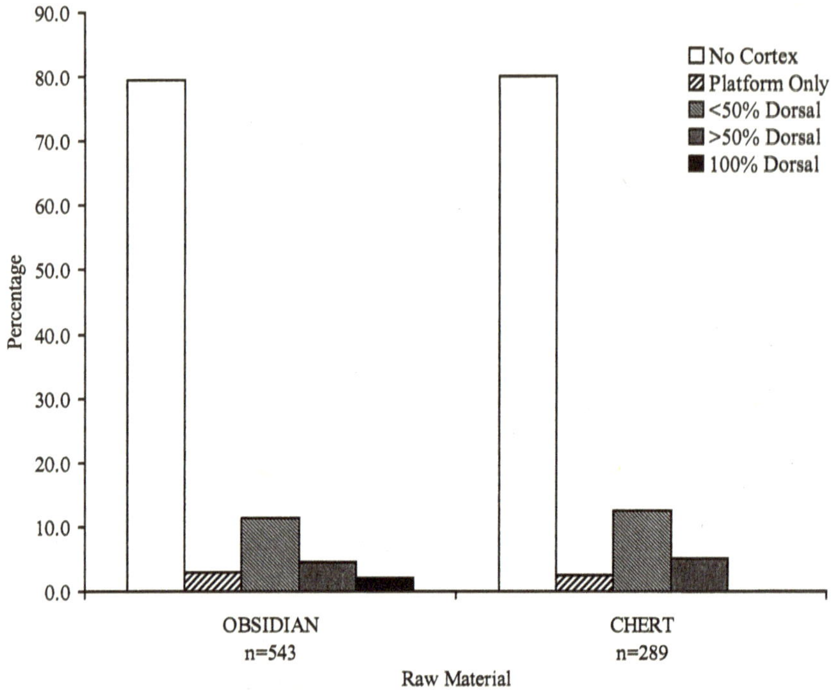

Fig. 9.7. Percentage of dorsal cortex for complete obsidian and chert flakes

However, the amount of dorsal cortex on flakes requires further commentary (Figure 9.7). Had obsidian possessed consistently less dorsal cortex than chert across the site, then it might have served as another line of evidence for the interpretation of late-stage reduction on obsidian rather than chert. Yet, 78.4 percent (*N*=543) of complete obsidian flakes have no cortex while 80.6 percent (*N*=289) of complete chert flakes have none. Rather than these similar values undermining the other evidence for later-stage obsidian reduction, the higher amounts of dorsal cortex on obsidian flakes indicate a smaller size of core from which these flakes were produced rather than a stage of reduction. Figure 9.4, introduced above, demonstrates the likely correlation of small nuclei and small size of debitage. If chert cores are larger than obsidian cores, then the likelihood of obtaining cortex-bearing flakes from the latter increases because of the greater ratio of surface area to mass. In the Rancho Petaluma collection, chert cores and unworked nodules are decidedly larger than obsidian cores and nodules. In addition, a currently unquantified amount of obsidian debitage displays evidence (e.g., impact fractures at both ends) of bipolar reduction. This indicates the probable small size of initial obsidian cores since knappers generally use bipolar technology to reduce small nuclei. The smaller size of obsidian raw materials makes even more telling the previously noted higher percentage of small cortex-free flakes compared to chert.

To complement these data, technological types help support the conclusion of obsidian and chert reduction patterns discussed above (see Table 9.2). Angular shatter provides the clearest evidence. For the site as a whole, obsidian contains only 16.5 percent angular shatter, whereas chert contains 50.4 percent. Angular shatter can be produced during numerous stages of lithic production, but it is strongly associated with core reduction. Some percentage differences between the two raw materials may be explained by the ease of recognizing flake features on obsidian or the typically less isotropic qualities of chert, but these aspects cannot explain this large of a difference. Raw material type and quality have a tremendous influence on the types of debitage produced during lithic reduction, and this aspect can complicate the relationships proposed between debitage morphology and reduction strategy. For this reason, I use this line of evidence as only secondary support for these interpretations, and I do so only because of the large discrepancy in percentages between obsidian and chert debitage classes. Although not as extreme, percentages also indicate that obsidian (41.7 percent) contains substantially more complete flakes than chert (24.4 percent). More complete flakes could indicate core reduction (Sullivan and Rozen 1985), but it is likely that they represent later stages of lithic production, if they show any relationship at all (Mauldin and Amick 1989:84–85). The combined effects of more cores in chert and more tools in obsidian further support the conclusion.

Finally, the obsidian-hydration data clarify the obsidian patterns slightly (Silliman 2002). Of the 111 obsidian artifacts returning a reliable hydration value, 75.3 percent of all debitage sampled for obsidian hydration derived from the historical period, while only 51.7 percent of formal tools did. This discrepancy suggests that more full-scale lithic production, rather than only trade in or use of formal tools, occurred at the site in the 1800s than had in pre-Contact times. It also seems to hint at a nineteenth-century proclivity of site residents to pick up and perhaps rework ancient tools found on or near the site.

In sum, then, the lithic data suggest that individuals used obsidian and chert for a variety of tools but that they directed these raw materials toward different intensities and uses. Obsidian was clearly preferred as the raw material for the production of formal bifaces and projectile points, a claim based on the discrepancies in tool representation and the debitage patterns between chert and obsidian. It is worth reiterating that I forward the conclusions based on debitage only after finding corroboration between different attribute constellations. Data on flake platforms, size, cortex, and dorsal scarring offer a clearer picture of stone tool production than do the typologies of shatter and flake, but the combination of them all seems to offer an enriched interpretation. Any one of these attributes alone would have been insufficient, and there would have been ample room for the classic logical error of affirming the consequent. Together, however, the variables point strongly toward these particular interpretations.

INTERPRETATIONS AND IMPLICATIONS

Evidence is abundant that Native-American people on the Rancho Petaluma continued their lithic technology, using obsidian and chert in quite different ways. The former conclusion did not require detailed lithic production analysis to demonstrate, but the latter did. However, what does this material and technological continuity mean? Is it evidence of metal scarcity, cultural "conservatism," a vestigial "pastime," resistance, negotiations of gender relations, or an expression of Native identity? Depending on one's theoretical stripe, any of these may seem like viable explanations. A related question is: How do these lithic practices demarcate social agents working through the colonial world of the California rancho? To produce or acquire stone tools as a Native American in such a colonial context is to make a statement. Even being "conservative" or having a favorite "pastime" is not a neutral or passive position—it is an active choice within the past and present conditions of one's social world. In addressing these questions here, I seek less of a single answer and more of a path that opens the possibility of tracing out continuity and discontinuity in lithic practices. This requires placing the rancho lithic practices in a broader context, one that includes the availability of and access to 1) lithic raw material and products in the wider landscape and 2) colonial mass-produced goods, particularly metal, in the rancho setting.

Lithic Raw Material Sourcing

The origins of the lithic materials at this rancho form the social and physical parameters for the on-site technical choices and practices. These factors implicate issues of raw material availability, social or physical effort involved in retrieving the material, and trading relations. Such aspects are as important in post-Contact archaeology as they are in pre-Contact ones where they are more traditionally studied.

As demonstrated above, Native individuals devoted obsidian to a variety of technological uses, from expedient flake tools to fully formed bifacial tools and projectile points. There is little evidence for this full range of production on the chert and other silicates, marked by the presence of only one chert formal tool and the debitage patterns vis-à-vis those in obsidian. This is intriguing because chert sources are relatively accessible around San Francisco Bay and northward, meaning that the raw material would not have been difficult to acquire. Many small outcrops are located within several kilometers of the Petaluma Adobe, although no direct sourcing efforts have been attempted.

On the other hand, the nearest known obsidian source is at least 20 km away and off the Rancho Petaluma proper (see Jackson 1986, 1989). Yet, this raw material proved to be the more important for manufacturing formal tools and other items for everyday use. It certainly offers better quality of raw material for knapping than the cherts and felsites discovered in the assemblage. Given the number of broken obsidian tools discarded into the refuse deposits, individuals must not have considered obsidian raw material scarce enough to conserve or rework extensively. The debitage evidence clearly suggests that individuals frequently manufactured obsidian bifaces and tools on-site rather than always trading in fully formed objects. This indicates that cores or rough blanks had to have been transported to the site for future working—but from where? The type of cortex suggests that these materials came from both primary sources and secondary stream deposits.

Energy-dispersive x-ray fluorescence analysis pinpointed the specific sources for these artifacts and the secondary "float" areas possibly associated with them (Silliman 2000b). For this discussion, I rely on a sample of 239 obsidian artifacts subjected to this geochemical technique, of which 111 have been subsequently dated by obsidian-hydration analysis (Silliman 2000a:219–225). Of the 78 dating to the historic period,* the results indicate the presence of ten different obsidian sources in the sampled assemblage, with two sources—Annadel (38.5 percent) and Napa Valley (41.0 percent)—in particularly high proportions (Table 9.4). These two well-represented sources are the closest large obsidian sources to the Petaluma Adobe (Figure 9.8). These two sources also comprise the majority of pre-Contact obsidian artifacts subjected to sourcing analysis in the general area (Jackson 1986) and all artifacts from the Petaluma Adobe State Historic Park (Silliman 1999:108, 2000a:224). The other large, regional obsidian sources of Mt. Konocti and Borax Lake are represented in the obsidian-hydration collection but as only one specimen each (1.3 percent), a cortex-free interior flake and a broken projectile point, respectively. The rest of the sourced obsidian includes a regionally restricted and little-recognized source (Franz Valley, 2.6 percent), a previously undiscovered source (Oakmont, 10.3

*Full discussion of this can be found in Silliman (2002). Percentages reflect a selection of already-sourced obsidian artifacts for hydration analysis. I boosted the representation of the rarer sources for hydration analysis to fine-tune chronology. In the original sample, Annadel and Napa Valley each occupied approximately 3–4 percent more with Oakmont dropping to about half of the percentage here. In other words, Annadel and Napa Valley obsidians are more common and the others slightly more rare than they appear here.

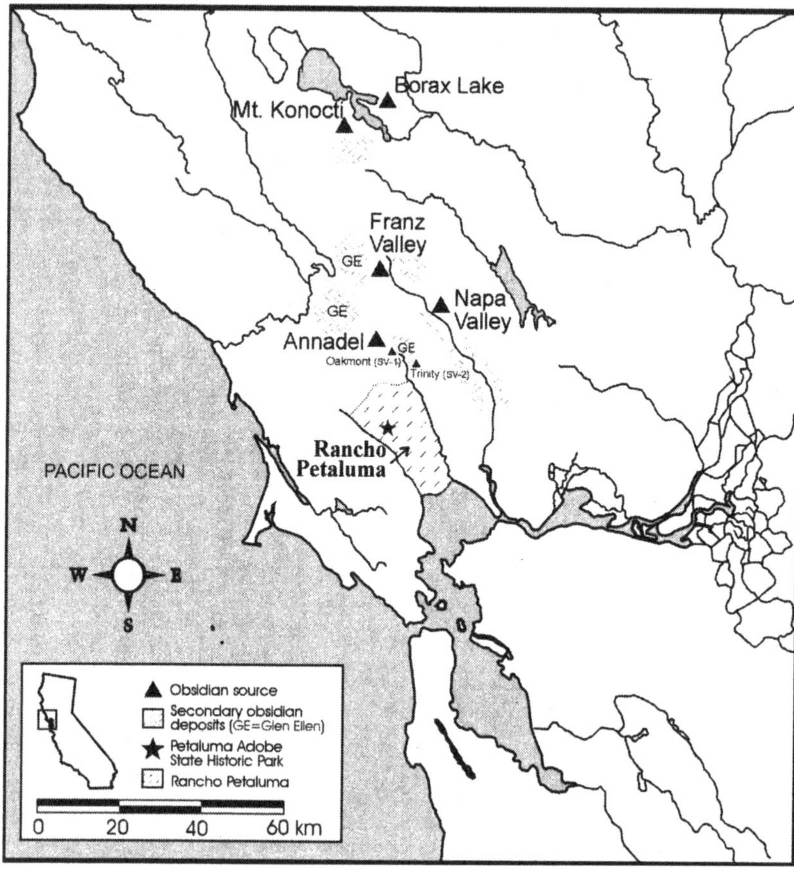

Fig. 9.8. Obsidian primary sources and secondary deposits in Northern California

percent), and currently unidentified sources that probably derive from the general area (Unknowns, 5.1 percent) (Silliman 2002). Other than a Franz Valley projectile point, these latter source samples are all debitage.

When compared to sequences at this site and in the area, the source representation is intriguing. New sources appeared in the archaeological record during the 1800s that are uncommon in the local cultural traditions or are completely novel for any Northern California archaeological site. In addition to raising a red flag about visual sourcing methods in California (Silliman 2000b), the sourcing data indicate a radical reshuffling of obsidian procurement and exchange. The shifts may indicate individuals from different homelands living in the area during the rancho period, individuals from villages far afield rotating through the Rancho Petaluma on seasonal rounds, laborers at the rancho altering their trade relations with outlying groups, or individuals modifying their

Table 9.4 Obsidian Source Frequency and Percentage for Analyzed Artifacts

Source	N	%
Annadel	30	38.5
Borax Lake	1	1.3
Franz Valley	2	2.6
Mt. Konocti	1	1.3
Napa Valley	32	41.0
Oakmont	8	10.3
Unknowns	4	5.1
Total	78	100.1

procurement in the obsidian landscape. Whatever the reasons, the residents on the Rancho Petaluma acquired obsidian in quite different ways than those who had resided in the area before, whether or not they were actual biological ancestors. They made active efforts to do so as part of their routine practices amidst required colonial duties, and it probably served as a node of social and economic connection among Native people in the rapidly changing colonial world. Native workers did not exclusively seek local cherts, indicating that obsidian retained or gained a high social and symbolic value.

Colonial Mass-Produced Goods

The acquisition of lithic raw material and the use of stone tools are particularly important when contextualized with the availability of colonial mass-produced goods. Numerous metal artifacts were recovered in the site deposits, and these indicate the general availability of this material to Native-American workers (Silliman 2000a:341–348, 360–363). Vallejo was a wealthy landowner who would have been well stocked with metal tools for use in cattle butchery, which, according to several descriptions across Mexican California, was an activity performed with metal knives (e.g., Robinson 1891:96; Sanchez 1929:47). This type of activity formed a core experience for many California Indian people, especially men, at colonial ranchos. Stone tools, whether formal or expedient, could have been used in the butchery process, but they would not have been the primary implements in the "production-line" nature of mass slaughter.

However, the lack of butchery tools such as knives or cleavers in the residential deposits is striking. I have argued that rather than these metal tools being completely unavailable to workers, the Native men who handled them as part of their required duties on the rancho did not opt to bring them into the household (Silliman 2000a:416–420). That is, they did not conscript the metal items as marks of affiliation with the colonial setting. Instead, Native individuals, primarily men, might have forged their way through the mid–1800s by staying connected to lithic procurement, manufacture, and use. It is certainly clear that stone tool use, primarily in obsidian form, ushered in a new political spin on a previously mundane activity. This strategy seems to have differed from that followed by some Native women at the Rancho Petaluma who brought colonial metal tools of their everyday required tasks, such as sewing, into the household (Silliman 2000a:416–420).

The trading relationships with outlying Native groups, the trips to obsidian sources for collection, and the use of stone implements for hunting helped constitute a response to the rancho labor regime. It might have been a strongly male response. With the amount of beef wasted after livestock were slaughtered by the thousands and the large quantities of harvested grains stored at the Petaluma Adobe, Native workers could have potentially subsisted on provisioned foods alone. Yet, hunting, gathering, and lithic raw material acquisition gave opportunities for getting out from under the yoke of colonial labor, for maintaining connections to the indigenous social and environmental landscape. These activities undoubtedly transpired in gendered ways.

In addition, the importance of lithic raw material cannot be overstated when one considers the relatively low percentage (4.9 percent) of the 2,896 glass artifacts that show unequivocal, intentional flaking (Silliman 2000a:339–340). The worked glass artifacts show no sign of formal tool manufacture, although some do have bifacial flaking to produce a sharp edge. In contrast to California's Spanish mission settings (Allen 1998; Hoover and Costello 1985) and the nearby coastal Russian colony of Ross (Silliman 1997) where formal tools had been crafted from bottle and window glass, glass-knapping technology at this Northern California rancho was focused more on expedient flakes and retouched bottle bases. The implication is that although handy for expedient use from time to time, glass came nowhere close to replacing obsidian or chert as a preferred raw material for making durable and sharp tools. That is, Native-American individuals wanted the rocks themselves and perhaps all the social connotations of their acquisition and use. Also, the Rancho Petaluma case with a mixture of formal and expedient obsidian tools contrasts sharply with the seemingly consistent preference for lithic flake and expedient tools in mission contexts (Allen 1998:82). The partiality for rocks seems to have been made possible by the availability of obsidian and chert, either as freshly quarried or gathered material or as objects recycled from sites, and by the focused efforts of Native-American workers to maintain the trading, access, and mobility patterns necessary to obtain the raw material. As demonstrated earlier, obsidian clearly garnered primary attention from the Native-American workers.

CONCLUSION

In conclusion, the analyses conducted for this paper attest to the continuity of lithic practices by Native-American people in this rancho context. The data make it clear that Native individuals remained committed to the practice of lithic technology in the face of new materials and social relations. However, this commitment was not a passive response to colonialism; it was an active negotiation. As Bamforth (1993:50) has stated: "Just having metal available does not determine how native people used it." Metal objects were surely available to Native laborers on the Rancho Petaluma, but individuals were selective in their choice of, or restricted in their access to, them. Any hope of addressing this issue must include a focus on indigenous choice and agency, which is made clearer by juxtaposing the selection and production of lithic tools with sourcing studies and colonial goods.

At the Rancho Petaluma, lithic use and manufacture were daily practices that became entangled in colonialism. This contrasts sharply with many Contact-period sites where Native Americans were not implicated in colonial labor regimes, at least on a daily basis. The entanglement in colonialism stems from the fact that labor regimentation directly impacted the times and opportunities for lithic production and use. However, given their abundance in the excavated areas, lithic artifacts frequently must have been the tools of choice in residential contexts. This is made more evident by the lack of certain metal tools—cleavers, knives, axes, etc.—that could have functionally replaced chipped-stone tools. Unless stone tools were employed in the daily required work duties on the rancho (and there is circumstantial evidence that metal tools probably served this purpose, although stone tools might have been conscripted occasionally for jobs that had more people to work than metal tools to work with), lithic practices served to demarcate materially the colonial working world from domestic spaces. At least, they seemed to do so for men since their rancho activities involving metal objects are the ones missing from the site record. On the other hand, Native women's rancho activities that took place with metal tools are visible in the form of needles, scissors, thimbles, and tableware. This means that the situation is doubly complex since gendered workers used stone tools perhaps in, but definitely in spite of, colonial work duties, and the continued use of stone tools for domestic and residential practices might have become a material expression of a gendered Native identity.

The Rancho Petaluma case has two serious implications for Contact-period and colonial lithic studies on the West Coast and elsewhere. First, considering lithic artifacts not as a stand-alone material class but as one component of a suite of material practices broadens archaeological interpretations. The details of lithic practice make more sense when compared and contrasted with other material goods and their uses than when considered in isolation. As demonstrated by the Petaluma case study, such a contextual approach is needed in historic-period settings where Native-American people were working through new colonial worlds. This contextual approach can help decipher not only lithic continuity but also the dissolution of lithic practices in Contact and post-Contact contexts. Second, lithic artifacts in Contact, colonial, or even post-Contact periods must be seen as something more than just functional responses or adaptations. This does not mean neglecting the realm of functionality, but it does mean not prioritizing it. This perspective on lithic technology casts the Petaluma materials in a new light. Lithics are part of material, social, and sometimes political practices, and they should be researched in that way (Bayman, chapter 7; Rosen 1996). Hudson (1993), in her study of Pawnee lithic practices, concluded that utilitarian lithic tools can take on symbolic meanings in episodes of culture contact. I concur, but I must modify that conclusion to say that lithics can take on new symbolic as well as social meanings in these Contact-period or colonial contexts. It is unlikely that lithic artifacts have ever been strictly utilitarian.

ACKNOWLEDGMENTS

My thanks go to a number of people who are unfortunately too numerous to name individually. I particularly want to thank Charlie Cobb for his invitation to join the "Liminal Lithics" session at the 2001 Society for American Archaeology meetings and for his dedication in collecting the papers for publication. I appreciate the comments offered on my presented paper by Doug Bamforth, my subsequent discussions with Jay Johnson and Mark Cassell, and the helpful commentaries and suggestions on the final version by Michael Nassaney and the anonymous manuscript reviewers. I also acknowledge Steve Shackley, Kathleen Hull, and Kent Lightfoot for their advice and discussion as I completed my lithic analyses. As always, I am indebted to the many students and volunteers who assisted in the field excavations between 1996 and 1998 and the laboratory processing between 1996 and 2000, the personnel of the California Department of Parks and Recreation who made this work possible, and the Federated Indians of Graton Rancheria for their continued support for this archaeological project.

10
Flint and Foxes

Chert Scrapers and the Fur Industry in Late-Nineteenth- and Early-Twentieth-Century North Alaska

Mark S. Cassell

In the late winter and early spring of 1892, about 80 Iñupiat Eskimos were preparing for the coming whale hunt at Point Belcher, Alaska, about 100 miles southwest of Point Barrow on the coast of the Chukchi Sea. It was an age-old practice; villagers in coastal north Alaska had spent this season getting ready for spring subsistence whaling for almost a thousand years under the leadership of *umialiit* (Eskimo "whaling captains"; see McLean 1980). The Eskimos at Point Belcher in 1892, however, were preparing for whaling under historical circumstances differing considerably from those of even a decade before. Like many people in north Alaska in 1892, they were *not* readying for subsistence whaling. They were preparing for the extraction of baleen, the fibrous material draping down from the upper jaws of the bowhead whale. Baleen was an industrial raw material, used in making buggy whips and corset stays (Stevenson 1907) and profitable on the open market in American manufacturing centers. Neither were they under Iñupiat *umialiit* leadership. These Eskimos were skilled laborers in the western Arctic commercial whaling industry. They were employees of American commercial whaler/trader John Kelly and worked at the shore whaling station Kelly established at Point Belcher in the fall of 1891 (Figure 10.1). And Kelly's station was not an Eskimo village. It was a little company town, a factory town, with storage facilities and workers' housing, a main office, and laborers and bosses, both native-born and immigrant. With tremendous support from the Iñupiat of the nearby village of Wainwright and from the Bureau of Land Management and the U.S. Fish and Wildlife Service, we excavated parts of Kelly's station only about 100 years after its brief 10-month occupation (Cassell 2000b).

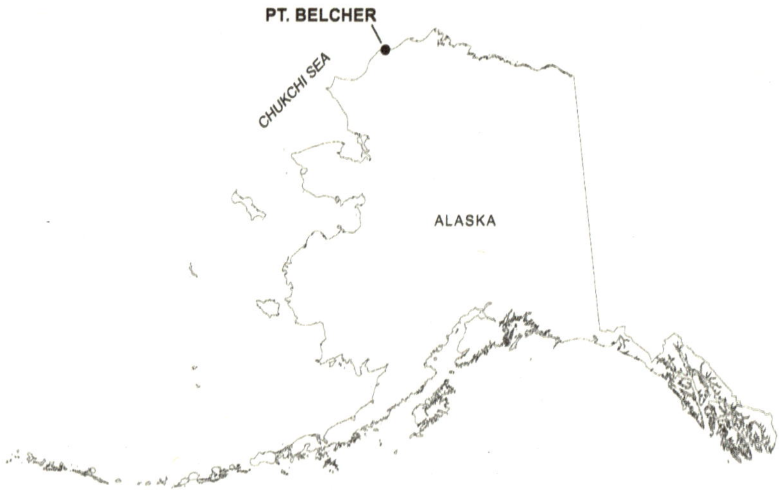

Fig. 10.1. Location of Point Belcher in Alaska (from Cassell 2000b)

COMMERCIAL WHALING AND ESKIMO LABOR IN NORTH ALASKA

John Kelly did not initiate the use of Eskimo labor in commercial shore whaling; that event can be attributed to Charles Brower just a few years before, in 1888. But in the short time between Brower's first hiring of Eskimos and the 1891 establishment of Kelly's Point Belcher station, Iñupiat labor became a near universal characteristic of the social landscape in north Alaska, and indeed all the western Arctic: virtually all able-bodied Iñupiat men and women worked to some degree for the commercial whaling industry within five years of Brower's initial commodification of Eskimo labor (Bockstoce 1986; Cassell 1988a).

Commercial whalers entered western Arctic waters through Bering Strait in 1848, reaching Point Barrow in 1854. While the commercial focus was whale oil in the early decades of the fishery, fashion trends and post–Civil War fossil fuels development led to an emphasis on baleen production. Prior to the late–1880s, commercial whaling in the Western Arctic was confined to the open sea, in ships with primarily Euro-American crews. Extant *umialiit* traded in baleen with commercial whalers for manufactured goods. At the time, commercial whalers had little use for Iñupiat labor.

In the 1880s, the whaling industry tried to offset reductions in the baleen supply caused by massive depletions of overhunted bowhead whale populations (Bockstoce 1980). Whalers instituted the practice of spring whaling from shore bases to complement summer open-sea harvest. Shore whaling was very similar to the Iñupiat method, using small boats to travel the narrow ice leads through which whales pass on their northward migration. Commercial shore whaling was conducted from stations established primarily in extant Iñupiat villages, which were settled initially because of their proximity to ice conditions favorable to spring whaling. The Iñupiat residents, knowledgeable about whaling, offered a prime source for labor to staff whaling stations and operate whaleboats.

Enter Charles Brower. Brower started shore whaling in Barrow in 1887 for the San Francisco-based Pacific Steam Whaling Company (PSWC). In the spring of 1887, Brower's Euro-American crew caught nothing, while village crews took 22 whales. After that unsuccessful 1887 season, Euro-Americans were never seriously considered for staffing shore stations, and in 1888 Brower began to organize crews using almost exclusively Eskimo labor (Bockstoce 1986). Although the village *umialiit* still maintained sufficient resources to control available labor, Brower was able to recruit some Iñupiat who had been temporarily restricted from village crews.

Brower left PSWC after the 1888 season and began his own operations. PSWC still maintained a station. While with PSWC, Brower "had discovered the simplicity of using native crews," and in 1889 he hired two families from Point Hope (Bockstoce 1980:234, 236). In addition, Brower "hired two more Eskimos from the village": "they were good enough men, and were glad to work for us, but they were taboo in native boats. . . . If we had not hired them, they could not have worked until the next spring" (Brower 1932:95).

The 1889 season was successful, and in 1890 more commercial shore whaling operations were begun at Barrow. That spring, villagers manned 40 boats while commercial operators fitted out ten. Although the whaling season was poor, the combined commercial profits of the baleen and fox fur trade were substantial (Bockstoce 1986:236; Libbey and Schneider 1987). These commercial profits enabled the American operators to continue offering material goods and foodstuffs as incentive and remuneration to encourage Iñupiat participation in commercial shore whaling. Use of Iñupiat labor spread rapidly at shore whaling stations established in native villages between Bering Strait and Point Barrow until the collapse of the baleen market around 1914 (Figure 10.2). According to ethnographer and explorer Vilhjalmur Stefansson (1922:60), the commercial whaling season was

> six weeks of fairly easy work at that. For all the rest of the year the men have nothing to do—are their own masters, and can go wherever they like, while their employers must not only pay them a year's wages for six weeks' work, but also furnish them houses to live in . . . , and rations for the entire year. . . . The employer supplies them with cloth for garments,

Fig. 10.2. Eskimo employees and baleen at a commercial whaling station near Point Hope, Alaska; note Euro-American in campaign hat at left (from Bockstoce 1986:253; courtesy of the California Academy of Sciences)

> and such suitable provisions as flour, tea, beans, rice, and even condensed milk, canned meats and fruit.

Stefansson's description details the ways in which Brower and other commercial whalers attempted to attract and maintain Iñupiat labor. Their ways mirrored those of extant *umialiit*. *Umialiit* had to ensure the feeding of their whaling crews and their families in the months of preparation for the hunt and during the hunt itself. Thus, the commercial operator had to have food resources to permit Iñupiat to forgo subsistence hunting during whaling. But while *umialiit* depended upon kin and the previous year's whale harvest to supply food to crews and their families, the whaler/trader relied on the supply ship which came every year with provisions from San Francisco. These annual shipments enabled the whaler/trader to provide a relatively steadier and more reliable supply of foodstuffs and other material goods in exchange for labor. This heightened ability to feed and supply crews and their families permitted the entry of the commercial into traditional leadership realms (e.g., Cassell 1988b, 2000a, 2000c).

Brower's actions of 1888 marked the first time Eskimos had been formally hired on by industry, the first time Eskimo labor had become a commodity itself. While it is true that Eskimos from Siberia and west and north Alaska had been hired occasionally by whalers as interpreters and seamstresses (Bockstoce 1986), Brower brought about a much larger scale of the sale of Eskimo labor power. Eskimos in north Alaska sold their labor power to the American whaling industry, receiving wages in return for their labor. It is important to locate late-nineteenth- and early-twentieth-century north Alaska in the broader historical context of Iñupiat interaction with and integration into the modern Euro-American world. Commercial whaling and the development of an Iñupiat wage labor force both by and for the industry was a landmark process in the social history of the Iñupiat because it marked the formal Euro-American exploitation of Alaskan Arctic natural and human resources, an exploitation seen today in petroleum-related extraction and employment. The wage remuneration for Eskimo labor power that began through participation in the whaling industry continues into the present-day in modern public and private economies (e.g., Chance 1990; Klausner and Foulks 1982; Jorgensen 1990).

JOHN KELLY'S 1891–1894 POINT BELCHER WHALING STATION

John Kelly (Figure 10.3) had whaled at Point Hope in 1889, and in 1890 he took his Point Hope employees north and built a large station in Barrow. In the 1891 whaling season, he and his 100 or so workers took 12 whales, while Brower's crews took five, and the Eskimo *umialiit* took one. In September 1891, Kelly's Barrow-bound supply ship became stuck in the ice off Point Belcher, and rather than move everything north by boat and sled, he set up his station there (Brower 1942:210). Charles Brower visited Kelly at the station in December of that year. According to Brower, "Kelley had built a long house of one thickness of lumber, banking it all with snow and sod. It was warm enough with all hands living there. No one had a great deal of room. . . . Kelley kept himself shut in his room all of the time. His house and every place in it was filled with Point Hope people. They mostly lived there, eating at the table" (Brower 1942:417, 418). He also observed what he felt were rather unpleasant surroundings inside during his December visit to the station, stating that "I never saw an Eskimo house in the condition that place was." Brower's Eskimo wife Toctoo "never wanted to visit Kelley again as long as he was in the country" (1942:418).

Kelly eventually had 80 Eskimos working for him at his station (Bockstoce 1986:238), sufficient for six or eight whaling crews. They caught no whales that spring, and in July 1892 Kelly dismantled the station and moved back to Barrow. There, in 1893, he had charge of 100 Eskimo employees and their family members, totaling about 500 people. In 1894, Kelly staffed 22 crews with nearly 200 employees, taking 11 whales (Bockstoce 1986:237–239).

As a commercial whaling operation, Kelly's Point Belcher station was a complete failure (no whales were taken), but Kelly did have brisk fur trade business there. Brower noted that "During the winter they caught several hundred fox. . . . Everyone that had furs had to go to Belcher and trade with Kelley" (1942:417, 416–417). The fur trade was burgeoning in north Alaska at the

Fig. 10.3. John W. Kelly (from Bockstoce 1986:237; courtesy of the Presbyterian Church of America)

time, and any labor not engaged in whaling at the station was likely devoted to acquiring fox furs. As will be shown below, this knowledge of Kelly's fur trade business has considerable bearing on the archaeology and social history of the place.

ARCHAEOLOGY AT KELLY'S STATION

Archaeological research at Kelly's station identified the original station building, at least three workers' houses, a possible warehouse structure, eight storage racks, and 12 middens (Figure 10.4). The main building is that referred to by Brower, in which Kelly and his workers lived. A midden identified under an apparent extension to the main building suggests the possibility that the extension was added as Kelly's room, separating him from his workers: Brower reported in

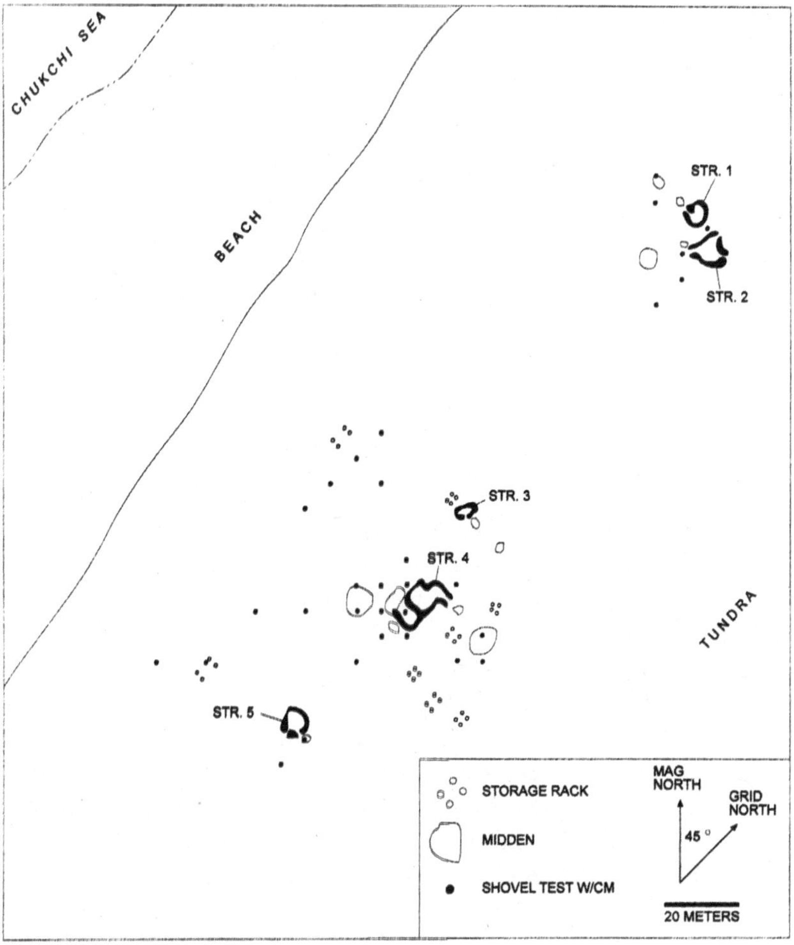

Fig. 10.4. Plan of Kelly's Station (from Cassell 2000b)

1888 that Kelly never liked to sleep in the same room with Eskimos (1942:311). The location of this main building in relation to the rest of the station provided Kelly with the capability of surveillance of his little industrial domain, a feature so characteristic of many nineteenth-century factories in America (e.g., Foucault 1979).

Excavation of nearly 500 shovel test pits identified the 12 middens. The spatial layout of the middens shows that specific middens were associated with specific structures; at least one midden was likely shared between two workers' houses. The main building was in close proximity with four large middens, one outside the primary entrance, two around the back, and one under the extension. All structures have a small midden just outside the entryway. Ten of the 12 middens became the focus of our excavations.

The midden and shovel test pit excavations yielded no material evidence that the property occupied by the station had ever been used or inhabited, either before Kelly's time there or afterwards. All recovered material was derived from nearly a full year of the lives and labors of Kelly and his Eskimo employees. This provides a very fine-grained temporal resolution of artifactual deposits at the site (*sensu* Binford 1978:483; Hall 1982). The bulk of recovered material consisted of burned and intact faunal elements, with coal ash, shotgun cartridges, burlap bag pieces, lamp and window glass, and miscellaneous iron fragments occurring in some frequency. Items of Eskimo style or manufacture were of limited variety and frequency, including an ivory harpoon finger rest, an ivory seal harpoon head with copper blade, and an iron *ulu* (semi-lunar knife).

The most intriguing Eskimo items recovered were also of limited variety but not frequency: 14 chipped chert endscrapers (Figure 10.5), known ethnographically to be used for hide scraping in making skin clothing. Murdoch (1892:295) wrote that, "Every woman owns one of these tools." Although gender association of endscraping activities with women is interesting, the sex composition of Kelly's staff is unknown. Endscrapers are classic material examples of traditional Iñupiat Eskimo lifeways (e.g., Murdoch 1892:Figures 289–298; see also Nelson 1899:Plate XLIX). The body of the endscraper usually rested inside a wooden or ivory handle that was custom-carved to fit the user's hand (Figure 10.6). The working edges of chert endscrapers are a studied balance of not-too-sharp yet not-too-dull. Fox hides are extremely delicate—the working edges of the endscrapers had to scrape fat and tissue from the hides without cutting into and damaging the hides (Robert Gal, personal communication 1993; also Murdoch 1892:294).

Endscrapers were recovered from the three largest middens only (middens 2–1, 4–1, and 4–2) (Figure 10.4). Discoid, T-shaped, and triangulate forms of endscrapers were present, all of which could be fitted into a handle. Most of the endscrapers show substantial use wear, and a few were broken opposite the working edge. All appear usable or salvageable. Whole endscrapers are rarely found in middens at Western Arctic sites predating commercial whaling, but they are found with some frequency within houses. The middens where whole endscrapers are found are those resulting from many years if not generations or centuries of deposition, such as those occurring at the Utqiagvik site in Barrow.

EMPIRICAL CONTEXTS OF ENDSCRAPER RECOVERY

I offer a few examples of endscraper recovery contexts from archaeological sites in the vicinity of Kelly's station. The sites include Nunagiak, Utqiagvik, and Siraagruk on the Chukchi Sea coast.

Fig. 10.5. Chert endscrapers recovered from Kelly's Station (the two small scrapers at bottom left are thumbnail scrapers rather than endscrapers, although they could conceivably be fitted into a handle) (from Cassell 2000b)

Ford (1959) excavated at Nunagiak and Utqiagvik (his "Utkiavik") in the 1930s, and his subsequent publication makes especial reference to the presence of chert endscrapers (1959:Table 12; Figures 90–92). The excavated deposits from both locations date prior to the advent of commercial whaling in the western Arctic. Nunagiak lies at Point Belcher, a few hundred meters away from Kelly's whaling station. Ford's excavations there recovered 10 endscrapers, at least seven of which were from within-house contexts; the contexts of the other three were uncertain and may be from middens or also from inside houses (Ford 1959:Table 12). Ford also excavated at Utqiagvik in present-day Barrow, where he recovered eight endscrapers from two houses (Ford 1959:Table 12).

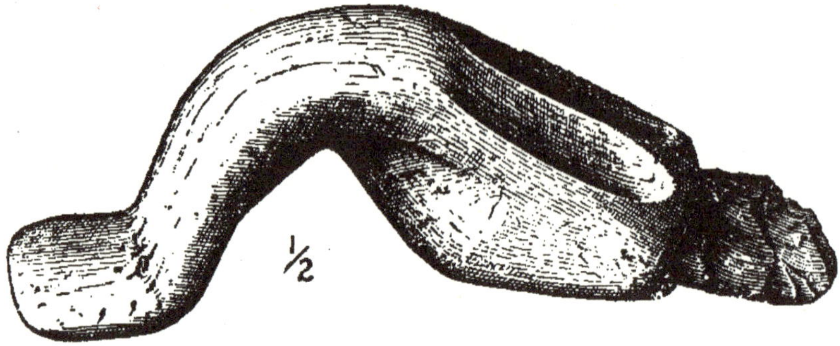

Fig. 10.6. Illustration of endscraper and handle

Dekin excavated at Utqiagvik in 1981–1983 (Cassedy et al. 1990; Dekin et al. 1990a, 1990b). The excavations were in deposits dating prior to and within the time during which commercial whalers were in the western Arctic. The Utqiagvik team recovered at least 70 chert endscrapers from within eight houses (the exact number is difficult to discern from the published reports). There was no endscraper recovery in the numerous tests excavated outside of six houses in which midden deposits did (or could) exist.

The third example is noteworthy because both the occupation of the site and the endscrapers recovered there date to the time of Kelly's station or shortly thereafter. Dale Slaughter excavated the site of Siraagruk in the early-1980s (Dale Slaughter, personal communication 1981, 2001), approximately three miles north of Kelly's station on the Chukchi Sea coast. The site consists of two houses. A small newspaper fragment was recovered at Siraagruk bearing an 1891 publication date (no month was present); the newspaper might have actually come from Kelly's station. The deposits from which endscrapers were recovered reflect a short-term occupation of perhaps a few years.

Slaughter recovered 14 chert endscrapers at Siraagruk, all from within-house deposits, one of which was observed to be very dulled. While it is true that no external midden deposits were excavated there, it is instructive to see that the pattern of endscrapers occurring inside houses matches the patterns found by Dekin and Ford at Utqiagvik and Nunagiak. Slaughter sees the presence of so many endscrapers as indicating that the inhabitants were heavily engaged in the fur trade and were possibly dealing directly with Kelly and his station (Dale Slaughter, personal communication 2001). There is no indication, however, that the people at Siraagruk were formal employees of Kelly (or any other commercial whaler-trader) at the time. Rather, they were likely acting as independent traders working within the fur trade networks but not for anyone in particular.

Given the substantial market that existed in the late nineteenth and early

Table 10.1 Context of Endscraper Recovery at Four North Alaskan Archaeological Sites

Site	Excavator	Internal to House	External to House	N =
Nunagiak	Ford	7	3?	10
Utkiavik	Ford	8	0	8
Utqiagvik	Dekin	70+	0	70+
Siraagruk	Slaughter	14	*	14
Kelly's Station	Cassell	*	14	14
	N =	99	17	116

*Data collected from one context.

twentieth centuries for furs from north Alaska, one would by no means be surprised to find that individual Eskimos trapped furbearing animals and traded the furs to both American and other Eskimos alike. Indeed, numerous recorded accounts exist of such Eskimo trapping and trading behaviors during the fur trade around the turn of the twentieth century (Libbey and Schneider 1987: 343–352). We can view the people at Siraagruk, then, as being *in* the fur trade, but not *of* it. Fur production was in the household context (production by household labor), not an industrial context (production by wage laborers in what was effectively a factory system). In terms of social relations involved in the capitalist fur trade, this distinguishes them from the employees at Kelly's station: at Siraagruk, fur was the commodity, while labor power was the commodity at the station. Use and exchange value drove the households at Siraagruk; surplus value drove Kelly's operation.

The combined data of recovery contexts internal or external to houses (including those from Kelly's Station) are provided in Table 10.1. It is readily apparent that, with the exception of Kelly's station, chert endscraper deposition largely occurs within houses, where endscrapers were curated.

The implication here is that endscrapers were not discarded after a few rounds of use but were kept, reworked, and used again. Recovery of 14 endscrapers from middens built up over less than a year at Kelly's station is thus in large measure inconsistent with traditional Eskimo material use and disposal patterns. It suggests that the industrial context of their use and users is a significant component in the interpretation of the place and time.

ENDSCRAPER PRESENCE IN AN INDUSTRIAL CONTEXT

The presence of the endscrapers at Kelly's station, together with their provenience, leads to a couple of conclusions. The first conclusion is that traditional

Eskimo skills and technologies were vital to Kelly's success in the fur trade. He would not have been able to capitalize (quite literally) on the productivity of the fur trade without the skin preparation know-how of the Eskimo employees and the technological development of the chert endscrapers. His season at Point Belcher would have been chalked up as a complete loss, much to the dismay of his financial backers. Indeed, the fur industry never was able to provide a functional replacement for chert endscrapers in hide preparation. Ethnologist Diamond Jenness wrote of Eskimos in north Alaska in 1918:

> Of their old implements only five are in everyday use, the snow shovel, the bow drill, the curved whittling knife, the woman's knife, and the skin scrapers, all of which . . . are more adapted to the purposes to which they are applied than any implement which we can supply. It is interesting to note that while the implement used for stretching and softening skins is generally an iron ferrule set in a short wood handle, the actual scraper, which is set on a similar handle, is still commonly made of flint. The scraper . . . [has] preserved the original type unchanged (Jenness 1918:93).

A 1935 study of Alaskan Eskimo material culture found that "The only ethnologically old tools and instruments still generally found in the Eskimo households studied are those used in the processes of tanning and working skins, such as scrapers. . . . " (Anderson and Eels 1935:131). That some aspects of Eskimo material culture should be more adaptive to certain tasks than introduced technologies is by no means a revelation; similar instances are known throughout North America (e.g., Hallowell 1957).

The second conclusion follows from the first: at Kelly's station, these endscrapers are not to be considered classic material hallmarks of traditional Eskimo lifeways. Rather, they are material indicators of Eskimo labor in an industrial world run by Euro-Americans. I suggest that the Eskimos working for Kelly and the fur industry might not have necessarily perceived those endscrapers in the same way they had when making and using endscrapers in a domestic context.

These chert endscrapers are material things. They have the characteristics of manufacture, use, discard, and, most importantly, meaning, based upon the social context of their presence, of who is using them, and why. McGuire (1992: 94–95) provides us with a material example of this idea of meaning and social context. While wine from the liquor store is a bought and sold commodity, the same wine in a communion cup is the sacred Blood of Christ. But the thing is still wine. What has changed is not the thing, but the social context of its presence.

For present purposes, the thing is still an endscraper; what changes is the meaning of the thing, the social context of its manufacture and use, the way it is perceived by those who made it and used it and threw it away. Things are nothing without the social context of their existence; they are meaningless if stripped of time and place and people.

These chert endscrapers, little but mightily functional pieces of chipped stone, were imbued with meaning by the Eskimos before, during, and after commercial whaling and the fur trade (e.g., Hodder 1986). The meaning shifted as chert endscrapers became used in social contexts differing from the original context. And meaning remained or shifted with individual endscrapers depending upon context and not with the category of "endscrapers." As individual chert endscrapers were made and used for the fur industry by industrial laborers, they were not perceived in the same way by their makers and users as if they had been made and used for skin clothing or boat covers or even the fur trade by the folks back home in the village or camp. They were consequently thrown away after use and were not curated as would normally have been the case.

CONCLUSION

I have attempted here to place the recovery of 14 chert endscrapers from Kelly's station in the contexts of prior archaeological data, of ethnography, and of social history. It is apparent that the use of lithic technologies in the form of endscrapers for the fur industry at Kelly's station (and elsewhere in the Arctic) was a boon to Kelly's success. No other technology satisfied the needs of fox hide processing as well as the traditional Eskimo endscraper. What is perhaps somewhat less apparent but nonetheless viable is the notion that Kelly's employees discarded their endscrapers rather than curate them because of the social context of endscraper use. In nonindustrial situations in north Alaska, endscraper curation would have been the general principle. But Kelly's employees were industrial laborers in Kelly's little factory town, wage workers in the capitalist fur trade in which they used the endscrapers in hide processing. The endscrapers were still endscrapers in and of themselves, but these particular chert endscrapers from Kelly's station were new tools for new laborers engaged in new work in a new age. And that seems to have made all the difference in the eyes of Kelly's Eskimo employees.

ACKNOWLEDGMENTS

My gratitude is extended to the Bureau of Land Management and the U.S. Department of Fish and Wildlife for logistics and supplies support; special thanks go to John Cook and Chuck Diters of those respective agencies. I wish to thank Bruce Mattioli for his professionalism, companionship, and camaraderie during the 1990 fieldwork at Kelly's station. I very much appreciate the editorial skills of Charles Cobb and the anonymous reviewers of this article. Finally, whatever success was achieved during the archaeological fieldwork at Point Belcher was due in large measure to the hospitality of the people of Wainwright, Alaska, and especially to Dempsey and Anna Mae Bodfish of that fine community.

11
Discussion

Douglas B. Bamforth

If there are still scholars who think that archaeological data do not add significantly to our understanding of the process of cultural change over the course of the Contact period in North America, the papers in this volume should change their minds. From documenting patterns of change that occurred beyond the reach of literate Europeans to focusing our attention on telling details of well-known periods in recent post-Contact history that the documentary record overlooks, the authors here show clearly how archaeology can expand traditional reconstructions of post-Contact changes in Native-American ways of life.

Like any collection of technically and geographically diverse archaeological analyses, this one has implications for a wide range of issues. I focus here on two of these: first, on a technical issue that these papers share with lithic analysis in general and, second, on the ways in which the papers here illustrate the complexity of the factors that influence technological change.

ONE TECHNICAL ISSUE: LITHIC TAPHONOMY

The majority of the papers here focus on Contact-period flaked-stone technology, and they draw on and highlight the technical sophistication of that domain of research in archaeology in general. However, they also demonstrate the lack of attention to taphonomic process by that domain of archaeology. Most of these papers report on one component of larger research projects that must focus on many classes of material culture, and a volume on, for example, the faunal analyses that parallel the studies included here would have considered taphonomy in detail. I make this point not because there are well-understood taphonomic processes that fundamentally alter the arguments made here but because all aspects of the archaeological record in all times and places reflect both the processes of human behavior that archaeologists want to understand and a variety of other processes as well. Lithic analysis has developed powerful ways of dealing with the first of these but has devoted remarkably little attention to the second, and it is time, and past time, for us to account for these processes in our work.

A multitude of processes, including use, intentional retouch, accidental technological effects, trampling, subsurface sediment movements, and careless handling during excavation and in the laboratory can damage the edges of flakes and other stone artifacts. On one hand, it is clear that the widespread argument that nonhuman processes produce random patterns of retouch (e.g., Tringham et al. 1974) is not correct—such processes unquestionably can produce patterns that mimic the results of intentional human action, readily producing pieces that can easily be classified as used or retouched (Bamforth 1998; McBrearty et al. 1998). On the other hand, although archaeologists have recognized such processes for over a century (e.g., Johnson 1978; Spurrell 1883; Warren 1923), it is equally clear that we lack widely used standards for distinguishing between the human processes we want to understand and the natural processes that can mimic these, particularly in the case of "utilized flakes" (Young and Bamforth 1990).

The fairly short period of time since the artifacts considered here were used limits the severity of the processes that might have operated on them, although the shallow burial of these sites suggests that they were likely vulnerable to trampling and agriculture in at least some cases. Nevertheless, unless we take these problems into account in our research designs and control for them in our analyses, we will not be able to understand how they affect our conclusions. This is an essential area for future work, and such work needs to address complex issues. To take only one example, trampling soon after discard may modify artifacts, and the likelihood that artifacts will be trampled depends, in part, on the intensity of human use of their discard location: other things being equal, artifacts recovered from intensively used locations (such as permanent communities that remained in the same location for centuries) will be more likely to bear traces of trampling than artifacts excavated from single- or short-term use locations.

LITHIC TECHNOLOGY AND CONTACT-PERIOD TRANSFORMATION

Regardless of how lithic analysis develops in the future, these papers have important implications for the present. Contact-period studies are clearly focused on transformation, with the end result of this transformation being catastrophic population loss, cultural disintegration, the removal of tribes from their traditional lands, and their forced incorporation into Euro-American society, albeit at the margins of that society. For many years, the clarity of the end result of this process of change has loomed far larger than either the complexity of the process itself or the diversity of ways in which that process played out in different areas. These papers follow the recent emphasis on understanding this complexity and diversity, and make important contributions to it in a number of areas.

Lessons for Everyone: Complex Causality

Archaeological interpretation relies on a combination of theory, imagination, and evidence to make sense of patterns in material culture. Text-aided archaeology like that reported here has the enormous advantage of being able to rely less on archaeological imagination and more on the documented historical context of change (although this varies over the course of the Contact period, as I note below). One important lesson that this advantage provides is a clear example of the diversity of the ways in which superficially similar societies responded to a single event. Kelly (2002:58) notes that "we have not as yet found any simple correlations between technology and other social, economic, or political variables." Kelly's comment refers to much of the literature of the 1980s and 1990s, particularly the literature on pre-Contact hunters and gatherers, which lacks the framework provided by documentary evidence and is replete with attempts to show just such correlations. The evidence here illustrates why such attempts have been unsuccessful: the causes and consequences of technological change are complex.

This is most evident in the range of initial responses to the availability of metal documented here. Cobb and Ruggiero (chapter 2) find that iron tools occur at the Early Contact-period King site as still-useable pieces found only in what seem to be relatively high-status graves, with little or no reorganization of stone technology. They contrast this with a pattern in comparable Onondaga sites in New York, where metal was recycled so intensively that the initial form of many pieces cannot be determined, and note that other sites in the vicinity of the King site have produced different assemblages of European implements than the one recovered from King. In contrast to both of these, Odell's paper (chapter 3) on the Lasley Vore site focuses on a baseline description of the lithic technology on the cusp of contact, but he notes that tools and other metal objects were recovered from much the same contexts as the lithic assemblage, suggesting that, even given the small numbers of tools available at the time the site was occupied, they were fairly widely integrated into daily life.

All of these cases report on the archaeology of settled horticulturalists, and the diversity of these responses is important cautionary information for arguments that attempt to link general aspects of societies—such as degrees of sedentism—simply and directly to even very general descriptions of technology. Interestingly, the King site case mirrors the basic pattern at the Chumash town of Helo' on the central California coast (Bamforth 1993), where extensive excavations in residential areas recovered no metal, but previous work in cemeteries found fairly large numbers of intact iron implements. In contrast to the horticultural cases reported here, Helo' was occupied by sedentary maritime hunter-gatherers, further emphasizing this point. The diverse ways in which Indian people altered indigenous technology in response to the constraints and opportunities of more sustained contact (documented here by Johnson [chapter 4] and by Carmody [chapter 5]) also highlight this issue, as does the persistence into the twentieth century of some stone tools in the Iñupiat case examined by Cassell (chapter 10).

The possibility raised by Cobb and Ruggiero that some initial responses to the availability of metal might have been conditioned by ideological factors is also important: in contexts like the Paleoindian period, where visually striking stone was often used for projectile points (and for other classes of tools), we may also wonder about ideology. Identifying the symbolic role played by utilitarian items can be extremely difficult (but see Apel [2001]), and it is essential to avoid assuming, even implicitly (as, for example, Rogers [1990] effectively does), that all traditional artifacts carried equal ideological weight. Evidence of use in clearly symbolic contexts or very specific comparisons of indigenous and imported materials may ultimately help to sort these problems out (for example, Cobb and Ruggiero's arguments about the importance of the color of metal may be strengthened by data on indigenous use of different colors of stone for different purposes). I return to this general issue below.

Stone or Steel?

Complex or not, though, the process of change at the center of this volume is the shift from stone to metal tools. As is true for Contact-period change in general, the outcome of this process is undoubted: metal replaced stone. However, as I note elsewhere (Bamforth 1993) and as the papers here illustrate, the course of post-Contact technological change occurred at different rates and involved different kinds of tools in different parts of North America. The papers here suggest at least some overall patterns that may help to understand some of this variability.

The pattern that seems most central here is, I think, driven significantly by the changing nature of the interactions between Indians and Whites. Perhaps the biggest change in archaeological and historical perceptions of the Contact period has been the recognition of the active role played by indigenous people in structuring these interactions. As the papers here note, Indians were victims of contact, but they were not simply passive victims (also see Coombs and Plog 1977; Rogers and Wilson 1993). Recognizing the active role played by Indian people in making choices throughout the Contact period is essential to understanding why post-Contact processes operated the way they did.

However, it is important to recognize that much of the interaction between

Indians and Whites reflected not just choices but also power and that power relations changed dramatically as the Contact period progressed. As the introductory chapter discusses, the cases presented here fall roughly into three groups with this issue in mind. The first includes the papers on the King and Lasley Vore sites (chapters 2 and 3), which focus on occupations during the very early periods of contact, when European goods, and Europeans, were relatively rare and indigenous ways of life were as yet little altered. Second, chapters 4 through 8 (including Johnson's work with the Chickasaw, Carmody's analysis of the Cameron site assemblage, Nassaney and Volmar on southern New England, Bayman on Hawai'i, and Wagner's paper on Potowatomi pipes) focus on groups who were, to varying degrees, independent of but closely interacting with and responding to White communities and White economies. Finally, chapters 9 and 10 (Silliman's examination of the lithic technology at Rancho Petaluma and Cassell's Iñupiat study) discuss groups late in the post-Contact period who were largely dependent clients of Whites.

These different kinds of interaction are important because (as Cobb also discusses in the Introduction), they imply very different degrees of control on the parts of both Indians and Whites. There is little doubt that the conceptual key to understanding post-Contact technological (and other) changes in North America lies in understanding how native groups made choices about interaction. However, while they were active participants in making those choices, they were not completely in control of the kinds of choices that were available for them to make; these were substantially in the hands of Whites (as the differing post-Contact availability of horses and guns in different areas of the Great Plains [Secoy 1952] shows so clearly). During the earlier periods of contact, Indian people had considerable control over the ways they could choose from the possibilities offered to them, and Whites were largely dependent on the goodwill of Indian groups. However, as they became more and more dependent on Whites for economic opportunity, replacement tools, and, often, even food, the balance of power must have shifted and, with it, the kinds of choices Indian people would make, and the reasons why they made them, must also have shifted.

Idiosyncratic, perhaps often ideological, issues (like the symbolic significance of a given metal's color) might well have been especially important during the earliest periods of contact, but technological changes evident in the cases addressing periods of more sustained contact appears to have been structured more by a complex balance of practical issues. The range of factors documented by the papers here includes the abundance of metal tools available, social factors within intact native communities affecting access to metal, the relative performance of metal and stone tools in use, the locations of raw material sources for stone tools, and the ideological importance of traditional technology for Indian people (an issue I consider in more detail later in this discussion).

Importantly, although a number of the papers note that metal often provided "functional replacements" for stone tools, the data presented here illustrate that we cannot understand any kind of technological change only in terms of the context in which tools are used. Technological choices also reflect procurement/replacement costs (as Bamforth and Bleed [1997] discuss in detail), and the shifting balance of power over the course of the transition from stone to metal must have altered these costs for both introduced and indigenous materials (as, for example, Chickasaw raw material use shifted as the tribe responded to altered post-Contact economic opportunities [chapter 4]). Population losses and population shifts resulting from contact must also have disrupted native economies in many ways, altering access to nonlocal materials and perhaps changing labor demands and allocations in ways that altered patterns of indigenous tool production. The possibility that one way of balancing procurement/replacement costs with use qualities was to accept metal tools first as replacements for stone tools used in tasks where metal made the greatest utilitarian difference (Bamforth 1993) finds some support in many of these papers, and this explanation may prove to be particularly useful for understanding the great variation in initial reactions of Indian groups to the availability of metal.

However, as several papers here note, objects, including tools, can be ideologically as well as practically important. Addressing the possible symbolic role of technological change is a major theme of this volume, and merits more detailed discussion.

What Do Stone Tools Mean?

Technological choices have immediate, concrete implications for all human groups, and it is certain that such choices cannot be understood without reference to those impacts. However, these choices may also be important in other ways, as the Amish rejection of most modern technology or master woodworker Adam Krenov's preference for hand-tools rather than power-tools (Krenov 1977) make clear.

Particularly in the later portions of the Contact period, as Native-American societies were progressively more and more disrupted, we may expect that all components of traditional ways of life, including stone technology, may well be increasingly valued, and the teachings of the Shawnee Prophet Tenskwatawa (discussed here by Wagner [chapter 8]), suggest that this was indeed so in at least some cases. Similar documentation of the ideological load carried by traditional technology, though, is not available in all of the cases considered here, and the general paucity of stone tools even at a site occupied by Tenskwatawa's followers implies that even strongly held ideologies may be tempered by other forces. It is perhaps telling that the two cases where the ideological meaning of stone objects is clearest (Wagner's work at the Windrose site [chapter 8] and

Nassaney and Volmar's work in southern New England [chapter 6]) involve nonutilitarian items. Furthermore, a number of these sacred items in both cases bear clear traces of having been manufactured using metal tools, suggesting that such prosaic issues as replacement costs and performance in the context of use might have been important even in cases where traditional material culture assumed an undoubted and important symbolic role.

This implies that we need to be cautious in arguing for an ideological role—and particularly for an active rather than an incidental ideological role—for everyday stone tools in cases where we lack documentary evidence supporting such an argument. My own work (Bamforth 1993) offers an example of this. The Chumash town of Helo', noted above, produced an assemblage of pre- and post-Contact stone tools that showed clear evidence both of functional replacement (metal knives replaced bifacial stone knives, for example) and of extensive technological continuity (projectiles appear to have been exclusively tipped with stone up until the forced abandonment of the site in 1803). I argued that the persistence of flaked-stone technology in this community represented a kind of resistance to incorporation into the Spanish mission system on the basis of two patterns. First, mission records indicated that fewer residents of Helo' were baptized than residents of adjacent Chumash communities: Helo' appears to have held itself apart from the mission. Second, past excavations in the cemeteries at Helo' produced fairly numerous metal tools that were placed in graves while still in serviceable condition: the residents of the town appear to have had adequate access to metal.

Taken together, these patterns suggest that the Helo' Chumash *chose* to use stone instead of metal, and that they might have done so as part of an overall reluctance to join the mission. However, it is also possible that access to metal was controlled by the Helo' elite, as Bayman argues here for post-Contact Hawai'i. If the Helo' collection derives from a nonelite area of the site, the technological persistence it shows might have been forced, not chosen. In addition, it is possible that reliance on stone technology might have been an incidental artifact of an overall resistance to Spanish domination rather than an active symbol of that resistance. Additional archaeological data on the distribution of metal tools within the Helo' cemeteries and on technological change in other Contact-era Chumash communities around Helo', as well as more detailed ethnohistoric data on the role of Helo' in the Chumash region during the Contact period, would help to assess these possibilities. While my argument plausibly accounts for the currently available evidence, lacking such additional data, it must be considered only one possible explanation for the patterns I saw.

The strength of my argument, though, lies in the documentation of the access Helo' had to metal and the mission-register data on low rates of baptism, which together provide a context for interpreting the technological data. To return to the issue of power in Contact-period relations, I argued in essence that the Helo' Chumash retained a relatively powerful, or at least independent, position in their relations with the Spanish until very late in the town's occupation. Most late-Contact situations, including some of the situations considered here, differ significantly from this. In these cases, it is possible that persistent use of stone tools may be evidence more of choices constrained by poverty, powerlessness, and lack of options than choices made to symbolize resistance. Recognizing the active role Indian people played in the Contact process is essential, but recognizing the point at which their victimization became a major factor structuring their lives is also essential; post-Contact archaeological material should document both of these. As in the Helo' example, clear archaeological and documentary information on the context in which technological choices were made is necessary to sort these possibilities out in specific cases.

CONCLUSION

Flaked- and ground-stone tools formed an essential part of the fabric of the everyday lives of pre-metal humans everywhere in the world. Their widespread neglect in Contact-era archaeology puts unnecessary limits on the insights that archaeology is capable of providing into the pattern of post-Contact change in the Americas, and these papers highlight this clearly. The diverse routes by which post-Contact changes led Indian people to a common end should be as richly recorded in the archaeological record as the many ways that the lives of Indian people changed prior to contact, and lithic analysis should play as important a role in unraveling this record in the former case as in the latter. At the same time, the framework of known changes provided by the documentary record of Contact provides an important control that illuminates the complexity of technological change in general. This volume should stand as an important contribution to lithic analysis in both of these areas.

ACKNOWLEDGMENTS

I particularly appreciate Charlie Cobb's invitation to participate in this volume, without which I probably would not have returned to many of the issues I have tried to address here. The high quality of the contributors' papers, though, was critical in focusing my thoughts and particularly in helping to suggest alternative interpretations of the data from Helo'.

References Cited

Aganstata, M.

1988 The Women Within a Circle. *Artifacts* 16(3–4):38–39.

Ahler, S. A.

1971 *Projectile Point Form and Function at Rodgers Shelter, Missouri.* Missouri Archaeological Society Research Series 8. University of Missouri and the Missouri Archaeological Society, Columbia.

Allen, R.

1998 *Native Americans at Mission Santa Cruz, 1791–1834: Interpreting the Archaeological Record.* Perspectives in California Archaeology 5. Institute of Archaeology, University of California at Los Angeles.

Amick, D. S., and Mauldin, R. P. (editors)

1989 *Experiments in Lithic Technology.* International Series 528. British Archaeological Reports, Oxford.

Anderson, H. D., and W. C. Eels

1935 *Alaska Natives: A Survey of their Sociological and Educational Status.* Stanford University Press, Stanford.

Andrefsky, W., Jr.

1998 *Lithics: Macroscopic Approaches to Analysis.* Cambridge Manuals in Archaeology. Cambridge University Press, Cambridge.

Apel, J.

2001 *Daggers, Knowledge, and Power.* Coast to Coast Book 3. Department of Archaeology and Ancient History, Uppsala, Sweden.

Atkinson, J. R.

1985 The Ackia and Ogoula Tchetoka Chickasaw Village Locations in 1736 during the French-Chickasaw War. *Mississippi Archaeology* 20:53–72.

Bamforth, D. B.

1988 Investigating Microwear Polishes with Blind Tests: The Institute Results in Context. *Journal of Archaeological Science* 15:11–23.

1993 Stone Tools, Steel Tools: Contact Period Household Technology at Helo'. In *Ethnohistory and Archaeology: Approaches to Postcontact Change in the Americas*, edited by J. D. Rogers and S. M. Wilson, pp. 49–72. Plenum, New York.

1998 Test Excavations at 5GA872, the Windy Ridge Quartzite Quarry. Report submitted to the USDA Forest Service, Routt National Forest, Steamboat Springs, Colorado.

Bamforth, D. B., and P. Bleed

1997 Technology, Flaked Stone Technology, and Risk. In *Rediscovering Darwin: Evolutionary Theory and Archaeological Explanation*, edited by G. Clark and M. Barton, pp. 109–141. Archaeological Papers of the American Anthropological Association No. 7. Washington, D.C.

Bamforth, D. B., G. R. Burns, and C. Woodman

1990 Ambiguous Use Traces and Blind Test Results: New Data. *Journal of Archaeological Science* 17:413–430.

Bancroft, H. H.

1888 *California Pastoral*. The History Company, San Francisco.

Barrera, W.

1971 Excavation of a Beach Midden Deposit at Anaeho'omalu Bay. Manuscript on file, Department of Anthropology, Bernice P. Bishop Museum, Honolulu, Hawai'i.

Barrera, W. M., Jr., and P. V. Kirch

1973 Basaltic-Glass Artifacts from Hawai'i: Their Dating and Prehistoric Uses. *The Journal of the Polynesian Society* 82:176–187.

Bath, J. E., and M. L. K. Rosendahl

1984 *Intensive Archaeological Survey and Testing, HelCo Sub-Station Project Area, Keahou-Kona Resort, Land of Kahalu'u, North Kona, Island of Hawai'i*. Submitted to Kamehameha Investment Corporation. Copies available from Hawaii State Historic Preservation Division Office, Honolulu, Hawaii.

Bayman, J. M., J. J. Moniz Nakamura, T. Rieth, and C. K. Paraso

2001 *The University of Hawai'i Archaeology Field School, Pôhakuloa, Island of Hawai'i: The 1998 & 1997 Seasons*. Copies available from the Hawai'i State Historic Preservation Division Office, Honolulu.

Beaudry, M. C., L. J. Cook, and S. A. Mrozowski

1991 Artifacts and Active Voices: Material Culture as Social Discourse. In *The Archaeology of Inequality*, edited by R. H. McGuire and R. Paynter, pp. 150–191. Basil Blackwell, Oxford.

Behm, J. A.

1983 Flake Concentrations: Distinguishing Between Flintworking Activity Areas and Secondary Deposits. *Southeastern Archaeology* 3:9–16.

Bell, E.

1929–30 Log of the Chatham. *Honolulu Mercury* 1:7–26, 55–69, 76–96; 2:80–91, 119–29.

Bennett, M.

1981 A Longhouse Pattern on the Cameron Site. *Chenango Chapter NSYAA Bulletin* 19(2). New Berlin, New York.

Bennett, M., and R. Bigford

1968 The Cameron Site. *Chenango Chapter NYSAA Bulletin* (10)2. New Berlin, New York.

Bennett, M., and D. Clark

1978 Recent Excavations on the Cameron Site. *Chenango Chapter NSYAA Bulletin* 17(4). New Berlin, New York.

Benton, C.

1957 *A Visitor to Chicago in Indian Days*, edited by P. M. Angle and J. R. Getz. Caxton Club, Chicago.

Berkson, A.

1992 Cultural Resistance of the Prairie Kickapoo at the Grand Village, McLean County, Illinois. *Illinois Archaeology* 4:107–205.

Binford, L. R.

1978 *Nunamiut Ethnoarchaeology*. Academic Press, New York.

1981 *Bones: Ancient Men and Modern Myths*. Academic Press, New York.

Blackburn, G.

1974 *The Illustrated Encyclopedia of Woodworking Hand Tools, Instruments, and Devices*. Globe Pequot Press, Chester, Connecticut.

Blakely, R. L. (editor)

1988 *The King Site: Continuity and Contact in Sixteenth-Century Georgia*. University of Georgia Press, Athens.

Blakely, R. L., and D. S. Mathews

1990 Bioarchaeological Evidence for a Spanish-Native American Conflict in the Sixteenth-Century Southeast. *American Antiquity* 55:718–744.

Bloch, M.

1989 *Ritual, History, and Power*. Athlone Press, London.

Bloom, H. S.

1883 History of Rockville Township. *Illustrated Atlas of Kankakee County, Illinois*. J. H. Beers, Chicago.

Bockstoce, J. R.

1980 A Preliminary Estimate of the Reduction of the Western Arctic Bowhead Whale Population by the Pelagic Whaling Industry, 1848–1915. *Marine Fisheries Review* 42(9–10):20–27.

1986 *Whales, Ice, and Men: The History of Steam Whaling in the Western Arctic*. University of Washington Press, Seattle.

Bourdieu, P.

1977 *Outline of a Theory of Practice*. Cambridge University Press, Cambridge.

1990 *The Logic of Practice*. Polity Press, Cambridge.

Bradley, J. W.

1987 *Evolution of the Onondaga Iroquois: Accommodating Change, 1500–1655*. Syracuse University Press, Syracuse.

Bradley, J. W., and S. T. Childs

1991 Basque Earrings and Panther's Tails: The Form of Cross-Cultural Contact in Sixteenth Century Iroquoia. In *Metals in Society: Theory Beyond Analysis*, edited by

R. M. Ehrenreich, pp. 7–17. MASCA Research Papers in Science and Anthropology Vol. 8, Pt. II. University of Pennsylvania, Philadelphia.

Bragdon, K. J.

1988 The Material Culture of the Christian Indians of New England, 1650–1775. In *Documentary Archaeology in the New World*, edited by M. Beaudry, pp. 126–131. Cambridge University Press, Cambridge.

1996a Gender as a Social Category in Native Southern New England. *Ethnohistory* 43: 573–592.

1996b *Native People of Southern New England, 1500–1650*. University of Oklahoma Press, Norman, Oklahoma.

Brain, J. P.

1988 *Tunica Archaeology*. Peabody Museum of Archaeology and Ethnology, Cambridge, MA.

Brandao, J. A.

1997 *Your Fyre Shall Burn No More: Iroquois Policy Toward New France and Its Native Allies to 1701*. University of Nebraska Press, Lincoln.

Braund, K. E. H.

1993 *Deerskins and Duffles: The Creek Indian Trade with Anglo-Americans, 1685–1815*. University of Nebraska Press, Lincoln.

Brenner, E. M.

1988 Sociopolitical Implications of Mortuary Remains in Seventeenth-Century Native Southern New England. In *The Recovery of Meaning*, edited by M. P. Leone and P. B. Potter, Jr., pp. 147–181. Smithsonian Institution Press, Washington, D.C.

Brigham, W. T.

1902 *Stone Implements and Stone Work of the Ancient Hawaiians*. Museum Memoirs Vol. 1, No. 4. Bernice P. Bishop Museum, Honolulu.

Brower, C. D.

1932 My Arctic Outpost. *The Blue Book Magazine* 54(6):86–101.

1942 *The Northernmost American: An Autobiography*. Unpublished typescript, Stefansson Library, Dartmouth College, Hanover, NH.

Brown, I. W.

1985 *Natchez Indian Archaeology: Culture Change and Stability in the Lower Mississippi Valley*. Archaeological Report No. 15. Mississippi Department of Archives and History, Jackson.

Brown, J. A., R. A. Kerber, and H. D. Winters

1990 Trade and the Evolution of Exchange Relations at the Beginning of the Mississippian Period. In *The Mississippian Emergence*, edited by B. D. Smith, pp. 251–280. Smithsonian Institution Press, Washington, D.C.

Buck, P. H., K. P. Emory, H. D. Skinner, and J. F. G. Stokes

1930 Terminology for Ground Stone Cutting-Implements in Polynesia. *The Journal of the Polynesian Society* 39:174–180.

Burton, W., and R. Lowenthal

1974 The First of the Mohegans. *American Ethnologist* 1:589–599.

Byron, G. A. L.

1826 *Voyage of the H.M.S. Blonde to the Sandwich Islands, in the Years 1824–1825*. Murray, London.

Callahan, E.

1979 The Basics of Biface Knapping in the Eastern Fluted Point Tradition: A Manual for Flintknappers and Lithic Analysts. *Archaeology of Eastern North America* 7:1–180.

Campisi, J.

Oneida. In *Handbook of North American Indians*, edited by W. C. Sturtevant, pp. 481–490. Smithsonian Institution, Washington, D.C.

Carmody, M. L.

1999 Tools of Contact: A Technological and Functional Analysis of the Cameron Site Chipped Stone Assemblage. Unpublished M.A. thesis, Department of Anthropology, State University of New York at Binghamton.

Cassedy, Daniel F., A. A. Dekin, Jr., J. N. Kilmarx, R. R. Newell, C. R. Polglase, G. A. Reinhardt, and B. L. Turcy

1990 *Excavation of a Prehistoric Catastrophe: A Preserved Household from the Utqiagvik Village, Barrow, Alaska*. The North Slope Borough Commission on Iñupiat History, Language, and Culture, Barrow, AK.

Cassell, M. S.

1988a Ethnohistory, Native Labor, and Commercial Whaling in the Beaufort Sea, 1889–1910. Unpublished M.A. thesis, Department of Anthropology, State University of New York at Binghamton.

1988b Farmers of the Northern Ice: Relations of Production in the Traditional North Alaskan Iñupiat Whale Hunt. *Research in Economic Anthropology* 10:89–116.

2000a Iñupiat Eskimo Labor and the Commercial Shore Whaling Industry in Late Nineteenth- Early Twentieth-Century North Alaska. *Pacific Northwest Quarterly* 91(3):115–123.

2000b "If They Did Not Work for the Station They Were in Bad Luck": Commercial Shore Whaling and Iñupiat Eskimo Labor in late Nineteenth-/Early Twentieth-Century North Alaska. Unpublished Ph.D. dissertation, Department of Anthropology, State University of New York at Binghamton.

2000c Feeding Industry: The Creation of an Industrial Labor Force in Late Nineteenth/ Early Twentieth Century North Alaska. *Anthropological Papers of the University of Alaska* 25(1):3–15.

Ceci, L.

1989 Tracing Wampum's Origins: Shell Bead Evidence from Archaeological Sites in Western and Coastal New York. In *Proceedings of the 1986 Shell Bead Conference: Selected Papers*, edited by C. F. Hayes III, pp. 63–80. Research Records No. 20. Rochester Museum & Science Center, Rochester.

1990 Native Wampum as a Peripheral Resource in the Seventeenth-Century World-System. In *The Pequots in Southern New England*, edited by L. M. Hauptman and J. D. Wherry, pp. 48–63. University of Oklahoma Press, Norman.

Chance, N. A.

1990 *The Iñupiat and Arctic Alaska: An Ethnography of Development*. Holt, Rinehart and Winston, Fort Worth.

Cheever, H. T.
1851 *The Island World of the Pacific*. Harper & Brothers, New York.

Chicago Historical Society
1833 *Indian Villages Around Chicago About 1833*. Indian Documents Collection, Chicago Historical Society, Chicago.

Chinen, Jon
1958 *The Great Mahele*. University of Hawaii Press, Honolulu.

Clark, J. T., and P. V. Kirch (editors)
1983 *Archaeological Investigations of the Mudlane-Waimea-Kawaihae Road Corridor, Island of Hawai'i: An Interdisciplinary Study of an Environmental Transect*. Department of Anthropology Report Series No. 83–1. Bernice P. Bishop Museum, Honolulu.

Clark, L.
2003 Beyond Status: Gender at an Early Seventeenth Century Oneida Village. Unpublished Ph.D. dissertation, Department of Anthropology, State University of New York at Binghamton.

Cleghorn, P.
1982 *The Mauna Kea Adze Quarry: Technological Analyses and Experimental Tests*. Ph.D. dissertation, University of Hawai'i, Honolulu. University Microfilms, Ann Arbor.
1984 An Historical Review of Polynesian Stone Adze Studies. *The Journal of the Polynesian Society* 93:399–421.
1986 Organizational Structure at the Mauna Kea Adze Quarry Complex, Hawai'i. *Journal of Archaeological Science* 13:375–387.
1992 A Hawaiian Adze Sequence or Just Different Kinds of Adzes. *New Zealand Journal of Archaeology* 14:129–149.

Cleghorn, P., T. Dye, M. Weisler, and J. Sinton
1985 A Preliminary Petrographic Study of Hawaiian Stone Adze Quarries. *The Journal of the Polynesian Society* 94:235–251.

Cleland, C. E.
1993 Economic and Adaptive Change Among the Lake Superior Chippewa of the Nineteenth Century. In *Ethnohistory and Archaeology: Approaches to Postcontact Change in the Americas*, edited by J. D. Rogers and S. M. Wilson, pp. 111–122. Plenum, New York.

Clifton, J. A.
1977 *The Prairie People*. The Regents Press of Kansas, Lawrence, Kansas.

Cobb, C. R.
1989 An Appraisal of the Role of Mill Creek Chert Hoes in Mississippian Exchange Systems. *Southeastern Archaeology* 8:79–92.
2000 *From Quarry to Cornfield: The Political Economy of Mississippian Hoe Production*. The University of Alabama Press, Tuscaloosa.

Cobb, C. R., and M. Pope
1998 Sixteenth-Century Flintknapping Kits from the King Site, Georgia. *Journal of Field Archaeology* 25:1–18.

Comaroff, J., and J. Comaroff
1992 *Ethnography and the Historical Imagination*. Westview, Boulder.

Cook, J.

1967 Journal of Captain Cook: The Third Voyage. In *The Journals of Captain James Cook on His Voyages of Discovery*, edited by J. C. Beaglehole, 3:1–491 [1778–79]. Cambridge University Press for the Hakluyt Society, Cambridge.

Cook, S. F.

1941 The Mechanism and Extent of Dietary Adaptation Among Certain Groups of California and Nevada Indians. *Ibero-Americana* 18:1–59.

1943 The American Invasion, 1848–1870. *Ibero-Americana* 23:1–115.

Coombs, G., and F. Plog

1977 The Conversion of the Chumash Indians: An Ecological Perspective. *Human Ecology* 5:309–328.

Cordy, R.

1981 *A Study of Prehistoric Social Change: The Development of Complex Societies in the Hawaiian Islands*. Academic Press, New York.

Cross, J.

1990 Specialized Production in Non-stratified Society: An Example from the Late Archaic in the Northeast. Unpublished Ph.D. dissertation, Department of Anthropology, University of Massachusetts, Amherst.

Cusick, J. G.

1998a Historiography of Acculturation: an Evaluation of Concepts and Their Application in Archaeology. In *Studies in Culture Contact: Interaction, Culture Change, and Archaeology*, edited by J. G. Cusick, pp. 126–145. Occasional Paper No. 25. Center for Archaeological Investigations, Southern Illinois University at Carbondale.

1998b Introduction. In *Studies in Culture Contact: Interaction, Culture Change, and Archaeology*, edited by J. G. Cusick, pp. 1–20. Occasional Paper No. 25. Center for Archaeological Investigations, Southern Illinois University at Carbondale.

Davis, W. H.

1929 *Seventy-Five Years in California 1831–1906*. John Howell, San Francisco.

Deetz, J.

1963 Archaeological Investigations at La Purísima Mission. *UCLA Archaeological Survey Annual Report* 5:163–208.

1977 *In Small Things Forgotten*. Anchor, New York.

Dekin, A. A., Jr., A. M. Jensen, J. N. Kilmarx, C. R. Polglase, G. W. Sheehan, and T. Webster

1990a *Additional Reports of the 1982 Investigations by the Utqiagvik Archaeology Project, Barrow, Alaska*. The North Slope Borough Commission on Iñupiat History, Language, and Culture, Barrow, AK.

Dekin, A. A., Jr., R. R. Newell, E. S. Hall, Jr., L. Brower, J. Cargill, R. Gill, R. Holloway, D. Libbey, J. Lobdell, J. Lothrop, R. Miraglia, R. Reanier, G. Reynolds, T. Smith, B. L. Turcy, C. G. Turner, C. Utermohle, and T. Webster

1990b *The 1981 Excavations at the Utqiagvik Site, Barrow, Alaska*. The North Slope Borough Commission on Iñupiat History, Language, and Culture, Barrow, AK.

Dincauze, D. F.

1968 *Cremation Cemeteries in Eastern Massachusetts*. Papers of the Peabody Museum of Archaeology and Ethnology Vol. 59, No. 1. Harvard University, Cambridge, Massachusetts.

Dobres, M.-A.

2000 *Technology and Social Agency: Outlining an Anthropological Framework for Archaeology*. Blackwell, Oxford.

Dobres, M.-A., and C. R. Hoffman

1994 Social Agency and the Dynamics of Prehistoric Technology. *Journal of Archaeological Method and Theory* 1:211–258.

Dobres, M.-A., and J. E. Robb (editors)

2000 *Agency and Archaeology*. Routledge, London.

Dockall, J. E.

2000 Use, Maintenance, and Discard of Basalt Adzes: A Case Study from Ahahulu Valley. Paper presented at the 13th Annual Conference of the Society for Hawaiian Archaeology, Hawai'i Volcanoes National Park, Hawai'i Island.

Dowd, G. E.

1992 *A Spirited Resistance*. Johns Hopkins University Press, Baltimore, Maryland.

Doyle, E. M.

1953 *Makua Laiana*. Advertiser, Honolulu.

Duff, R.

1959 Neolithic Adzes of Eastern Polynesia. In *Anthropology in the South Seas: Essays Presented to H. D. Skinner*, edited by J. D. Freeman and W. R. Geddes, pp. 121–147. Thomas Avery & Sons Limited, New Plymouth, New Zealand.

Dye, D. H.

1995 Feasting with the Enemy: Mississippian Warfare and Prestige-Goods Circulation. In *Native American Interactions: Multiscalar Analyses and Interpretations in the Eastern Woodlands*, edited by M. S. Nassaney and K. E. Sassaman, pp. 289–316. University of Tennessee Press, Knoxville.

Dye, T. S., and E. Komori

1992 A Pre-Censal Population History of Hawai'i. *New Zealand Journal of Archaeology* 14:113–828.

Earle, T. K.

1978 *Economic and Social Organization of a Complex Chiefdom: The Halelea District, Kaua'i, Hawai'i*. Anthropological Papers No. 63. Museum of Anthropology, University of Michigan, Ann Arbor.

Edmunds, R. D.

1983 *The Shawnee Prophet*. University of Nebraska Press, Lincoln.

1984 *Tecumseh and the Quest for Indian Leadership*. Little, Brown, and Co., Boston.

Edwards, N. W.

1870 *Illinois from 1778 to 1833; and the Life and Times of Ninian Edwards*. Springfield, Illinois.

Emerson, T. E.

1982 *Mississippian Stone Images in Illinois*. Circular No. 6. Illinois Archaeological Survey, Urbana, Illinois.

Emory, K. P.

1968 Easy Polynesian Relationships as Revealed Through Adzes. In *Prehistoric Culture in Oceania: A Symposium*, edited by I. Yawata and Y. H. Sinoto, pp. 151–169. Bernice P. Bishop Museum Press, Honolulu.

Emory, K. P., and Y. H. Sinoto

1969 *Age of the Sites in the South Point Area, Ka'ū, Hawai'i.* Pacific Archaeological Records No. 8. Bernice P. Bishop Museum Press, Honolulu.

Englebrecht, W.

1985 New York Iroquois Political Development. In *Cultures in Contact: The European Impact on Native Cultural Institutions in Eastern North America* A.D. 1000–1800, edited by W. W. Fitzhugh, pp. 163–183. Smithsonian Institution Press, Washington, D.C.

Engels, F.

1972 [1884] *The Origins of the Family, Private Property and the State.* International Publishers, New York.

Feest, C. F., and R. D. Edmunds

1993 *Indians of the Changing Frontier: The Art of George Winter.* Indiana Historical Society, Indianapolis.

Folmer, H.

1941 Contraband Trade between Louisiana and New Mexico in the Eighteenth Century. *New Mexico Historical Review* 16:249–274.

Ford, J. A.

1959 Eskimo Prehistory in the Vicinity of Point Barrow, Alaska. *Anthropological Papers of the American Museum of Natural History* 47(1):1–272.

Foster, G. M.

1960 *Culture and Conquest: America's Spanish Heritage.* Quadrangle Books, Chicago.

Foucault, M.

1979 *Discipline and Punishment: The Birth of the Prison.* Vintage, New York.

Fox, D. E.

1979 *The Lithic Artifacts of Indians at the Spanish Colonial Missions, San Antonio, Texas.* Special Report No. 8. Center for Archaeological Research, University of Texas, San Antonio.

Frankie, W.

1997 *Guide to the Geology of Kankakee River State Park Area, Kankakee County, Illinois.* Illinois State Geological Survey, Champaign.

Freycinet, L. de

1829 *Voyage Autour du Monde (Corvettes "L'Uranie" et "La Physicienne"): Historique.* Vol. 1. Atlas, Paris.

Fredrickson, D. A.

1984 The North Coastal Region. In *California Archaeology*, by M. J. Moratto, pp. 471–527. Academic Press, Orlando.

Fried, M. H.

1979 Economic Theory and First Contact. In *New Directions in Political Economy: An Approach from Anthropology*, edited by M. B. Leons and F. Rothstein, pp. 3–17. Greenwood, Westport, CT.

Frierman, J. D. (editor)

1982 *The Ontiveros Adobe: Early Rancho Life in Alta California.* Copies available from Greenwood and Associates, Pacific Palisades, CA. Report submitted to Redevelopment Agency. Santa Fe Springs, CA.

Galloway, P. K.
1996 Ougoula Tchetoka, Ackia, and Bienville's First Chickasaw War: Whose Strategy and Tactics? *Journal of Chickasaw History* 2:3–10.

Garrett, J.
1988 Status, the Warrior Class, and Artificial Cranial Deformation. In *The King Site: Continuity and Contact in Sixteenth Century Georgia*, edited by R. L. Blakely, pp. 35–46. University of Georgia Press, Athens.

Gasco, J.
1993 Socioeconomic Change within Native Society in Colonial Soconusco, New Spain. In *Ethnohistory and Archaeology: Approaches to Postcontact Change in the Americas*, edited by J. D. Rogers and S. M. Wilson, pp. 163–180. Plenum Press, New York.

Gero, J.
1991 Genderlithics: Women's Role in Stone Tool Production. In *Engendering Archaeology*, edited by J. M. Gero and M. W. Conkey, pp. 163–194. Basil Blackwell, Oxford.

Gibson, S. G. (editor)
1980 *Burr's Hill: A Seventeenth Century Wampanoag Burial Ground in Warren, Rhode Island*. Studies in Anthropology and Material Culture Vol. 2. Haffenreffer Museum of Anthropology, Brown University, Providence.

Giddens, A.
1984 *The Constitution of Society*. University of California Press, Berkeley.

Goldstein, P. M.
1993 Tiwanaku Temples and State Expansion: A Tiwanaku Sunken-Court Temple in Moquegua, Peru. *Latin American Antiquity* 3:22–47.

Good, M. E.
1972 Guebert Site: An Eighteenth Century Historic Kaskaskia Indian Village. *Central States Archaeological Society Memoir No. 2*. Wood River, Illinois.

Greenwood, R. S.
1989 The California Ranchero: Fact and Fancy. In *Columbian Consequences, Volume 1: Archaeological and Historical Perspectives on the Spanish Borderlands West*, edited by D. H. Thomas, pp. 451–465. Smithsonian Institution Press, Washington, D.C.

Grumet, R. S.
1995 *Historic Contact: Indian People and Colonists in Today's Northeastern United States in the Sixteenth through Eighteenth Centuries*. University of Oklahoma Press, Norman.

Guilday, J. E., P. W. Parmalee, and D. P. Tanner
1962 Aboriginal Butchering Techniques at the Eschelman Site (36LA12), Lancaster County, Pennsylvania. *Pennsylvania Archaeologist* 32:59–83.

Gundersen, J. N., G. A. Waselkov, and L. K. Pollock
2002 Pipestone Argillite Artifacts from Old Mobile and Environs. *Historical Archaeology* 36(1):105–116.

Gunnerson, J. H., and D. A. Gunnerson
1988 *Ethnohistory of the High Plains*. Bureau of Land Management, Denver, Colorado.

Haddon, A. C., and J. Hornell
1975 *Canoes of Oceania*. Vol. I, *The Canoes of Polynesia, Fiji, and Micronesia*. Benice P. Bishop Museum Special Publication No. 27, Honolulu.

Hall, E. S., Jr.

1982 The Potential Significance of Small, Single Component Archaeological Sites for Elucidating the Culture History of Northern Alaska. *Anthropological Papers of the University of Alaska* 20(1–2):7–13.

Hallowell, A. I.

1957 The Impact of the American Indian on American Culture. *American Anthropologist* 59:201–217.

Hally, D. J.

1970 *Archaeological Investigation of the Potts' Tract Site (9-Mu-103), Carters Dam, Murry County, Georgia.* Laboratory of Archaeology Series Report No. 6. University of Georgia, Athens.

1988 Archaeology and Settlement Plan of the King Site. In *The King Site: Continuity and Contact in Sixteenth Century Georgia*, edited by R. L. Blakely, pp. 3–16. University of Georgia Press, Athens.

1993 The 1992 and 1993 Excavations at the King Site (9FL5). *Early Georgia* 21(2): 30–44.

1994 The Chiefdom of Coosa. In *The Forgotten Centuries: Indians and Europeans in the American South, 1521–1704*, edited by C. Hudson and C. C. Tesser, pp. 227–253. University of Georgia Press, Athens.

Hally, D. J., and J. L. Rudolph

1986 *Mississippi Period Archaeology of the Georgia Piedmont.* Laboratory of Archaeology Series Report No. 24. University of Georgia, Athens.

Hamell, G.

1983 Trading in Metaphors. In *Proceedings of the 1982 Glass Trade Bead Conference*, edited by C. F. Hayes III, pp. 5–28. Research Records No. 16. Rochester Museum and Science Center, Rochester, New York.

Handsman, R. G.

1988 Algonkian Women Resist Colonialism. *Artifacts* 16(3–4):29–31.

Hartley, J. D., and A. F. Miller

1977 *Archaeological Investigations at the Bryson-Paddock Site: an Early Contact Period Site on the Southern Plains.* Oklahoma River Basin Survey, Archaeological Site Report No. 32. University of Oklahoma, Norman.

Hasenstab, R. J.

1999 Fishing, Farming, and finding the Village Sites: Centering Late Woodland New England Algonquians. In *The Archaeological Northeast*, edited by M. A. Levine, K. E. Sassaman, and M. S. Nassaney, pp. 139–153. Bergin & Garvey, Westport, CT.

Hatley, M. T.

1989 The Three Lives of Keowee: Loss and Recovery in Eighteenth Century Cherokee Villages. In *Powhatan's Mantle*, edited by P. H. Wood, G. A. Waselkov and M. T. Hatley, pp. 223–248. University of Nebraska Press, Lincoln.

Hawley, M. F., and C. E. Haury

1994 Lower Walnut Great Bend: Investigations of Sites near Arkansas City, Kansas, Background and Preliminary Results. *Kansas Anthropologist* 15:1–45.

Hay, D., A. E. Haun, P. H. Rosendahl, and C. Severance

1986 *Kahalu'u Data Recovery Project: Excavations at Site 50–10–37–7702, Kahalu'u Habitation Cave, Land of Kahalu'u, North Kona, Island of Hawai'i.* Submitted to Office of Housing and Community Development, County of Hawai'i. Copies available from Hawaii State Historic Preservation Division Office, Honolulu.

Helms, M. W.

1988 *Ulysses' Sail: An Ethnographic Odyssey of Power, Knowledge, and Geographical Distance.* Princeton University Press, Princeton.

Hester, T. R.

1977 The Lithic Technology of Mission Indians in Texas and Northeastern Mexico. *Lithic Technology* 6(1–2):9–13.

1989 Perspectives on the Material Culture of the Mission Indians of the Texas-Northeastern Mexico Borderlands. In *Columbian Consequences, Vol. 1: Archaeological and Historical Perspectives on the Spanish Borderlands West,* edited by D. H. Thomas, pp. 213–229. Smithsonian Institution Press, Washington, D.C.

Hickerson, H.

1973 Fur Trade Colonialism and the North American Indians. *Journal of Ethnic Studies* 1:15–44.

Hill, J. D.

1998 Violent Encounters: Ethnogenesis and Ethnocide in Long-Term Contact Situations. In *Studies in Culture Contact: Interaction, Culture Change, and Archaeology,* edited by J. G. Cusick, pp. 146–171. Occasional Paper No. 25. Center for Archaeological Investigations, Southern Illinois University at Carbondale.

Hodder, I.

1986 *Reading the Past: Current Approaches to Interpretation in Archaeology.* Cambridge University Press, Cambridge.

Hoffman, C.

1991 *A Handbook of Indian Artifacts from Southern New England.* Revised from original text of William S. Fowler. Special Publication No. 4. Massachusetts Archaeological Society, Middleborough.

Holen, S. R.

1991 Bison Hunting Territories and Lithic Acquisition among the Pawnee: An Ethnohistoric and Archaeological Study. In *Raw Material Economies among Prehistoric Hunter-Gatherers,* edited by A. Montet-White and S. Holen, pp. 399–411. Publications in Anthropology, 19. University of Kansas, Lawrence.

Holmes, T.

1981 *The Hawaiian Canoe.* Editions Limited, Honolulu, Hawai'i.

Hommon, R. J.

1986 Social Evolution in Ancient Hawai'i. In *Island Societies: Archaeological Approaches to Evolution and Transformation,* edited by P. V. Kirch, pp. 55–68. Cambridge University Press, Cambridge.

Hoopes, C. L.

1965 The Petaluma Adobe. Manuscript on file, California Department of Parks and Recreation, Sacramento.

Hoover, R. L., and J. G. Costello

1985 *Excavations at Mission San Antonio 1976–1978*. Monograph XXVI. Institute of Archaeology, University of California at Los Angeles.

Hudson, C.

1976 *The Southeastern Indians*. University of Tennessee Press, Knoxville.

Hudson, C., M. Smith, D. Hally, R. Polhemus, and C. DePratter

1985 Coosa: A Chiefdom in the Sixteenth-Century Southeastern United States. *American Antiquity* 50:723–737.

Hudson, L.

1993 Protohistoric Pawnee Lithic Economy. *Plains Anthropologist* 38:265–277.

Hundterfund, J.

1996 King Site Projectile Points: A Functional and Spatial Analysis. Unpublished Senior Honors Thesis, Department of Anthropology, State University of New York at Binghamton.

Jackson, T. L.

1986 Late Prehistoric Obsidian Exchange in Central California. Unpublished Ph.D. dissertation, Department of Anthropology, Stanford University, Stanford, CA.

1989 Late Prehistoric Obsidian Production and Exchange in the North Coast Ranges, California. In *Current Directions in California Obsidian Studies*, edited by R. E. Hughes, pp. 79–94. Contributions of the University of California Archaeological Research Facility 48. Archaeological Research Facility, University of California, Berkeley.

Jenness, D.

The Eskimos of Northern Alaska: A Study in the Effect of Civilization. *The Geographical Review* 5(2):89–101.

Jennings, J. D.

1941 Chickasaw and Earlier Indian Cultures of Northwest Mississippi. *Journal of Mississippi History* 3:155–226.

Jensen, H. P.

1963 Pipes from Illinois. In *Reports on Illinois Prehistory: I, Illinois Archaeological Survey Bulletin No. 4.*, edited by E. A. Bluhm, pp. 107–118. Rantoul Press, Rantoul, Illinois.

Jesuit Relations

1896–1901 *Jesuit Relations and Allied Documents: Travels and Explorations of the Jesuit Missionaries in New France, 1610–1791*, edited by Reuben Gold Thwaites. Burrows Brothers, Cleveland.

Johnson, E. S.

1993 "Some by Flatteries and Others by Threatenings": Political Strategies Among Native Americans of Seventeenth-Century Southern New England. Unpublished Ph.D. dissertation, Department of Anthropology, University of Massachusetts, Amherst.

1999 Community and Confederation: A Political Geography of Contact Period Southern New England. In *The Archaeological Northeast*, edited by M. A. Levine, K. E. Sassaman, and M. S. Nassaney, pp. 155–168. Bergin & Garvey, Westport, CT.

2000 The Politics of Pottery: Material Culture and Political Process among Algonquians of Seventeenth-Century Southern New England. In *Interpretations of Native North American Life: Material Contributions to Ethnohistory*, edited by M. S. Nassaney and E. S. Johnson, pp. 118–145. The Society for Historical Archaeology and the University Press of Florida, Gainesville.

Johnson, J. K.

1997 Stone Tools, Politics, and the Eighteenth Century Chickasaw in Northeast Mississippi. *American Antiquity* 62:215–230.

Johnson, L.

1978 A History of Flint-knapping Experimentation, 1838–1976. *Current Anthropology* 19:337–372.

Johnson, M. A.

1989 Conceptions of Agency in Archaeological Interpretation. *Journal of Anthropological Archaeology* 8:198–211.

1996 *An Archaeology of Capitalism*. Blackwell, Oxford.

Jorgensen, J. P.

1990 *Oil Age Eskimos*. University of California Press, Berkeley.

Juel-Jensen, H. J.

1994 *Flint Tools and Plant Working: Hidden Traces of Stone Age Technology*. Aarhus University Press, Denmark.

Kamakau, S.

1964 *Ka Po'e Kahiko: The People of Old*. Bernice P. Bishop Museum Special Publication No. 51. Bernice P. Bishop Museum, Honolulu.

Kay, M.

1996 Microwear Analysis of Some Clovis and Experimental Chipped Stone Tools. In *Stone Tools: Theoretical Insights into Human Prehistory*, edited by G. H. Odell, pp. 315–344. Plenum Press, New York.

Keeley, L. H.

1980 *Experimental Determination of Stone Tool Uses*. University of Chicago Press, Chicago.

Keeley, L. H., and M. H. Newcomer

1977 Microwear Analysis of Experimental Flint Tools: a Test Case. *Journal of Archaeological Science* 4:29–62.

Keesing, R. M.

1987 Anthropology as Interpretive Quest. *Current Anthropology* 28:161–176.

Kelly, R. L.

2002 Lithic Analysis: Stone Tools and Waste Flakes in Archaeology. In *Archaeology: Original Readings in Method and Practice*, edited by P. Peregrine, C. Ember, and M. Ember, pp. 48–61. Prentice Hall, Upper Saddle River, NJ.

King, J.

1967 Supplement to Cook's Journal. In *The Journals of Captain James Cook on His Voyages of Discovery*, edited by J. C. Beaglehole, 3:493–718. Cambridge University Press for the Hakluyt Society, Cambridge.

Kirch, P. V.

1972 Five Triangular Adzes from Haiku, Maui, Hawaiian Islands. *New Zealand Archaeological Association Newsletter* 15:140–143.

1992 *ANAHULU: The Anthropology of History in the Kingdom of Hawaii*. Vol. 2, The Archaeology of History. University of Chicago Press, Chicago.

2000 *On the Road of the Winds: An Archaeological History of the Pacific Islands Before European Contact*. University of California Press, Berkeley.

Klausner, S. Z., and E. F. Foulks

Eskimo Capitalists: Oil, Politics, and Alcohol. Allenheld, Osmun, Publishers, Totowa, NJ.

Knight, V. J., Jr.

1986 The Institutional Organization of Mississippian Religion. *American Antiquity* 51: 675–687.

Koldehoff, B.

1987 The Cahokia Flake Tool Industry: Socioeconomic Implications for Late Prehistory in the Central Mississippi Valley. In *The Organization of Core Technology*, edited by J. K. Johnson and C. A. Morrow, pp. 151–185. Westview Press, Boulder.

Koldehoff, B., and J. Seidel

1990 The Recent Discovery of a Tube Pipe and Filter. *Illinois Antiquity* 19:11–13.

Krenov, J.

1977 *The Fine Art of Cabinetmaking*. Van Nostrand, New York.

Kuykendall, R. S.

1938 *The Hawaiian Kingdom: 1778–1854*. University of Hawai'i, Honolulu.

Kvamme, K. L.

1997 Patterns and Models of Debitage Dispersal in Percussion Flaking. *Lithic Technology* 22:122–138.

Ladd, E. J.

1986 *Ki'ilae Village Test Excavations: Archeology at Pu'uhonua o Honaunau National Historical Park*. Publications in Anthropology No. 35. Western Archaeological and Conservation Center, Tucson.

Landes, R.

1970 *The Prairie Potawatomi: Tradition and Ritual in the Twentieth Century*. The University of Wisconsin Press, Madison.

Langford, J. B., Jr., and M. T. Smith

1990 Recent Investigations in the Core of the Coosa Province. In *Lamar Archaeology: Mississippian Chiefdoms in the Deep South*, edited by M. Williams and G. Shapiro, pp. 104–116. University of Alabama Press, Tuscaloosa.

Lass, B.

1994 *Hawaiian Adze Production and Distribution: Implications for the Development of Chiefdoms*. Monograph No. 37. Institute of Archaeology. University of California, Los Angeles.

1998 Crafts, Chiefs, and Commoners: Production and Control in Precontact Hawai'i. In *Craft and Social Identity*, edited by C. L. Costin and R. P. Wright, pp. 19–30.

Archaeological Papers No. 8. American Anthropological Association, Washington, D.C.

Lawrence, R. A.

1979 Experimental Evidence for the Significance of Attributes used in Edge Damage Analysis. In *Lithic Use-Wear Analysis*, edited by B. Hayden, pp. 113–121. Academic Press, New York.

Leach, H. M.

1993 The Role of Major Quarries in Polynesian Prehistory. In *The Evolution and Organisation of Prehistoric Society in Polynesia*, edited by M. W. Graves and R. C. Green, pp. 33–42. Monograph No. 19. New Zealand Archaeological Association, Auckland.

Leacock, E.

1972 Introduction. In *Origins of the Family, Private Property and the State*, by F. Engels, pp. 7–67. International Publishers, New York.

Leone, M. P.

1995 A Historical Archaeology of Capitalism. *American Anthropologist* 97:251–268.

Leone, M. P., Parker P. B., and P. A. Shackel

1987 Towards a Critical Archaeology. *Current Anthropology* 28:283–302.

Lewis, A.

1924 La Harpe's First Expedition in Oklahoma, 1718–1719. *Chronicles of Oklahoma* 2:331–349.

Libbey, D., and W. Schneider

Fur Trapping on Alaska's North Slope. In *Le Castor Fait Tout: Selected Papers of the Fifth North American Fur Trade Conference, 1985*, edited by B. G. Trigger, T. Morantz, and L. Dechene, pp. 335–358. Lake Saint Louis Historical Society, Montreal.

Lightfoot, K. G.

1995 Culture Contact Studies: Redefining the Relationship Between Prehistoric and Historical Archaeology. *American Antiquity* 60:199–217.

Lightfoot, K. G., and S. W. Silliman

1997 Chronology of Archaeological Deposits from the Fort Ross Beach and Native Alaskan Village Sites. In *The Archaeology and Ethnohistory of Fort Ross, Volume 2: The Native Alaskan Neighborhood, A Multiethnic Community at Colony Ross*, edited by K. Lightfoot, A. Schiff, and T. Wake, pp. 337–354. Contributions of the Archaeological Research Facility 55. University of California, Berkeley.

Lightfoot, K. G., A. Martinez, and A. M. Schiff

1998 Daily Practice and Material Culture in Pluralistic Social Settings: An Archaeological Study of Culture Change and Persistence from Fort Ross, California. *American Antiquity* 63:199–222.

Linnekin, J.

1990 *Sacred Queens and Women of Consequence: Rank, Gender, and Colonialism in the Hawaiian Islands*. The University of Michigan Press, Ann Arbor.

Loren, D. D. P.

1999 Creating Social Distinction: Articulating Colonial Policies and Practices Along the

Eighteenth-Century Louisiana/Texas Frontier. Unpublished Ph.D. dissertation, Department of Anthropology, State University of New York at Binghamton.

Lothrop, M. L.

1932 The Indian Campaigns of General M. G. Vallejo. *Quarterly, the Society of California Pioneers* 9(3):161–205.

Lyman, R. Lee

1987 Archaeofaunas and Butchery Studies: A Taphonomic Perspective. In *Advances in Archaeological Method and Theory*, Vol. 10, edited by M. B. Schiffer, pp. 249–337. Academic Press, San Diego.

McBrearty, S., L. Bishop, T. Plummer, R. Dewar, and N. Conard

1998 Tools Underfoot: Human Trampling as an Agent of Lithic Artifact Edge Modification. *American Antiquity* 63:108–131.

McCoy, I.

1840 *History of the Baptist Indian Missions.* William M. Morrison, Washington.

McCoy, P. C.

1990 Subsistence in a Non-Subsistence Environment: Factors of Production in a Hawaiian Alpine Desert Adze Quarry. In *Pacific Production Systems: Approaches to Economic Prehistory*, edited by D. E. Yen and J. M. M. Mummery. Occasional Papers in Prehistory No. 18. The Australian National University, Canberra.

Macdonald, G. A., A. T. Abbott, and F. L. Peterson

1983 *Volcanoes in the Sea: The Geology of Hawaii.* University of Hawai'i Press, Honolulu.

McGuire, J. D.

1899 Pipes and Smoking Customs of the American Aborigines, Based on Material in the U.S. National Museum. *Annual Report of the United States National Museum, 1896–97*, pp. 351–645. Washington, D.C.

McGuire, R. H.

1992 *A Marxist Archaeology.* Academic Press, San Diego.

McLean, E. A.

1980 *Abridged Inupiaq and English Dictionary.* University of Alaska Native Language Center, Barrow, North Slope Borough Iñupiat Language Commission, Fairbanks.

McMullen, A.

1986 Shantok Pots. Mohegan Woman and Power. Paper presented at the 3rd Annual symposium on Northeastern Aboriginal Ceramics. Peabody Museum, Yale University, New Haven.

1995 Post-Contact. Prepared for the National Archaeological Survey Initiative, System-wide Archaeological Inventory Program. Copies available from the National Museum of the American Indian, Suitland, MD.

MacNeish, R. S.

1952 The Archaeology of the Northeastern United States. In *Archaeology of Eastern United States*, edited by J. B. Griffin, pp. 46–58. University of Chicago Press, Chicago.

Malo, D.

1951 *Hawaiian Antiquities.* Bernice Bishop Museum Special Publication No. 2. Bernice P. Bishop Museum, Honolulu, Hawai'i.

Malone, P. M.

1991 *The Skulking Way of War: Technology and Tactics Among the Indians of Southern New England, 1600–1677.* Madison Books, Lanham, MD.

Margry, P. (editor)

1879–88 *Decouvertes et établissements des Francais dans 1'ouest et dans le sud de l'Amérique Septentrionale, 1614–1754.* Mémoires et Doucements Originaux. 6 vols. Jouest et Sigaux, Paris.

Mason, R. J.

1986 Rock Island: Historical Archaeology in the Northern Lake Michigan Basin. *Midcontinental Journal of Anthropology Special Paper No. 6.* Kent State University Press, Ohio.

Mathieu, J. R., and D. A. Meyer

1997 Comparing Axe Heads of Stone, Bronze, and Steel: Studies in Experimental Archaeology. *Journal of Field Archaeology* 24:333–351.

Mauldin, R. P., and D. S. Amick

1989 Investigating Patterning in Debitage from Experimental Bifacial Core Reduction. In *Experiments in Lithic Technology,* edited by D. S. Amick and R. P. Mauldin, pp. 67–88. International Series 528. British Archaeological Reports, Oxford.

Miller, C., and G. Hamell

1986 A New Perspective on Indian-White Contact: Cultural Symbols and Colonial Trade. *Journal of American History* 73:311–328.

Milner, G. R., C. S. Larsen, D. L. Hutchingson, M. A. Williamson, and D. A. Humpf

2000 Conquistadors, Excavators, or Rodents: What Damaged the King Site Skeletons? *American Antiquity* 65:355–363.

Miroir, M. P., R. King Harris, J. C. Blaine, and J. McVay

1973 Bénard de la Harpe and the Nassonite Post. *Bulletin of the Texas Archaeological Society* 44:113–167.

Moore, J. L.

1992 Spanish Colonial Stone Tool Use. In *Current Research on the Late Prehistory and Early History of New Mexico,* edited by B. Vierra, pp. 239–244. Special Publication 1. New Mexico Archaeological Council, Albuquerque.

Morgan, L. H.

1851 *League of the Ho-De'-No-Sau-Nee, Iroquois.* Sage Brothers, New York and Boston.

Morrow, T. A.

1997 A Chip Off the Old Block: Alternative Approaches to Debitage Analysis. *Lithic Technology* 22:51–69.

Morse, D. F., and P. A. Morse

1983 *Archaeology of the Central Mississippi Valley.* Academic Press, San Diego.

1990 The Spanish Exploration of Arkansas. In *Columbian Consequences: Archaeological and Historical Perspectives on the Spanish Borderlands East,* edited by D. H. Thomas, pp. 197–210. Smithsonian Institution Press, Washington, D.C.

Muller, V.

1985 Origins of Class and Gender Hierarchy in Northwest Europe. *Dialectical Anthropology* 10:93–105.

Murdoch, J.

1892 Ethnological Results of the Point Barrow Expedition. *9th Annual Report of the Bureau of American Ethnology for the Years 1887–1888*, pp. 19–441. U.S. Government Printing Office, Washington, D.C.

Nassaney, M. S.

1989 An Epistemological Enquiry into Some Archaeological and Historical Interpretations of Seventeenth Century Native American-European Relations. In *Archaeological Approaches to Cultural Identity*, edited by S. J. Shennan, pp. 76–93. Unwin Hyman, London.

1996 The Role of Chipped Stone in the Political Economy of Social Ranking. In *Stone Tools: Theoretical Insights into Human Prehistory*, edited by G. H. Odell, pp. 181–224. Plenum Press, New York.

2000 Archaeology and Oral Tradition in Tandem: Interpreting Native American Ritual, Ideology, and Gender Relations in Contact-Period Southeastern New England. In *Interpretations of Native North American Life: Material Contributions to Ethnohistory*, edited by M. S. Nassaney and E. S. Johnson, pp. 412–431. The Society for Historical Archaeology and the University Press of Florida, Gainesville.

2001 Men and Women, Pipes and Power in Native New England. Paper presented at the 66th Annual Meeting of the Society for American Archaeology, New Orleans.

2002 *The Material Lives of Native Men and Women in Seventeenth-Century Southeastern New England*. Copies available from the John Nicholas Brown Center for the Study of American Civilization, Brown University, Providence.

Nelson, E. W.

The Eskimo About Bering Strait. *18th Annual Report of the Bureau of American Ethnography for the Years 1896–1897*, pp. 3–518. U.S. Government Printing Office, Washington, D.C.

Newcomb, W. W., and W. T. Field

1967 An Ethnohistoric Investigation of the Wichita Indians in the Southern Plains. In *A Pilot Study of Wichita Indian Archeology and Ethnohistory*, assembled by R. Bell, E. Jelks, and W. Newcomb, pp. 240–354. National Science Foundation, Washington, D.C.

Odell, G. H.

1975 Micro-wear in Perspective: A Sympathetic Response to Lawrence H. Keeley. *World Archaeology* 7:226–240.

1981 The Morphological Express at Function Junction: Searching for Meaning in Lithic Tool Types. *Journal of Anthropological Research* 37:319–342.

1992 Bewitched by Mechanical Site Testing Devices. *American Antiquity* 57:692–703.

1996 *Stone Tools and Mobility in the Illinois Valley: from Hunting-Gathering Camps to Agricultural Villages*. International Monographs in Prehistory, Ann Arbor, MI.

1998 The Protohistoric Period in Eastern Oklahoma: Evidence from the Lasley Vore Site. *Bulletin of the Oklahoma Anthropological Society* 47:83–117.

1999 The Organization of Labor at a Protohistoric Settlement in Oklahoma. *Journal of Field Archaeology* 26:407–421.

2001 The Use of Metal at a Wichita Contact Settlement. *Southeastern Archaeology* 20: 173–186.

2002 *La Harpe's Post: A Tale of French-Wichita Contact on the Eastern Plains*. University of Alabama Press, Tuscaloosa.

Odell, G. H., and F. Odell-Vereecken

1980 Verifying the Reliability of Lithic Use-Wear Assessments by 'Blind Tests': the Low Power Approach. *Journal of Field Archaeology* 7:87–120.

Odell, G. H., J. C. Dixon, K. E. Dickerson, and K. L. Shingleton, Jr.

1990 *An Archaeological Investigation of the Arkansas River Bluffline between Jenks and Bixby, Eastern Oklahoma*. Contributions in Archaeology, No. 17. Department of Anthropology, University of Tulsa.

Olson, L. G.

1983 Hawaiian Volcanic Glass Applied "Dating" and "Sourcing": Archaeological Context. In *Archaeological Investigations of the Mudlane-Waimea-Kawaihae Road Corridor, Island of Hawai'i: An Interdisciplinary Study of an Environmental Transect*, edited by J. T. Clark and P. V. Kirch, pp. 325–340. Department of Anthropology Report Series No. 83–1. Bernice P. Bishop Museum, Honolulu.

Orser, C. E., Jr.

1996 *A Historical Archaeology of the Modern World*. Plenum Press, New York.

Otto, M. P.

1992 A Prehistoric Menagerie: Ohio Hopewell Effigy Pipes. In *Proceedings of the 1989 Smoking Pipe Conference: Selected Papers*, edited by C. F. Hayes III, pp. 1–13. Research Records No. 22. Rochester Museum & Science Center, Rochester, New York.

Parry, W. J., and R. L. Kelly

1987 Expedient Core Technology and Sedentism. In *The Organization of Core Technology*, edited by J. Johnson and C. Morrow, pp. 285–304. Westview Press, Boulder.

Paynter, R.

1988 Steps to an Archeology of Capitalism. In *The Recovery of Meaning: Historical Archaeology of the Eastern United States*, edited by M. P. Leone and P. B. Potter, Jr., pp. 407–433. Smithsonian Institution Press, Washington, D.C.

Pohlemus, R. R.

1990 Dallas Phase Architecture and Sociopolitical Structure. In *Lamar Archaeology: Mississippian Chiefdoms in the Deep South*, edited by M. Williams and G. Shapiro, pp. 125–138. University of Alabama Press, Tuscaloosa.

Portlock, N.

1789 *A Voyage Around the World; But More Particularly to the North-West Coast of America: Performed in 1785, 1786, and 1788*. Stockdale and Goulding, London.

Powers, H. A.

1939 *Hawaiian Adz Materials in the Haleakala Section of Hawaii National Park*. Proceedings of the Hawaiian Academy of Science 14th Annual Meeting, 1938–39. Bernice P. Bishop Museum Special Publication No. 34. Bishop Museum Press, Honolulu.

Pratt, P.

1976 *Archaeology of the Oneida Iroquois Vol. 1.* Occasional Publications in Northeastern Anthropology No. 1. Man in the Northeast, Georges Mill, NH.

1983 Glass Trade Beads Among the Iroquois: A Perspective. *Proceedings of the 1982 Glass Trade Bead Conference*, edited by C. F. Hayes, III, pp. 213–217. Research Records No. 16. Rochester Museum and Science Center, Rochester, New York.

Puikui, M. K.

1939 *The Canoe Making Profession in Ancient Times.* Papers No. 20. Hawaiian Historical Society, Honolulu.

Quimby, G. I.

1966 *Indian Culture and European Trade Goods.* University of Wisconsin Press, Milwaukee.

Rafferty, S. M.

2001 "They Pass Their Lives in Smoke, and at Death, Fall into the Fire": Smoking Pipes and Mortuary Ritual During the Early Woodland Period. Unpublished Ph.D. dissertation, Department of Anthropology, State University of New York at Binghamton.

Ramenofsky, A. F.

1987 *Vectors of Death: the Archaeology of European Contact.* University of New Mexico Press, Albuquerque.

1998 Evolutionary Theory and the Native American Record of Artifact Replacement. In *Studies in Culture Contact: Interaction, Culture Change, and Archaeology*, edited by J. G. Cusick, pp. 77–101. Occasional Paper no. 25. Center for Archaeological Investigations, Southern Illinois University at Carbondale.

Rawls, J.

1984 *Indians of California: The Changing Image.* University of Oklahoma Press, Norman.

Resnick, S., and R. Wolff

1987 *Knowledge and Class.* University of Chicago Press, Chicago.

Rice, P.

1998 Contexts of Contact and Change: Peripheries, Frontiers, and Boundaries. In *Studies in Culture Contact: Interaction, Culture Change, and Archaeology*, edited by J. G. Cusick, pp. 44–66. Occasional Paper No. 25. Center for Archaeological Investigations, Southern Illinois University at Carbondale.

Richter, D. K.

1992 *The Ordeal of the Longhouse: Peoples of the Iroquois League in the Era of European Colonization.* University of North Carolina Press, Chapel Hill.

Riconda, D.

1972 Historical Archaeology of Makaha Valley: A Preliminary Report. In *Makaha Valley Historical Project Interim Report No. 3*, edited by E. J. Ladd and D. E. Yen, pp. 3–21. Pacific Anthropological Records No. 18. Bernice P. Bishop Museum, Hawai'i.

Ritzenthaler, R.

1953 The Potawatomi Indians of Wisconsin. *Bulletin of the Public Museum of the City of Milwaukee* 19:99–174.

Robinson, A.

1891 *Life in California During a Residence of Several Years in That Territory*. William Doxey, San Francisco.

Robinson, P. A.

1990 The Struggle Within: The Indian Debate in Seventeenth Century Narragansett Country. Unpublished Ph.D. dissertation, Department of Anthropology, State University of New York at Binghamton.

Robinson, P. A., M. A. Kelley, and P. E. Rubertone

1985 Preliminary Biocultural Interpretations from a Seventeenth-Century Narragansett Indian Cemetery in Rhode Island. In *Cultures in Contact*, edited by W. W. Fitzhugh, pp. 107–130. Smithsonian Institution Press, Washington, D.C.

Rogers, J. D.

1990 *Objects of Change: The Archaeology and History of Arikara Contact with Europeans*. Smithsonian Institution Press, Washington, D.C.

1993 The Social and Material Implications of Culture Contact on the Northern Plains. In *Ethnohistory and Archaeology: Approaches to Postcontact Change in the Americas*, edited by J. D. Rogers and S. M. Wilson, pp. 73–88. Plenum Press, New York.

Rogers, J. D., and S. Wilson (editors)

1993 *Ethnohistory and Archaeology: Approaches to Postcontact Change in the Americas*. Plenum Press, New York.

Rohn, A. H., and A. M. Emerson

1984 *Great Bend Sites at Marion, Kansas*. Publications in Anthropology, No. 1. Department of Anthropology, Wichita State University, Wichita, Kansas.

Rosen, S. A.

1996 The Decline and Fall of Flint. In *Stone Tools: Theoretical Insights in Human Prehistory*, edited by G. H. Odell, pp. 129–158. Plenum Press, New York.

1997 *Lithics after the Stone Age: A Handbook of Stone Tools from the Levant*. Altamira Press, Walnut Creek, CA.

Rowlandson, M.

1953 [1682] *The Narrative of the Captivity and Restoration of Mrs. Mary Rowlandson*. 1953 Lancaster Tercentenary. Ed. Chapman Billies, Sandwich, Massachusetts.

Rubertone, P. E.

2001 *Grave Undertakings: An Archaeology of Roger Williams and the Narragansett Indians*. Smithsonian Institution Press, Washington, D.C.

Ruggiero, D. A.

2000 Lithics in a Household Context: An Examination of Lithic Reduction, Tools and Activity Areas in a King Site (9FL5) House. Unpublished M.A. thesis, Department of Anthropology, State University of New York at Binghamton.

Sacks, K.

1974 Engels Revisited: Women, the Organization of Production, and Private Property. In *Woman, Culture, and Society*, edited by M. Z. Rosaldo and L. Lamphere, pp. 207–222. Stanford University Press, Stanford.

Sahlins, M. D.

1981 *Historical Metaphors and Mythical Realities: Structure in the Early History of the*

Sandwich Islands Kingdom. ASAO Special Publications No. 1. University of Michigan Press, Ann Arbor.

1990 The Political Economy of Grandeur in Hawaii from 1820 to 1830. In *Culture Through Time: Anthropological Approaches*, edited by E. Ohnuki-Tierney, pp. 26–56. Stanford University Press, Stanford.

1992 *ANAHULU: The Anthropology of History in the Kingdom of Hawaii*, Vol. No. 1, *Historical Ethnography*. University of Chicago Press, Chicago.

Saitta, D. J.

1994 Agency, Class, and Archaeological Interpretation. *Journal of Anthropological Archaeology* 13:201–227.

Salisbury, N.

1982 *Manitou and Providence: Indians, Europeans, and the Making of New England, 1500–1643*. Oxford University Press, New York.

Salisbury, R. F.

1962 *From Stone to Steel: Economic Consequences of a Technological Change in New Guinea*. Cambridge University Press, London.

Sanchez, N. V. de Grift

1929 *Spanish Arcadia*. Powell, San Francisco.

Saraydar, S., and I. Shimada

1971 A Quantitative Comparison of Efficiency Between a Stone Axe and a Steel Axe. *American Antiquity* 36:216–217.

Sassaman, K. E.

1999 A Southeastern Perspective on Soapstone Vessel Technology in the Northeast. In *The Archaeological Northeast*, edited by M. A. Levine, K. E. Sassaman, and M. S. Nassaney, pp. 75–95. Bergin & Garvey, Westport, CT.

Scarry, J. F.

1990 Beyond Apalachee Province: Assessing the Evidence for Early European-Indian Contact in Northwest Florida. In *Columbian Consequences: Archaeological and Historical Perspectives on the Spanish Borderlands East*, edited by D. H. Thomas, pp. 93–105. Smithsonian Institution Press, Washington, D.C.

Schiff, A. M.

1997 Lithic Assemblage at the Fort Ross Beach and Native Alaskan Village Sites. In *The Archaeology and Ethnohistory of Fort Ross, Volume 2: The Native Alaskan Neighborhood, A Multiethnic Community at Colony Ross*, edited by K. Lightfoot, A. Schiff, and T. Wake, pp. 213–237. Contributions of the Archaeological Research Facility, 55. Archaeological Research Facility, University of California, Berkeley.

Seckinger, E. W., Jr.

1972 Social Complexity During the Mississippian Period in Northwest Georgia. Unpublished M.A. thesis, Department of Anthropology, University of Georgia, Athens.

Secoy, F.

Changing Military Patterns on the Great Plains. American Ethnological Society Monograph 21. J. J. Augustin, New York.

Seeman, M. F.

1984 Craft Specialization and Tool Kit Structure: A Systemic Perspective on the Midcontinental Flint Knapper. In *Lithic Resource Procurement: Proceedings from the Second Conference on Prehistoric Chert Exploitation*, edited by S. C. Vehik, pp. 7–36. Occasional Paper No. 4. Center for Archaeological Investigations, Southern Illinois University at Carbondale.

Shackel, P. A.

1993 *Personal Discipline and Material Culture: An Archaeology of Annapolis, Maryland, 1695–1870*. University of Tennessee Press, Knoxville.

Sharp, L.

1952 Steel Axes for Stone Age Australians. In *Human Problems in Technological Change: A Casebook*, edited by E. H. Spicer, pp. 69–81. Russell Sage Foundation, New York.

Shoemaker, N. (editor)

1995 *Negotiators of Change: Historical Perspectives on Native American Women*. Routledge, New York.

Shott, M. J.

1994 Size and Form in the Analysis of Flake Debris: Review and Recent Approaches. *Journal of Archaeological Method and Theory* 1:69–110.

Silliman, S.

1997 European Origins and Native destinations: Historical Artifacts from the Native Alaskan Village and Fort Ross Beach Sites. In *The Archaeology and Ethnohistory of Fort Ross, Volume 2: The Native Alaskan Neighborhood, A Multiethnic Community at Colony Ross*, edited by Kent Lightfoot, Ann Schiff, and Thomas Wake, pp. 136–178. Contributions of the Archaeological Research Facility 55. Berkeley: Archaeological Research Facility, University of California.

1998 An Investigation of Native California Indian Labor at the Mexican Rancho. *Proceedings of the Society for California Archaeology* 11:37–42.

1999 *Beneath Historic Floors: Archaeological Investigations of the Petaluma Adobe Seismic Retrofit Project*. Submitted to California Department of Parks and Recreation, Sacramento. Copies available from California Department of Parks and Recreation, Sacramento.

2000a *Colonial Worlds, Indigenous Practices: The Archaeology of Labor on a Nineteenth-Century California Rancho*. Ph.D. dissertation, Department of Anthropology, University of California, Berkeley. University Microfilms, Ann Arbor.

2000b Obsidian Studies in the Archaeology of Nineteenth-Century California. *Society for California Archaeology Newsletter* 34(1):1, 26–29.

2001 Agency, Practical Politics, and the Archaeology of Culture Contact. *Journal of Social Archaeology* 1:184–203.

2002 Archaeological Obsidian Studies and the Historic Period: Insights and Implications from Northern California. Manuscript on file at Department of Anthropology, University of Massachusetts, Boston.

Simmons, W. S.

1970 *Cautantowwit's House: An Indian Burial Ground on the Island of Conanicut in Narragansett Bay*. Brown University Press, Providence.

1978 Narragansett. In *Handbook of North American Indians, Vol. 15, The Northeast,* edited by B. G. Trigger, pp. 190–197. Smithsonian Institution Press, Washington, D.C.

1986 *Spirit of the New England Tribes: Indian History and Folklore, 1620–1984*. University Press of New England, Hanover.

Sinton, J. M., and Y. H. Sinoto

1997 A Geochemical Database for Polynesian Adze Studies. In *Prehistoric Long-Distance Interaction in Oceania: An Interdisciplinary Approach*, edited by M. I. Weisler, pp. 194–204. New Zealand Archaeological Association Monograph No. 21.

Skinner, A.

1926 The Mascoutens or Prairie Potawatomi Indians. *Bulletin of the Public Museum of the City of Milwaukee* 6(2):263–326.

Smith, F. T.

2000 *The Wichita Indians: Traders of Texas and the Southern Plains, 1540–1845*. Texas A&M University Press, College Station.

Smith, M. T.

1975 European Materials from the King Site. *Southeastern Archaeological Conference Bulletin* 18:63–66.

1987 *Archaeology of Aboriginal Culture Change in the Interior Southeast: Depopulation during the Early Historic Period*. University Press of Florida, Gainesville.

2000 *Coosa: The Rise and Fall of a Mississippian Chiefdom*. University Press of Florida, Gainesville.

Smith, R. A.

1958–59 Account of the Journey of Bénard de la Harpe: Discovery Made by Him of Several Nations Situated in the West. *Southwestern Historical Quarterly* 62:246–259, 371–385, 525–541.

Snow, D. R.

1992 Disease and Population Decline in the Northeast. In *Disease and Demography in the Americas*, edited by J. W. Verano and D. H. Ubelaker, pp. 177–186. Smithsonian Institution Press, Washington D.C.

1994 *The Iroquois*. Blackwell, Cambridge.

1995 Migration in Prehistory: The Northern Iroquoian Case. *American Antiquity* 60: 59–79.

Spear, R. L.

1987 *Archaeological Data Recovery, Pu'ueo Agricultural Lots, Land of Pu'ueo, Ka'ū, Island of Hawai'i*. Submitted to R. M. Towill Corporation. Copies available from Hawaii State Historic Preservation Division Office, Honlulu.

Spinden, H. J.

1950 *Tobacco is American*. New York Public Library, New York.

Spurrell, F.

1883 Paleolithic Knapping Tools and Modes of Using Them. *Journal of the Royal Anthropological Institute* 13:109–118.

Stahl, A. B.

2001 *Making History in Banda. Anthropological Visions of Africa's Past*. Cambridge University Press, Cambridge.

Stannard, D.

1989 *Before the Horror: The Population of Hawai'i on the Eve of Western Contact*. Social Science Research Institute, University of Hawai'i, Honolulu.

Stefansson, V.

1922 *My Life with the Eskimo*. MacMillan, New York.

Stevenson, C. H.

Whalebone: Its Production and Utilization. Bureau of Fisheries Document No. 626. U.S. Government Printing Office, Washington, D.C.

Stoler, A. L.

1989 Rethinking Colonial Categories: European Communities and the Boundaries of Rule. *Comparative Studies in Society and History* 13(1):134–161.

Stoler, A. L., and F. Cooper

1997 Between Metropole and Colony: Rethinking a Research Agenda. In *Tensions of Empire: Colonial Cultures in a Bourgeois World*, edited by F. Cooper and A. L. Stoler, pp. 1–56. University of California Press, Berkeley.

Sudbury, B.

1975 Ka-3, the Deer Creek Site, an Eighteenth Century French Contact Site. *Bulletin of the Oklahoma Anthropological Society* 24:1–135.

Sugden, J.

1997 *Tecumseh*. Henry Holt and Company, New York.

2000 *Blue Jacket*. University of Nebraska Press, Lincoln.

Sullivan, III, A. P., and K. C. Rozen

1985 Debitage Analysis and Archaeological Interpretation. *American Antiquity* 50: 755–779.

Summers, C. C.

1999 *Material Culture: The J. S. Emerson Collection of Hawaiian Artifacts*. Bernice P. Bishop Museum Press, Honolulu.

Swanton, J. R.

1922 *Early History of the Creek Indians and Their Neighbors*. Bureau of American Ethnology Bulletin No. 73. Smithsonian Institution, Washington, D.C.

1928 Religious Beliefs and Medical Practices of the Creek Indians. *Bureau of American Ethnology, Annual Report* 42:473–672. Smithsonian Institution, Washington, D.C.

Tanner, H. H. (editor)

1987 *Atlas of Great Lakes Indian History*. University of Oklahoma Press, Norman.

Tays, G.

1937 Mariano Guadalupe Vallejo and Sonoma: A Biography and a History. *California Historical Society Quarterly* 16:99–121, 216–254, 348–372.

Teltser, P. A.

1991 Generalized Core Technology and Tool Use: A Mississippian Example. *Journal of Field Archaeology* 18:363–375.

Temple, W.

1975 Atlas Supplement, Indian Villages of the Illinois Country. *Illinois State Museum Scientific Papers, Vol. II, Pt. 1*. Illinois State Museum, Springfield.

Thomas, L. A.

2000 Images of Women in Native American Iconography. In *Interpretations of Native North American Life: Material Contributions to Ethnohistory*, edited by M. S. Nassaney and E. S. Johnson, pp. 321–357. Society for Historical Archaeology and the University Press of Florida, Gainesville.

Thorbahn, P. F.

1988 Where Are the Late Woodland Villages in Southern New England? *Bulletin of the Massachusetts Archaeological Society* 49(2):46–57.

Tomka, S. A.

1989 Differentiating Lithic Reduction Techniques: An Experimental Approach. In *Experiments in Lithic Technology*, edited by D. S. Amick and R. P. Mauldin, pp. 137–161. International Series 528. British Archaeological Reports, Oxford.

Townsend, W. H.

1969 Stone and Steel Tool Use in a New Guinea Society. *Ethnology* 8:199–205.

Trigger, B.

1978 Northern Iroquoian Contacts with Europeans. In *Handbook of North American Indians*, edited by W. C. Sturtevant, pp. 344–356. Smithsonian Institution Press, Washington D.C.

Trigger, B., and W. R. Swagerty

1996 Entertaining Strangers: North Americans in the Sixteenth Century. In *The Cambridge History of the Native Peoples of the Americas, Vol. 1, Pt. 1*, edited by B. G. Trigger and W. E. Washburn, pp. 325–398. Cambridge University Press, NY.

Tringham, R., G. Cooper, G. Odell, B. Voytek, and A. Whitman

1974 Experimentation in the Formation of Edge Damage: A New Approach to Lithic Analysis. *Journal of Field Archaeology* 1:171–195.

Trubowitz, N. L.

1992 Thanks, But We Prefer to Smoke Our Own: Pipes in the Great Lakes-Riverine Region During the Eighteenth Century. In *Proceedings of the 1989 Smoking Pipe Conference: Selected Papers*, edited by C. F. Hayes III, pp. 97–111. Research Records No. 22. Rochester Museum & Science Center, Rochester, New York.

1994 *Understanding Trade in the Colombian Exchange: Archaeological Models from the Southeast and Midwest*. Paper presented at the joint meeting of the Southeastern Archaeological Conference and Midwest Archaeological Conference, Lexington, Kentucky.

Trumbull, J. H. (editor)

1866 *A Key into the Language of America*, by Roger Williams [1643]. Publications of the Narragansett Club, 1st series 1:31–282. Providence.

Tuck, J. A.

1971 *Onondaga Iroquois Prehistory*. Syracuse University Press, Syracuse.

1978 Northern Iroquoian Prehistory. In *Handbook of North American Indians*, edited by W. C. Sturtevant, pp. 344–356. Smithsonian Institution Press, Washington, D.C.

Tucker, S. J.

1942 Atlas, Indian Villages of the Illinois Country. *Illinois State Museum Scientific Papers, Vol. II, Pt. 1*. Illinois State Museum, Springfield.

Tuma, S. J., Jr.

1985 *Contact Period (1500–1675) Burials in Southern New England.* Unpublished M.A. thesis, History and Historical Archaeology Program, University of Massachusetts, Boston.

Turnbaugh, W. A.

1975 Tobacco, Pipes, Smoking and Rituals Among the Indians of the Northeast. *Quarterly Bulletin of the Archaeological Society of Virginia* 30(2):59–71.

1976 The Survival of a Native Craft in Colonial Rhode Island. *Man in the Northeast* 11:74–79.

1977 Elements of Nativistic Pipe Ceremonialism in the Post-Contact Northeast. *Pennsylvania Archaeologist* 47(4):1–7.

1980 Native American Smoking Pipes. *Archaeology* 33(1):15–22.

1984 *The Material Culture of RI-1000, A Mid–Nineteenth-Century Narragansett Indian Burial Site in North Kingstown, Rhode Island.* Department of Sociology and Anthropology, University of Rhode Island, Kingston, Rhode Island.

1992 Post-Contact Smoking Pipe Development: The Narragansett Example. In *Proceedings of the 1989 Smoking Pipe Conference: Selected Papers*, edited by C. F. Hayes III, pp. 113–124. Research Records No. 22. Rochester Museum & Science Center, Rochester, NY.

1993 Assessing the Significance of European Goods in Seventeenth Century Narragansett Society. In *Ethnohistory and Archaeology: Approaches to Postcontact Change in the Americas*, edited by J. D. Rogers and S. M. Wilson, pp. 133–160. Plenum Press, New York.

van den Bogart, H. M.

1988 The Journal of Harmen Meyndertsz van den Bogart. In *A Journey into Mohawk and Oneida Country, 1634–1635*, edited by C. T. Gehring and W. A. Starna. Syracuse University Press, Syracuse.

Vaughan, P. C.

1985 *Use-Wear Analysis of Flaked Stone Tools.* University of Arizona Press, Tucson.

Vehik, S. C.

1992 Wichita Culture History. *Plains Anthropologist* 37:311–332.

1994 Cultural Continuity and Discontinuity in the Southern Prairies and Cross Timbers. In *Plains Indians,* AD *500–1500: The Archaeological Past of Historic Groups*, edited by K. Schlesier, pp. 239–263. University of Oklahoma Press, Norman.

Villiers du Terrage, B. M. de

1934 *An Explorer of Louisiana: Jean-Baptiste Bénard de La Harpe (1683–1765).* Translated by Samuel Dorris Dickinson. Imprimeries Oberthur, Rennes.

Volmar, M. A.

1992 The Conundrum of Effigy Pestles. Unpublished M.A. thesis, Department of Anthropology, University of Massachusetts, Amherst.

1998 The Micromorphology of Landscapes: An Archaeological Approach in Southern New England. Unpublished Ph.D. dissertation, Department of Anthropology, University of Massachusetts, Amherst.

von Gernet, A. D.

2000 North American Indigenous Nicotiana Use and Tobacco Use and Tobacco Shamanism: The Early Documentary Record, 1520–1660. In *Tobacco Use by Native Americas: Sacred Smoke and Silent Killer*, edited by J. C. Winter, pp. 59–80. University of Oklahoma Press, Norman.

Wagner, G.

2000 Tobacco in Prehistoric Eastern North America. In *Tobacco Use by Native North Americans*, edited by J. C. Winter, pp. 185–201. University of Oklahoma Press, Norman.

Wagner, M. J.

1998 Some Think It Impossible to Civilize Them at All: Cultural Change and Continuity Among the Early Nineteenth-Century Potawatomi of Northeastern Illinois. In *Studies in Culture Contact: Interaction, Culture Change, and Archaeology*, edited by James G. Cusick, pp. 430–456. Occasional Paper No. 25. Center for Archaeological Investigations, Southern Illinois University at Carbondale.

2001 The Windrose Site (11Ka336): An Early Nineteenth Century Potawatomi Settlement in the Kankakee River Valley of Northeastern Illinois. *Report of Investigations No.* 36. Illinois State Museum, Springfield, Illinois.

Wallace, A. F. C.

1969 *The Death and Rebirth of the Seneca*. Vintage Books, New York.

Wallace, W. J., and E. T. Wallace

1958 Indian Artifacts from the Hugo Reid Adobe. *Lasca Leaves* 8(4):74–80.

Wallerstein, I.

1974 *The Modern World-System I: Capitalist Agriculture and the Origins of the European World-Economy in the Sixteenth Century*. Academic Press, New York.

1980 *The Modern World-System II: Mercantilism and the Consolidation of the European World-Economy, 1600–1750*. Academic Press, New York.

Warren, S.

1923 Subsoil Pressure Flaking. *Proceedings of the Geologists' Association* 34:153–175.

Waselkov, G. A.

1989 Seventeenth-Century Trade in the Colonial Southeast. *Southeast Archaeology* 8:117–133.

Wedel, M. M.

1971 J.-B. Bénard, Sieur de La Harpe: Visitor to the Wichitas in 1719. *Great Plains Journal* 10:37–70.

1978 *La Harpe's 1719 Post on Red River and Nearby Caddo Settlements*. Bull. 30. Texas Memorial Museum, Austin.

1981 *The Deer Creek Site, Oklahoma: A Wichita Village Sometimes Called Ferdinandina, an Ethnohistorian's View*. Series in Anthropology No. 5. Oklahoma Historical Society, Oklahoma City.

1982 The Wichita Indians in the Arkansas Basin. In *Plains Indian Studies*, edited by D. Ubelaker and H. Viola, pp. 118–134. Smithsonian Institution Press, Washington, D.C.

Wedel, W. R.

1959 *An Introduction to Kansas Archeology*. Smithsonian Institution, Bureau of American Ethnology, Bulletin 174.

Weisler, M. I.

1990 A Technological, Petrographic, and Geochemical Analysis of the Kapohaku Adze Quarry, Lana'i, Hawaiian Islands. *New Zealand Journal of Archaeology* 12:29–50.

Weisler, M. I., and J. Sinton

1997 Towards Identifying Prehistoric Exchange Systems in Polynesia. In *Prehistoric Long-Distance Interaction in Oceania: An Interdisciplinary Approach*, edited by M. I. Weisler, pp. 173–194. New Zealand Archaeological Association Monograph No. 21.

Welch, P. D.

1991 *Moundville's Economy*. University of Alabama Press, Tuscaloosa.

Wells, P. S.

1991 Metal and Meaning. In *Metals in Society: Theory Beyond Analysis*, edited by R. M. Ehrenreich, pp. 89–92. MASCA Research Papers in Science and Anthropology Vol. 8, Pt. II, University of Pennsylvania, Philadelphia.

1998 Culture Contact, Identity, and Change in the European Provinces of the Roman Empire. In *Studies in Culture Contact: Interaction, Culture Change, and Archaeology*, edited by J. G. Cusick, pp. 316–334. Occasional Papers No. 25. Center for Archaeological Investigations, Southern Illinois University at Carbondale.

West, G. A.

1934 Tobacco, Pipes, and Smoking Customs of the American Indians. *Bulletin of the Public Museum of Milwaukee* 17:1–994.

Wheeler-Voegelin, E.

1974 *Anthropological Report on the Ottawa, Chippewa, and Potawatomi Indians*. Garland, New York.

White, R.

1991 *The Middle Ground: Indians, Empires, and Republics in the Great Lakes Region, 1650–1815*. Cambridge University Press, Cambridge.

Whittaker, J. C.

1994 *Flintknapping: Making and Understanding Stone Tools*. University of Texas Press, Austin.

Whittaker, J. C., and L. Fratt

1984 Continuity and Change in Stone Tools at Mission Tumacacori, Arizona. *Lithic Technology* 13:11–19.

Wilbur, C. K.

1978 *The New England Indians*. Globe Pequot Press, Chester, CT.

Williams, M., and G. Shapiro (editors)

1990 *Lamar Archaeology: Mississippian Chiefdoms in the Deep South*. University of Alabama Press, Tuscaloosa.

Williams, M. B., and J. Bendremer

1997 The Archaeology of Maize, Pots, and Seashells: Gender Dynamics in Late Woodland and Contact-Period New England. In *Women in Prehistory: North America and Mesoamerica*, edited by C. Claassen and R. A. Joyce, pp. 136–149. University of Pennsylvania Press, Philadelphia.

Williams, R.

1973 *A Key into the Language of America*, edited by J. J. Teunissen and E. J. Hinz. Wayne State University Press, Detroit.

Williams, S., and J. P. Brain

1983 *Excavations at the Lake George Site, Yazoo County, Mississippi, 1958–1960*. Papers of the Peabody Museum of Archaeology and Ethnology 74. Harvard University, Cambridge.

Willoughby, C. C.

1973 *Antiquities of the New England Indians with Note on the Ancient Cultures of the Adjacent Territory*. Peabody Museum of Archaeology and Ethnology, Harvard University, Cambridge, Massachusetts.

Winter, J. C.

2000a Botanical Description of the North American Tobacco Species. In *Tobacco Use by Native Americans: Sacred Smoke and Silent Killer*, edited by J. C. Winter, pp. 87–127. University of Oklahoma Press, Norman.

2000b Traditional Use of Tobacco by Native Americans. In *Tobacco Use by Native North Americans*, edited by J. C. Winter, pp. 9–58. University of Oklahoma Press, Norman.

2000c Food of the Gods: Biochemistry, Addiction, and the Development of Native American Tobacco Use. In *Tobacco Use by Native North Americans*, edited by J. C. Winter, pp. 305–328. University of Oklahoma Press, Norman.

Winter, J. C. (editor)

2000d *Tobacco Use by Native North Americans*. University of Oklahoma Press, Norman.

Winters, H. D.

1969 The Riverton Culture: A Second Millennium Occupation in the Central Wabash River Valley. *Illinois State Museum Report of Investigations* 13. Springfield, Illinois.

Witthoft, J.

1966 A History of Gunflints. *Pennsylvania Archaeologist* 36:12–49.

Wolf, E. R.

1982 *Europe and the People Without History*. University of California Press, Berkeley.

Wonderley, A.

2002 Oneida Ceramic Effigies: A Question of Meaning. *Northeast Anthropology* 63:23–48.

Wood, W.

1977 [1634] *New England's Prospect*. University of Massachusetts Press, Amherst.

Worthen, A. H.

1883 *Geological Survey of Illinois, Vol. VII*. H. W. Rokker, Springfield, Illinois.

Wray, C., M. L. Sempowski, and L. P. Saunders

1991 *Tram and Cameron: Two Early Contact Era Seneca Sites*. Research Records No. 21. Rochester Museum and Science Center, Rochester, New York.

Wyckoff, D. G.

1993 Gravel Sources of Gravel Alibates Silicified Dolomite. *Geoarchaeology* 8:35–58.

Wylie, H. G.

1975 Tool Microwear and Functional Types from Hogup Cave, Utah. *Tebiwa* 17:1–31.

Yerkes, R. W.
1983 Microwear, Microdrills, and Mississippian Craft Specialization. *American Antiquity* 48(3):499–518.

Young, D., and D. Bamforth
1990 On the Macroscopic Identification of Used Flakes. *American Antiquity* 55:403–409.

Zymroz, D. D.
1997 The Titicut Site Burials: An Alternative Perspective on Native Actions and Experiences in Southern New England during the Contact Period. Unpublished M.A. thesis, History and Historical Archaeology Program, University of Massachusetts, Boston.

Contributors

Douglas B. Bamforth received his B.A. from the University of Pennsylvania and his M.A. and Ph.D. from the University of California, Santa Barbara. His interests are in human ecology—particularly early Holocene hunter-gatherer responses to long-term environmental change on the North American Great Plains—and flaked stone technology. He has worked with lithic assemblages from Texas, Colorado, Nebraska, California, and Ireland.

James M. Bayman is an Assistant Professor and Director of the Archaeological Field School at the University of Hawai'i. He received his Ph.D. degree from Arizona State University in 1994. He also held a post-doctoral fellowship at the Smithsonian Institution and a fellowship sponsored by the Wenner-Gren Foundation. His research currently focuses on craft economies in the Hawaiian Islands and in the North American Southwest. He has conducted fieldwork in several areas of North America, the Hawaiian Islands, and Southeast Asia.

Michael L. Carmody received his B.A. from the University of Virginia and his M.A. from Binghamton University. He currently serves as Preservation Program Coordinator for the Virginia Department of Transportation. His research interests include Contact-period archaeology, the Late Woodland period in the Northeast, lithic technology, and functional analysis.

Mark S. Cassell received his Ph.D. in anthropology from Binghamton University. He has been conducting archaeological and documentary research in the western Arctic for over 20 years.

Charles R. Cobb is Professor of Anthropology at Binghamton University, New York. His interests include political economy, lithic studies, culture contact, and the late prehistoric Southeast. He is the author of *From Quarry to Cornfield: The Political Economy of Mississippian Hoe Production* (2000). He is current editor of the journal, *Northeast Anthropology*.

JAY K. JOHNSON is a Professor of Anthropology and the Director of the Center for Archaeological Research at the University of Mississippi. He received his Ph.D. from Southern Illinois University in Carbondale and has been working in Southeastern archaeology since he was an undergraduate at Florida State University in the late 1960s. A long-time interest in lithic analysis led to the coediting of *The Organization of Core Technology* (1987), a collection of essays on stone tools. He received the Award for Excellence in Lithic Studies from the Society for American Archaeology in 1996. A symposium organized for the American Association for the Advancement of Science resulted in *The Development of Southeastern Archaeology* (1993), an edited volume in which specialists chronicled changes in the way that archaeology has been done in their subdisciplines since the mid–nineteenth century. Other research interests include remote sensing, geographic information systems analysis, and ethnohistory.

MICHAEL S. NASSANEY is Associate Professor of Anthropology at Western Michigan University. His research interests include social archaeology, political economy, ethnohistory, culture contact, and material analysis in eastern North America. He currently directs the Fort St. Joseph Archaeological Project, an interdisciplinary study of the archaeology and history of the fur trade in southwest Michigan. He recently co-edited *Interpretations of Native North American Life: Material Contributions to Ethnohistory* (2000) and *The Archaeological Northeast* (2000).

GEORGE H. ODELL has worked extensively in the Old World and the New, specializing in lithic, and particularly use-wear, analysis. He is currently engaged in muddying up the prehistoric record of eastern Oklahoma.

DINO A. RUGGIERO is an Archaeologist and Lab Manager for TRC Garrow and Associates in Durham, North Carolina. His research interests include the organization of technology and lithic studies in the eastern United States.

STEPHEN SILLIMAN is an Assistant Professor in the Department of Anthropology at the University of Massachusetts, Boston. He specializes in the archaeological study of Native Americans before and after European contact, with a geographical focus on California and the Northeast. His topical interests include labor and social agency. His most recent publications can be found in the *Journal of Social Archaeology* and *Journal of Anthropological Archaeology*.

MICHAEL VOLMAR is Curator at the Fruitlands Museum in Harvard, Massachusetts. He began his anthropological career doing archaeology in Connecticut, Rhode Island, and Massachusetts in 1986. He completed his graduate work at the University of Massachusetts at Amherst. His interests include Native American history and interactive learning technology.

MARK J. WAGNER is a staff archaeologist at the Center for Archaeological Investigations, Southern Illinois University, Carbondale. In addition to culture contact studies, his research interests include the Native American rock art of Illinois.

Index